M000240484

COMIC BOOK HEROES of the Screen

WILLIAM SCHOELL

Design by Steven Brower

A CITADEL PRESS BOOK
PUBLISHED BY CAROL PUBLISHING GROUP

Copyright © 1991 by William Schoell
All rights reserved. No part of this book may be reproduced in any form,
except by a newspaper or magazine reviewer who wishes to quote brief
passages in connection with a review.

A Citadel Press Book
Published by Carol Publishing Group

Citadel Press is a registered trademark of Carol Communications, Inc.
Editorial Offices: 600 Madison Avenue, New York, N.Y. 10022
Sales & Distribution Offices: 120 Enterprise Avenue, Secaucus, N.J. 07094
In Canada: Musson Book Company, a division of General Publishing
    Company, Ltd., Don Mills, Ontario M3B 2T6

Queries regarding rights and permissions should be addressed to Carol
Publishing Group, 600 Madison Avenue, New York, N.Y. 10022

All stills in this book are from private collections.
All comics covers/illustrations in this book are from the author's private collection and
are reproduced strictly for historical purposes.

All DC Comics characters, related logos, and indicias are trademarked and
copyrighted by DC Comics Inc.
All Marvel Comics characters, related logos, and indicias are trademarked and
copyrighted by Marvel Entertainment Group, Inc.
The Spirit is copyrighted by Will Eisner and published by Kitchen Sink Press.
American Flagg! is copyrighted by Howard Chaykin, Inc., and First Comics, Inc.
Conan the Barbarian is copyrighted by Conan Properties, Inc., and published by
Marvel Comics.
Doc Savage is copyrighted by Condé Nast Publications and published by DC Comics.

"Super-heroes" is a joint trademark of Marvel and DC Comics.

Carol Publishing Group books are available at special discounts for bulk
purchases, for sales promotions, fund raising, or educational purposes.
Special editions can be created to specifications. For details contact:
Special Sales Department, Carol Publishing Group, 120 Enterprise Avenue,
Secaucus, N.J. 07094

Manufactured in the United States of America

10 9 8 7 6 5 4 3 2 1

Library of Congress Cataloging-in-Publication Data

Schoell, William,
    Comic book heroes of the screen / by William Schoell.
      p.   cm.
    ISBN 0-8065-1252-0
    1. Comic strip characters in motion pictures.   I. Title.
PN1995.9.C38835   1991
791.43'652--8820   91-27057
                                                          CIP

It would be easy to be brave if we had superpowers; not so easy when we're merely mortal. Maria Hernandez saw that something had to be done when her Queens neighborhood was overrun with crack dealers and gave her life in an effort to make it safe again for her children and neighbors. It is to her—and to others like her—that this book is dedicated. They *are the real "heroes."*

CONTENTS

ACKNOWLEDGMENTS

The author tenders his appreciation to:

Allan J. Wilson, Matthew Bialer, Lawrence J. Quirk, Doug McClelland, Mike Ritzer, Arthur Tower, John A. Guzman, Robert Heide, John Gilmam, Caroline and William T. Schoell.

The author also wishes to thank the following firms and individuals for their assistance and cooperation:

Kitchen Sink Press (Doreen Riley, Denis Kitchen); Marvel Entertainment Group (Steven P. Sheffler, Kay Shadley); First Comics (Rick Obadiah); DC Comics (Patricia Mach); The staff of the Billy Rose Theatre Collection at Lincoln Center; Jerry Ohlinger's Movie Material Store; Hal Prince; Paul Ronald; National Screen Service Corp.; ABC-TV; CBS-TV; NBC-TV; RKO Pictures; Fleischer Studios; Columbia Pictures; Lippert Pictures, Inc.; Warner Bros.; Warner Bros. Television; Cannon Films; Tri-Star Pictures; Republic Pictures; Walt Disney Co.; Paramount Pictures; Universal; MGM; Arena Productions; King Features; Orion Pictures; Lucas Film Ltd.; Dino De Laurentiis; Famous Artists Ltd.; United Artists; 20th Century Fox; Fox Television; Clark/Bergman Productions; Danjag S.A.; Sarecky Productions; Eon Productions; Pet Fly Productions; Edward R. Pressman Productions; Greenway Productions; Mattel; *Time* Magazine; Condé Nast Publications; Conan Properties, Inc. New York *Sunday News*.

In addition to those mentioned in the bibliography, the work of the following writers provided further insights or directions for further research:

Paul M. Sammon, Allen Malmquist, Judith P. Harris, Tom Sciacca, Gregory J. M. Catsos, Dan Scapperotti, Andy Mangels, Stephen Rebello, Bill Florence, Marc Shapiro, Roy Kinnard.

INTRODUCTION

Icarus flew too high.

He wanted to escape from Crete, from his fate, his daily existence, but he flew too close to the sun—the symbol of hope, power, and adventure—and the wax with which his wings were fastened melted and he dropped into the sea. He became a victim to the rapture and fantasy of flying, of rising above mundane, mortal fates and soaring like no man ever had before. He paid the price for daring to challenge the gods.

All of us at one time or another have fantasies of flying—under our own power—or of having abilities that set us apart from other humans. Because the attaining of superhuman powers has proven an impossibility, we have created our own heroes and given them the gifts that we covet: flight, strength, priceless beauty, endless youth, invulnerability. The power to see things that others only dream of. The power to walk among others without being seen. Power. The power of being different, special, unordinary.

Through our heroes we can vicariously experience what Icarus did—the rapture of flying, of being *above* the earth and its concerns—without the danger. Super-heroes provide an escape that is devoid of the fear of falling into the sea. They are a safe avenue through which to savor the closest thing to godhood.

The appeal of super-heroes is easy to understand. The human race is constantly barraged with a variety of appalling vulnerabilities: crime, drugs, the fragility of our bodies. Heroes never have to worry about street gangs or plane crashes: Batman can trash a street gang in ten seconds flat and Superman can survive a plane crash. Even the more ordinary heroes have an uncanny ability to survive whatever may be thrown at them. Think of it: being able to deal with virtually every dangerous situation, to have the power to save yourself under any circumstances, and to always protect your loved ones from harm. It is a giddy sensation, to imagine that you can take on whatever the world can throw at you and come out fighting. A sensation that few of us feel in reality. It is also seductive to imagine that there are heroes out there who are fighting against the odds to make the world a better, safer place. There are heroes like that in the real world; but our imaginary superhumans have a better chance of winning.

Super-heroes take us into a world of pure escapism; we know too well that life is never that easy. That's why films and comics that feature super-heroes have always been so popular, and perhaps never more popular than now. Oddly, our super-hero material has taken on a grim reality. Politics, drugs, and street crime figure in the stories even more than before. The fantasy element is provided by the heroic vigilante (Batman, The Punisher) or outré law enforcement agent (Robocop) who deals with problems that aren't terribly different (if at all) from the ones we face every day. This "new" reality in our comic books and movies has been both applauded and vilified.

Super-heroes are nothing new. In the days of the ancient Greeks and Romans, the gods of mythology were the opiate of the masses. Zeus and his cohorts were not only superpowerful, but capable of changing the course of history and affecting the lives of every trembling citizen. Their deeds were of truly heroic proportions. Stories abounded of "ordinary" mortals whose lives would interact with those of the gods, who would indeed even challenge the Lions of Olympus and risk their towering wrath. Hercules and his Twelve Labors. Jason and his quest for the Golden Fleece. Theseus and the Minotaur. Over the decades, more legends grew about superhuman characters, such as Sindbad, whose voyages took him to the seven seas of awe and wonder and back.

Many years later the art of oral storytelling was replaced by bound pages of black print and the legends became popular fiction. Heroes of all types became the stars of cheap pulp magazines that were devoured by the thousands: *The Shadow, The Spider, G-8 and His Battle Aces, Doc Savage.* Heroes proliferated in newspaper comic strips as well: *Buck Rogers, Dick Tracy, Flash Gordon, Mandrake the Magician, The Phantom.* Reprints of comic strips were bound together to make the first comic books. When these proved successful, original material was tried and the first true comic books were born. It wasn't long before they in turn gave birth to the first *true* super-hero (as we know him today): *Superman.* The seeds were sown for an explosion of colorful costumed characters who would not sit still when the lives of others were threatened by petty hoodlums, corrupt politicians, or warmongering reprobates. The heroes were here to stay!

Soon, these heroes were adapted into the film medium. Comic strip characters like Dick Tracy proved a sensation in cliff-hanger serials, and Captain Marvel flew for Republic Pictures like he had never flown before—out of the comic and onto the movie screen. He was followed by other popular characters, such as Superman, Batman, and Captain America. In the fifties, the serials gave way to television, and the *Adventures of Superman* became a hit across the nation. "Camp" took over in the sixties, with *Batman* and a multitude of imitations parading in low comedy across the television screen. The seventies gave birth to the super-hero motion picture "epic," blazing with sophisticated effects and Dolby stereo; the superhuman feature entered a new era: no more tacky dummies and trampolines, Superman *really* flew. The eighties brought us the glossy upscale *film noir* of megabuck, box office-smashing *Batman* and the nineties ushered in the sizzling razzle-dazzle of *The Flash.* And the end isn't in sight.

From the first there was always a link between comic books and films, with the two providing inspiration for, and feeding off, each other. Veteran artist Jack Kirby, cocreator of *Captain America,* spent much of his childhood in movie houses. He liked the way that a story was told in a succession of pictures, and he has been credited with being the first artist to bring a dynamic visual flair to the comic book page. Mort Meskin, a DC Comics artist in the forties, was heavily influenced by Orson Welles's *Citizen Kane,* as were many other artists of the period.

Welles's story of a fabulously rich and successful man who has never gotten over the betrayal and abandonment he felt at being sent away by his parents as a boy (represented by "Rosebud," his sled) is a work of genius on every

Above: *Secret Origins* #1. Copyright © 1973 National Periodical Publications.

level. Although his and Herman Manciewicz's screenplay remains as strong and timely as ever, it is the visual quality of *Citizen Kane* that has fascinated viewers over the years. Welles made a film that is extremely stylish and imaginative in presentation, employing different cinematic methods for each sequence. The disintegrating relationship between Kane and his wife is shown entirely at the same table as the years go by, with a fixed camera and a series of wipe-dissolves, for instance. Each scene was directed in a unique and riveting manner.

For artists like Jack Kirby, each page of a comic book became a different "scene." Comic scripts—like screenplays) were divided into long and medium shots, and close-ups. There were wide angles and narrow focuses. A comic page even had its own kind of "editing." A series of small, similar panels would be the equivalent of quick, successive shots in a movie. A full-page panel was the equivalent of a long-held, or establishing, shot. Comic artists had their own version of *mise en scène*: the layout of each page. Each page could have one, six, eight, ten panels, or more, or less. The borders could be straight and uniform, or irregular, even circular or jagged. The panels could each be the same size, or different sizes, squares, rectangular, oval, or oblong. In this way they would "direct" a comic just as a film director would decide how to cover the action in each scene: long shot, close-up, over-the-shoulder shot, etc. Filmmaker and comic artist could also choose the angles they wanted, with the camera—or the artist's human eye—high above the characters, at shoulder level, or down at the floor looking upward. In this way, comic books (and strips) were just like the movies.

One of the most cinematic artists of all was Will Eisner, who drew stories of his creation, *The Spirit*. Not only did Eisner play around with, stretch and invigorate all the conventions of the comic strip (just as Welles had done in the film medium) but he made many of his Spirit tales amusing and clever parodies of popular movies of the forties. Each splash page in a Spirit

Top: *Citizen Kane* the unlikely inspiration for many comic book artists.

Bottom: A striking shot from *Citizen Kane*.

11

adventure was a riot of imaginative visuals; Eisner would even make the title of the story part of the art, with The Spirit leaning against the letters, or the words dripping snow, ice, or blood, or crumpling as if they were a headline in a crushed, discarded newspaper. His layouts and angles were full of filmic energy, and his pages dripped with an atmosphere that might be termed "comic *noir*."

But while the artists were busy making the early tales of super-heroes and adventurers wonderful to look at (although few artists were on the level of Kirby or Eisner), the writers were crafting stories that were one-tenth imagination and nine-tenths contrivance. The feeling was that children didn't particularly care about logic or storytelling values—although even in the forties many comic readers were adults—and what was the difference if not everything made sense? Super-hero stories had always required a certain suspension of disbelief, but some comics asked for too much. We might "accept" that no one could *ever* recognize a best friend, fiancé, or relative just because he or she put on a costume and mask, but how could a plane fly from the United States to Europe in a matter of *minutes*? We "understood" that villains (who in real life just would have shot the hero and been done with it) had to give megalomaniacal speeches so the hero could escape, but how come the hero developed a convenient *new* power every time he was in a trap? Comic books gave birth to new types of

conventions; thus, stories took place in an alternate universe where a certain dopiness and implausibility were tolerated, if not encouraged.

Hence we call "comic bookish" those other kind of stories that take place in that aforementioned alternate universe: spy stories (particularly of the gadget-y variety); action-adventure films (like *Die Hard 2*); even, of all things, soap operas. We make allowances for their indiscretions, as long as they don't go *too far*. The external logic may be lacking, but the *internal* logic—a dead character cannot pop up alive without explanation, for instance—had better be sacrosanct.

While remaining at least partially in that alternate universe, comic books have gradually started entering the real world also. It began with the relevancy kick of the late sixties and seventies. Green Arrow discovered that his ward, Speedy, was a junkie. Green Lantern was encouraged to stop flying off into space and see what he could do for the poor and oppressed on Planet Earth. The Justice League of America got after bigwigs who were dumping nerve gas in the ocean, and Spider-Man learned that his best friend was a dope addict. These stories gave the

Bottom: *Fantasy Masterpieces* #3. Copyright © 1966 Zenith Books (Marvel Comics).

Top: The famous breakfast table sequence from *Citizen Kane* Orson Welles and Ruth Warrick.

comics genre the shot in the arm it needed. Teenagers no longer felt they had to stop reading comics, at say, age fifteen, while adults, their curiosity piqued, took a peek and stayed for a second look.

The eighties brought the growth of many independent comic book companies, as well as the proliferation of comic specialty stores across the nation. Each Thursday, stacks of new comics were delivered (earlier than to newsstands) to shops where adults and teens lined up to buy their weekly supply. With all these specialty outfits awaiting their products, the independent companies were ready and eager to give something different from and more daring than what the majors—Marvel and DC—were offering. Wary of competition, the majors countered with more innovative projects of their own. While super-heroes still dominate the marketplace, there are also horror, science fiction, satirical, political, sexual, and three-dimensional comic books available. Many are labeled "For Mature Readers" and are not sold to children.

Even the regular super-hero comics are more sophisticated than before. The characters suffer from angst; they have identity problems and neurotic hang-ups, even sex lives, like everyone else. Many fine writers work in the field, among them Chris Claremont, who has taken *The X-Men* from Marvel and made the characters three-dimensional human beings (or rather, mutants) with their own real problems and concerns and personalities. The better comic books increasingly present strong writing and characterizations, even when dealing with super-heroes (or "long-underwear characters," as they used to be called). Comics are not always as mindless as they are thought to be, at least not as mindless as certain sitcoms, slasher movies, action shows, or even comic book film adaptations. (As we will examine, generally the writing is better in comic books than in their TV and big screen translations.)

The new graphic nature and "dark" quality to many comic books has engendered attacks from the narrow-minded. The *New York Times Magazine* ran an ill-conceived piece on the "dangerous" immorality of today's comics that was obviously written by someone who had at best a cursory knowledge of his subject and who based his supposition on a handful of carefully selected examples. Critics of comic books will not accept that the industry had to expand and continue to attract adult readers or die a slow death. Comic books must compete with video games and the like for the short attention spans of children, so aiming at more adult readers was a partial solution to the problem.

As depicted in other media, the stereotypical comic book reader is a mentally deficient nerd in a baseball cap. In reality, comic book fans are often widely read and well educated, with comics being only a small percentage of their general reading. Like films, there are comics that are strictly for children or exclusively for adults or for both children and grown-ups. Super-hero *films* also appeal to a large cross section of viewers, including people who wouldn't be caught dead reading a comic book (but who feel absolutely no embarrassment waiting on line to see a picture like *Superman III*).

Above: *The Spirit* #5. Copyright © 1946, 1984 Will Eisner. Published by Kitchen Sink Press.

Comic books may not be great literature, but like escapist films of the better variety, they can be literate and well crafted. Like films (and television), comics have also been accused of contributing to the demise of legitimate reading. In some ways, this criticism may have validity; in others, it's much too simplistic. Comics not only are useful in teaching people how to read, but can even stimulate an interest in more "serious" reading.

One thing that comic books and comic book adaptations have in common for the most part is that they're *fun.* That in itself gives them some validity.

This overview covers films *from* comic books as well as those that are "comic bookish" (a term that is less derogatory the more sophisticated comic books become). It examines the origins, careers, and highlights of many comic book and comic strip characters. In these pages, you will find the likes of Superman, Batman, Captain Marvel, and Captain America. Wonder Woman, The Hulk, and Spider-Man. Not to mention Robocop, James Bond, and Indiana Jones, and many other characters whose filmic personas have been profoundly influenced by comic books.

Although super-hero comics and films are still dominated by men and women of little ethnicity and much physical perfection, comic books, at least, have tried to change with the times. There are super-heroes in comics who are black, Hispanic, Jewish, gay, and Oriental. Perhaps one day Hollywood will follow their lead and present heroes who are diverse and truly special, heroes who may not possess classic faces and figures, but who have compassion and courage of the heart, the most important qualities that any hero can possess.

Above: Superman made the cover of *Time* Magazine in 1988—a *super*-man of the year? Illustration by John Byrne and Jerry Ordway. Copyright © 1988 DC Comics.

CHAPTER ONE
KRYPTON'S SON: SUPERMAN

uperman!"

There's hardly a man, woman, or child who doesn't know the story of Superman: how the great planet Krypton failed to heed the warnings of its leading scientist Jor-El, who claimed the planet was due to explode; how he built an escape rocket ship, large enough only for his infant son, as a way of ensuring that both his seed and Krypton's would survive; how the baby Kal-El started a long voyage to the distant planet Earth as Krypton began to shake in its death throes.

On Earth, Jonathan and Martha Kent from Smallville in Middle America see the rocket falling, find the baby Kal-El, take him first to an orphanage, and then adopt little Clark, as they call him. Soon they learn of his amazing powers, due to Earth's different gravity (later the rays of a yellow sun would also be offered as an additional explanation for his abilities). Clark grows up to become Superman, the champion of the great city, Metropolis, and of the world. He becomes a reporter in his human identity, and acquires a girlfriend (and rival) Lois Lane, a boss,

Perry White, and a younger buddy, Jimmy Olsen.

All of these developments did not come at once, of course, and there have been many inconsistencies over the years. The *Daily Planet* was first named the *Daily Star*. Before Perry White, there was editor George Taylor. Superman could only leap great distances at first, not fly. And originally the world first learned of his existence when he reached adulthood; it was only later that we learned he had a whole career as Superboy back when he was a Smallville teenager and that he even had a rather nosy childhood sweetheart, Lana Lang. As the years went by, the myths grew, and so did the number of discrepancies, some to be explained away years later.

Superman is one of the few comics characters to survive the public's waning interest in super-heroes in the early 1950s and to be continuously published over the years (Batman and Wonder Woman, also published by DC, are the others). In 1956, DC Comics decided to revive some of its other super-heroes, such as Flash and Green Lantern, using the same names but giving them whole new origins, identities, and costumes; only the basic concept, the powers, remained the same (such as Flash's superspeed). The successful revival of these characters created a new interest in the originals. These were brought back in some stories as guest stars with the explanation that there was more than one Earth—the golden-age heroes came from Earth-2 and the new versions from Earth-1. They could cross

Top: *Action Comics* #1. The first appearance of the first real "super-hero." Copyright © 1938, DC Comics.

Opposite: Superman (Christopher Reeve) saves a train in *Superman*.

Above: *Secret Origins* #1 (second series) retold the origin of the "Earth-2" Superman and became an instant collectible. Copyright © 1986 DC Comics.

dimensional barriers to come into contact with each other.

This was an easy way of clearing up some of Superman's inconsistencies, too. The Earth-2 Superman (the original) began his career as an adult and worked for the *Daily Star*; the Earth-1 Superman, who came into being at the same time as the new versions of those other heroes, started out as Superboy and worked for the *Daily Planet*.

In time, DC Comics felt all these double worlds and double characters were confusing and put out a superb twelve-issue maxiseries, *Crisis on Infinite Earths*, in which time itself (the past included) was altered, with the result that only one Earth remained (by that time there were several), and one definitive version of each character, usually the silver-age version. The Earth-2 Superman, who had married Lois Lane,[1] promptly ceased to exist, and in fact, had never existed.

If that is confusing, imagine what happens when applied to virtually every hero created by DC Comics. Instead of clearing up matters, the maxiseries only created a thousand more questions. What makes it even more futile is that Marvel Comics, DC's main competitor, started *playing up* the alternate Earth/multiple character bit at about the same time as *Crisis on Infinite Earths* appeared. As far as story (Len Wein) and art (George Perez) go, *Crisis* is an excellent comic series, but could never be considered one of DC's wisest moves.[2]

Superman first appeared in *Action* #1 in 1938, the brainchild of artist Joe Shuster and writer Jerry Siegel. He was in part wish-fulfillment: the kind of guy boys would admire and look up to and girls would go crazy over. For inspiration, Shuster and Siegel turned to Philip Wylie's 1930 novel *Gladiator* (about a man who slowly discovers he has a variety of special powers that add up to his being a superman) and Kenneth Robeson's pulp hero Doc Savage, whose first name was Clark and who even had a Fortress of Solitude years before Superman did.

The artwork in that first story is primitive, but attractive and well composed. Superman is depicted as being a rather gruff, no-nonsense figure. He smashes a wifebeater into a wall in fury, and orders people about with disarming directness. (Probably a more accurate portrait of the way a superman would act than the big Boy Scout we have now.) This first story gives short shrift to his Kryptonian origin (one page, no mention of the Kents, and a brief explanation for his superstrength, which suggests *all* Kryptonians possessed it) and gets down to business. Superman has already tracked down a woman who committed a murder for which another person, scheduled to be executed that night, has been accused.[3] The story establishes Clark Kent's "weakling" role, as well as Lois Lane's courage and taunting "bitchiness" toward Clark.

[1]This was not a big event, as by that time the original or "Earth-2" Superman was only relegated to guest-star status, and was not the major character the Earth-1 or "real" Superman was.

[2]Apparently DC wanted to bow to the demands of its younger fans, who couldn't care less about Golden Age counterparts. Marvel, on the other hand, understood and respected that its audience appreciated continuity and that they often kept reading their favorite comics well into adulthood.

[3]When this story was reprinted in the first issue of *Superman,* new pages were added at the beginning which showed how Superman captured the woman.

Above: *DC Comics Presents* Annual #1 teamed up both Earth-1 and Earth-2 Superman. Copyright © 1982 DC Comics.

Early stories indicated that Shuster and Siegel wanted to use their derivative creation to right the wrongs of the world; the stories are morality tales in which Superman intervenes when some manner of venality threatens decent people. He places a greedy industrialist in the middle of the war the latter helped start for profit, and in the same story forces the generals of the two opposing armies to battle each other, only they can't even remember why the factions they represent are fighting. (This is a recurrent theme in these pre-World War II stories: wars are started to promote the sales of munition.) In another excellent tale, Superman traps a callous mine owner and his mindlessly partying friends in a cave-in so that they can experience—and understand—the kind of terror the miners face when they work in unsafe conditions. Some of Superman's actions are questionable, illegal, or downright idiotic, but others are satisfying, such as when he kills a nasty character who has just tried to electrocute him by putting his hand on the bad guy's shoulder and letting the electricity pass from his invulnerable body to the other's much more vulnerable one.

Superman became a big hit and in no time took over *Action* Comics, eventually being awarded his own book. Other comic book companies rushed to create imitations of him, while DC itself came out with many other different super-heroes. Single-handedly, Superman revolutionized the industry and brought into being a slew of superhuman characters who would dominate the comics medium for several years in the forties, reappearing in the late fifties where they quickly regained ascendancy and have ruled benevolently ever since.

Superman's universe began expanding, particularly under the editorship of Mort Weisinger. Lois Lane and Jimmy Olsen got their own books. A Supergirl was created, appearing in backup stories until she received her own. There also was Krypto, the Super Dog, and memorable villains such as Lex Luther and Braniac (who shrank the city of Kandor, which Superman keeps in a bottle in his Fortress of Solitude). Then there was the comical Bizarro race with imperfect duplicates of Superman and Lois who populate their own literally square world and do everything backward.

Apparently feeling that Republic Studios would do everything backward, DC Comics put too many constrictions on the studio when it tried to do a serial based on the exploits of the Man of Steel. When Republic dropped the project (the full-size dummy it built was later used in *The Adventures of Captain Marvel*), DC shopped around for another way to get the Man of Steel into movie theaters and found Max Fleischer's cartoon studio.

An ad for the Superman cartoons from the Fleischer Studios.

Seventeen seven-minute cartoons were directed by Fleischer during the early 1940s, the best of which were directed by Dave Fleischer. These include the first cartoon, *The Mad Scientist*, which briefly shows Superman's origin and uses certain famous phrases ("jumps tall buildings"... "mild-mannered reporter"...) that were later adapted and slightly revised for the 1950s TV program. *The Mad Scientist* is a very effective cartoon (even though said scientist's voice sounds like Popeye's) and ends with a great sequence in which Superman *climbs up* a deadly Electrothanasia Ray by punching it repeatedly as if it were solid!

Equally exciting is *The Magnetic Telescope*, which draws a fireball and then a deadly rain of comets to Metropolis. Superman halts the mass destruction first by batting away the comets and then using his own body as a conduit for the electricity that is needed to start the telescope working again. (Throwing the "reverse" lever saves the day.)

Less effective is *The Mummy Strikes*, in which an Egyptologist's female assistant is accused of murdering him, but the real culprit is simply a poisoned needle secreted in a sarcophagus the doctor was examining. Unaccountably, some twelve-foot-tall mummies come to life but these are quickly dispatched by Superman in a pedestrian manner. Seymour Kneitel's direction is substandard and the story poor and confusing. Other Superman cartoons include *The Bulleteers, Volcano,* and *Underground World.*

In spite of some crudeness and jerkiness, these cartoons are infinitely superior to and more fluid than today's Saturday morning TV animated fare. They are very stylized and detailed, and more "realistic," although there is some Popeye-like unreality or surrealism now and then, such as a scene in which Superman saves a crumbling building that seems to bend back and forth as if made of rubber.

Lois Lane is a pretty, black-haired Bonita Granville type; Perry White is portly, red-headed, and younger than he is usually portrayed in later serials and films. Clark/Superman is as handsome and determined as ever. There is no real characterization to speak of. Bud Collyer, who was the voice of Superman in some of the cartoons, later starred in the radio series.

It wasn't until 1948 that there was a live-action serial based on Superman, this one put out by Columbia Pictures. The serial depicts the destruction of Krypton, Superman's arrival on Earth, and his going to Metropolis years later to become a reporter. The main story deals with his various struggles against the villainess, the Spider-Lady,[4] who wants to get her hands on a Relativity Reducer Ray that will make her the most powerful woman in the world. At one point, she urges a scientist to use the ray to blow up a jail cell holding two henchmen. "Hurry—there are two useless people to be wiped out!" As played by Carol Forman, the Spider-Lady, Queen of the Underworld, comes off like a hooker or "B girl" who accidentally wandered onto a movie set. Initially ludicrous, the character

The Spider-Lady (Carol Forman) in *Superman* looked more like a hostess in a clip joint than a super-villainess.

eventually grows on you, always supremely confident even when the odds are against her. She certainly manages to keep Superman and his pals hopping for fifteen episodes. In one that's particularly exciting, she uses an electromagnetic net or web hanging in her lair to kill anyone who crosses her. At one point she puts on a brunette wig and masquerades as Lois Lane. Her reason for not killing Lois on her web after threatening to do so—"I just want her to know my power"—is pretty feeble, however.

The actor selected to play Superman in the serial was Kirk Alyn, a perfect choice. Like Superman in the comic books, Alyn is virile if "square-looking," playing the character a touch more menacingly than George Reeves in the subsequent television series, and more than willing to strong-arm a bad guy if he has to. He widens his eyes at criminals as if warning them that he's a little bit crazy and may not be responsible for what happens. Oddly enough, Alyn's "tougher" Superman (as in the early stories) is also happy-go-lucky and boyish, as opposed to George Reeves's more authoritative, manly portrayal. This is not to say that Alyn's Superman is a wimp, however. Alyn himself was given little publicity for his role as Superman; originally his name didn't even appear in the credits. It was as if fans were meant to believe there really was a Superman!

Noel Neill plays Lois Lane. Although she was cute and attractive, her lack of standard Hollywood "beauty" led her to be labeled the "dopey-looking" Lois (as opposed to the "smarter" Phyllis Coates), but her portrayal is perhaps the best remembered. Neill understood the key to the character: Lois is competent, self-reliant, brave, sometimes foolhardy, and occasionally condescending, but she isn't a "bitch."[5] She always follows her putdowns of "cowardly" Clark with a little smile. She's sweet, vulnerable, and likable—but never saccharine.

[4]One assumes the character was christened with the silly moniker "Spider-Lady" so as to avoid confusion with Gale Sondergaard's "Spider Woman."

[5]Although she was pretty much depicted as a bitch in her early comic book appearances.

Above: A publicity pose of Kirk Alyn.

She's spunky—but never insolent or obnoxious. Neill also played Lois beginning with the second season of the *Adventures of Superman* TV series.

Tommy Bond, who had appeared in "Our Gang" featurettes as a youngster, plays Jimmy Olsen. He's a little older than as depicted in the comics, but this makes his gutsy assertiveness more believable. By the time of the second serial, however, Bond seemed like a creepy, over-age anthropoid. Pierre Watkin is Perry White; he has as much "bite" as gruff John Hamilton in the television series, but is a little more likable in the part.

The powers of Superman which are established and illustrated in the serial include flying, invulnerability, super-strength, X-ray vision, freeze breath, supersensitive hear-

ing, and supersight. Superman also keeps repeating "This is a job for—*Superman!*" and "Up, up, and away!" until it's a wonder criminals didn't surrender just at the sight of him. Although Superman is rarely shown talking to others, he is somehow considered a "friend" of Clark, Jimmy, and Lois.

While the cliff-hangers in *Superman* are not very compelling, they are distinguished by the fact that most of them do not cheat by revealing missing information in the following chapter. The one exception is the cliff-hanger at the end of chapter eleven, where a packing crate inside which Jimmy is hiding is riddled with bullets. Chapter twelve reveals that Superman flew into the create and took Jimmy's place before a bullet was fired. Other cliff-hangers include Superman—in his Clark Kent guise—apparently dropping dead after being exposed to Kryptonite (he recovers, of course); Lois being locked or tied up and menaced by fires or bombs (on several occasions); and Jimmy heading toward a furnace on a conveyor belt. In all cases, Superman saves the day.

The flying effects were done with cartoon animation. Actor Alyn would pose on the edge of a window sill, but a cartoon Superman would fly out of the building. The animation in these sequences is certainly fluid, but too unrealistic, the Superman figure too supple and "cartoony" to blend well with the live action. The filmmakers tried to use a wire and harness to get Alyn into the air, but an early accident convinced them to go a different route. Alyn was "floating" near a prop airplane engine that was on fire, when sparks from the engine caused his chest hair to smolder. The combination of animation and live action works best when cartoon bullets are shown bouncing off of Alyn's manly chest.

Opposite top: Clark (Kirk Alyn) feels faint at the sight of Kryponite in *Superman*.

Opposite bottom: Kirk Alyn tells it like it is in *Superman*.

Top : Superman demonstrates his great strength to save Lois Lane again.

Lower middle: Superman confers with the authorities.

Some of Superman's superfeats are recorded in live action: Alyn lifts up the back of a car in several chapters and keeps it from moving forward, and runs up to a back-projected train in chapter nine and stops the train before it can reach a wrecked portion of the tracks. The producers put Alyn through his paces. In chapter one, in which he fixes another damaged track ahead of a train, he was almost sucked up and swept away by the real passing train as he knelt by the track in costume. (One wonders why it was necessary for Clark to change to Superman just to repair the track.) Although Alyn had been assured that he was not in any danger, he couldn't help noting that the camera had been put on automatic and the crew had retreated to a safer vantage point.

The first *Superman* serial is modestly amusing and essentially mediocre. Director Spencer Bennet lacks the knockout action knowhow of a William Witney, who worked on *Adventures of Captain Marvel* and many others. There are no real standout sequences in the entire serial, the plot and script lack invention, and even the cliff-hangers are relatively uninspired. Although the orchestral opening theme is rousing, the rest of the music is pretty dreary, a real kiss of death for an action movie. The three-note Superman theme that plays whenever Clark changes into the Man of Steel is anticlimactic, with the last two repeated notes being lower than the first. The sleazy Spider-Lady with her tinny voice and the sensuality of a poor man's Veronica Lake is the first—and often only—thing people remember about the serial. Nevertheless this Superman adventure was successful enough to engender a sequel.

Atom Man vs. Superman was unleashed in 1950, with the same star, cast, and director. This time the villain was not some ridiculous Spider-Lady, but Superman's archenemy Lex Luthor. The story begins in Metropolis, which has been hit by a crime wave. In addition, Luthor is trying to extort money from the city by threatening it with destruction, and creating potentially devastating sound waves on the bridge to show he means business. As it buckles and sways like taffy, Superman shows up to stop the vibrations and track them back to their source. This is only the beginning of his fifteen-chapter battle with Lex Luthor.

An interesting aspect of the serial is that Lex Luthor technically is locked up in jail during the early chapters and the villain is presumed to be the mysterious Atom Man. Actually Luthor has created special coins that can

Opposite: Kirk Alyn pops in in *Superman*.

Left: Kirk Alyn pretends to fly as Superman. A background would later be added.

Right: Bullets bounce off the amazing Man of Steel.

instantly teleport a person from one place to another by using a matter-transmission machine that can supposedly project whole armies. By using one of these coins, Luthor can zap himself from jail to his headquarters and back again. As Atom Man, Luthor wears a ludicrous, oversize, masklike headpiece and a voluminous black cloak, and

speaks with a positively dreadful Italian accent. Atom Man is never actually unmasked as Lex Luthor; late in the serial it just seems to be understood by all the principals that the two are one and the same.

The transmitter coins make for some entertaining sequences. In one, two of Luthor's cronies jump from the roof of the *Daily Planet* building and disappear in midair. Of course, such an act of teleportation would hardly have saved them in real life. When they materialized back at Luthor's headquarters, they still would have been "falling" and the impact with the floor—even if they were level with it—would at least have broken an ankle. Later, a coin is delivered to Lois inside a gift-wrapped box, and when she touches it, Luthor is able to spirit her away to his lair.

Another major subplot in the serial deals with the "Empty Doom," into which Luthor projects all those who displease him. The Empty Doom is actually a limbo comprised of spheroid planets and white dots that are stand-ins for stars. Luthor's first attempt to send Superman into the Doom is a failure. The machine doesn't work on Superman because, as he says, "I moved so rapidly I became invisible to the naked eye." We can only assume he doesn't use his superspeed more often because he'd get things done so fast there wouldn't be much of a story left to tell.

Luthor next uses his machine on two of his underlings who have fouled up, incurring his wrath. When they plead for a second chance, Luthor "mercifully" says that he'll only send one of them—which one will it be? When one hood inexplicably volunteers, Luthor decides to send the one who kept silent, but brings him back to earth from the Empty Doom shortly thereafter.

Several chapters later, Luthor finally succeeds in sending his enemy into the void of the Empty Doom and the results are among the more (unintentionally) hilarious sequences in the serial. Superman returns from the Doom, but only as an immaterial spirit. While the Man of Steel is trying in vain to get somebody's attention, Perry White is wondering where Clark Kent has disappeared to. Superman and Clark, both missing at the same time? Do you suppose...? After voicing his suspicions to Lois, Perry orders her to write a story entitled "Is Clark Kent Superman?" The fact that no self-respecting paper would ever print such a story without having hard evidence or at least waiting to question Clark never occurs to the screenwriter. Luckily Jimmy, who may or may not think Clark and Superman are the same, decides to disguise his voice as Kent's and phone Perry, who hearing the missing reporter's voice on the other end of the line, kills the story.

Above: Superman prepares to get the drop on some crooks.

Superman, still in his ghostly form, finally communicates with Lois by mentally manipulating the keys of her typewriter. At first, Lois thinks the machine is malfunctioning. ("These newfangled typewriters," she says in regard to a museum piece that must have been one of the first electric typewriters off the assembly line.) Finally, she understands what's happening. "I'm in the Empty Doom," types Superman—as if Lois would immediately know what that is. She soon learns where she has to go to free Superman from his unearthly prison, and sets out to rescue him—with Jimmy, of course. Lois is always stupidly putting herself in unnecessary danger because she wants to get a scoop. Couldn't she have brought a cop along?

Naturally, she and Jimmy are captured by Luthor, or rather Atom Man, who forces her to make a decision. If she flicks the right switch on Luthor's machine, she'll save Superman. If she flicks the wrong one, she'll destroy him. Instead Lois flicks both switches and knocks herself and Jimmy unconscious. Superman finally escapes from the Empty Doom when Luthor sends a man into limbo to look for him. Luthor mistakenly believes, simply because he has seen newsreel footage of Superman on TV, that his foe has returned to Earth.

The screenplay is riddled with additional contrivances, inconsistencies, and inanities. After trying to destroy the entire city, Luthor is released from prison after an incredibly short period of time. Although it may make sense for Luthor to commit his future crimes as Atom Man while pretending that he has gone straight as a legitimate businessman and TV station owner, the Atom Man character is so ridiculous that it would have been better if it had been dropped entirely, with Luthor just being his villainous self throughout.

In chapter seven, Superman, incapacitated by Kryptonite being held in a box by a man standing several feet away, remains powerless even after the felon has departed, and shows no signs of recovering during the time it takes to put him into the ambulance. Yet in an earlier chapter, Clark was able to get up from the floor and recover when exposed to Kryptonite secreted in a water cooler only a couple of feet away.

In chapters nine and ten, Jimmy's foot is caught on the rail as a train is approaching. Instead of using his superstrength and superspeed to free his young friend, Superman throws himself against the train to stop it (a feat repeated from the previous serial) without regard for the inevitable injuries it will inflict on the passengers on board.

However, *Atom Man vs. Superman* also has some highlights. In chapter five, Superman gets a would-be thief to talk by hauling him out of Perry White's office window and repeatedly throwing him high into the air. "If you won't play ball with me, I'll play ball with you," he warns. On another occasion, Superman knocks out a crook who's shooting at him by using his invulnerable palm to deflect a bullet to a light fixture over the gunsel's head. The light crashes down, landing on the hoodlum's noggin. The best sequence of all is in chapter twelve, in which the not-so-respectable Luthor sends two henchmen after Lois to retrieve a notepad that she had lifted from his office. What ensues is an amusing, well-executed, and well-edited chase scene, with a clever Lois ducking in and out of buildings and up and down fire escapes in a successful effort to elude her pursuers.

The cliff-hangers are somewhat more exciting than the ones in the preceding serial. Lois falls from a window when some crooks try to snatch a transmitter coin from her. (Although the room that she enters appears to be at sidewalk level, the window manages to be near the top of the building.) A kidnapped Jimmy is inadvertently driven by his captor onto an air force bombing range. Superman intervenes when Luthor turns his destructive ray on the *Daily Planet* building, and falls onto some power lines in apparent defeat.

Cartoon animation again was used to show Superman flying, but this time the producers wisely added some effective process shots showing Kirk Alyn against various backgrounds. In chapter three, he climbs onto the wing of a plane that has caught on fire with Jimmy and Lois on board. In chapter fourteen, when Luthor sends a rocket hurtling toward Metropolis, Alyn is seen straddling the missile, with racing clouds in the background. There is also a shot of the rocket, sans Superman, flying over the city as he sends it into the sea where it explodes.

The special effects department didn't strain itself coming up with Luthor's flying vehicles. A flying saucer that appears in chapter thirteen is a cartoon in every sense of the word. And the tacky spaceship in which he tries to escape at the climax looks like an ambitious, finned version of one of those old-fashioned sugar shakers found now and then in diners. There is also a liberal use of stock footage throughout the serial, such as when a dam breaks in chapter eleven (Lois is swept over a cliff in her van) and every conceivable kind of wartime and disaster footage is used as a backdrop. When Luthor turns on his "sonic vibrator" in the final chapters, however, causing an earthquake on the east side of Metropolis, some effective scenes and use of props are blended in with the stock material.

The only major new performer in *Atom Man vs. Superman* is Lyle Talbot as Lex Luthor. Talbot is a road-show villain, underplaying so much that he borders on the dull. Lex isn't given an origin in this, but we learn that he knows so much about Superman because Jor-El's messages to Earth were picked up on a ship's wireless. The captain gave these messages to Lex, who was able to translate them and knows all there is to know about his enemy—except his secret identity.

Although *Atom Man vs. Superman* is not without its entertaining moments, too much of it is pretty inane and illogical. (Superman knows Luthor's lair is in the mountains, and with all of Metropolis at stake, why doesn't he simply find Lex by smashing into the hills at superspeed? And wouldn't the lead-lined walls of the hideout be a dead giveaway to Superman, only calling attention to the very thing Luthor was trying to hide?) While the serial is never quite wretched, for long stretches it's unbearably dumb and slapdash. It is not the Man of Steel's shining hour.

The following year, DC Comics, encouraged by the response to the two serials, decided it might be a good idea to have a Superman television series. However, the publisher, Jack Leibowitz, suggested a feature-length film be tried first to test audience reaction. Alyn, who once had the audacity to ask for more money, was passed over in favor of George Reeves. Reeves had had a small part in *Gone With the Wind* and a somewhat larger one several years later in *So Proudly We Hail*, but was primarily known for a number of appearances in "B" movies. With a new Superman, a new Lois Lane was required; the part went to Phyllis Coates, who had appeared in serials, Westerns, and assorted undistinguished vehicles.

The new feature was entitled *Superman and the Mole Men* and was released in 1951. Its story takes place in the small town of Silsby, the location of the deepest oil well ever drilled. Clark Kent and Lois Lane have come to Silsby to do a piece on the well but find it closed down for "confidential" reasons. The foreman has discovered that certain oil samples glow in the dark and may be radioactive, and has also found living organisms in samples scraped from the drill head after it was six miles down. The drill has broken into a subterranean world inhabited by humanoid creatures, who climb up the well to see what's what.

The creatures have oversize craniums with monks' tonsures, and midget bodies. The "little people" who play the mole men are talented mimes who effect a nice, hesitant way of walking, slightly hunched over, as if they were used to traveling through narrow tunnels with low ceilings. While exploring the town as advance scouts, two of the mole men come into contact with a little girl who falls ill. Soon the whole town is caught in the grip of panic and hysteria.

One of the townspeople, Luke Benson (Jeff Corey), organizes a search-and-destroy party to hunt down the mole men. Originally, Benson was supposed to be the father of the ill child, which would explain his rage and ruthlessness, but this angle was eliminated (through overdubbing) to make the little people more sympathetic. The trouble is that Benson subsequently comes off as an irredeemable and one-dimensional hothead without any shadings of humanity. At the same time, the picture manages to work up some suspense and audience involvement just *because* the bad guy is so heinous—you want to see Superman give him his comeuppance. Although the villainy in the picture may seem a touch overstated, one has to wonder if the behavior is really all that exaggerated, given what we know of human nature.

Clark unsuccessfully tries to calm the frightened townspeople before they go off shooting at shadows, and doesn't have any more luck when he switches to Superman. Not only do the townspeople fail to listen to him, but they are also dubious about his abilities. Superman seems more legend to them than reality. (You would think seeing a man fly would take their minds off a couple of silly midget mole men!) He does convince Lois, though, not to file a story about the alien mole men because it might spread the panic nationwide.

After trying to shoot Superman, Benson takes his mob and starts to hunt down the two frightened mole men. They corner one of the little fellows at a dam and aim their rifles. Although Superman warns them that the alien is radioactive and may contaminate the reservoir if he falls into it, the members of the mob are stupid enough to shoot at the little guy anyway. Superman saves him and flies him to the hospital, the head of which is a nice, compassionate fellow. He takes one look at the mole man and tells Superman he wants "that thing" taken out of his hospital immediately. Superman is not easily intimidated, however.

Benson and his buddies try to roast the second alien in a toolshed where he's hiding, but he escapes through the floorboards and makes his way back to the oil well. Soon he returns with two other mole men and a weird vacuum cleaner-type weapon (a modified Electrolux) that had even the film's cast in stitches. The mole men are not a pitiful strike force, however; they simply want their hospitalized pal returned to them. Trigger-happy Benson shoots at the aliens and they turn their ray gun on him. Superman steps in front of Benson and saves his worthless hide.

It turns out that the mole men aren't radioactive, after all; they only leave traces of "harmless phosphorescence." They return to their underground home and destroy the well behind them. If the dastardly Benson is arrested for the attempted murder of Superman, we never see it.

Superman and the Mole Men is a rather silly kiddie feature that does attempt to say something about prejudice within its contrived story line. The trouble—and irony—is that many kids (and their parents) find it easier to feel sympathy for "mole men" and "mutants" (in the *X-Men* and other comics series) than they do for blacks, Jews, gays, or whatever real-life minority may be suggested by some fantastic counterparts.

George Reeves is fine and authoritative as Superman, without being crude or macho. His Clark Kent is a man worthy of respect, even if Lois Lane doesn't think so. Phyllis Coates's Lois hasn't any of Noel Neill's affectionate exasperation toward or intolerance of Clark. When he goes out to handle the mob, she sneers, "You?" When he says that the doctor who took the bullet out of the mole man has courage, she snaps, "I wish you did!" One can only wish he had eventually given Lois a piece of his mind. Coates's Lois is tough, brave, and uncompromising, but she's also a hardhearted bitch. Of course, she has her side of it. "He always does that!" she hollers. "Gets himself into a jam and then runs away!"

Although it is claimed that Superman does not fly in *Superman and the Mole Men*, that is not the case. (Perhaps when the sixty-minute feature later was chopped into two parts for airing on the TV series, the flying scenes were deleted.) There is a quick shot of Superman jumping up or being pulled into the sky about midway through the picture, followed by a shot of the ground rushing by as Superman flies overhead. During the dam sequence, two different techniques are used to show Superman flying. Cartoon animation (as in the serials), superimposed over the background of the dam, shows the mole man falling and Superman flying in toward him from the left. Then there is a medium live-action shot of Superman (Reeves) catching the little guy and flying off.

Generally, the production values of the movie are about on the level of the television series: cheesy, but acceptable. Perhaps the best thing about the movie is the performance by Jeff Corey as the evil Luke Benson. (Corey is a fine actor whose career suffered by blacklisting during the McCarthy era. He continues to ply his trade

Above: An ad for *Superman and the Mole Men*.

Opposite top: Lois Lane (Phyllis Coates) and Superman (George Reeves) confront villain Jeff Corey.

Opposite bottom: Superman (George Reeves) confers with the doctor in *Superman and the Mole Men*.

and has become a noted acting coach.)

The film was received kindly by the critics. *Variety* wrote: "Juve idol makes ok impression in full-length pic bow. Although limited in his first screen adventure to some routine 'superhuman' stunts, Superman should please his fans and build a following for inevitable sequels. He's sock moppet bait. [Reeves] is effective in both roles and Jeff Corey projects plenty of intolerance as the mob leader."

The television program premiered in the late afternoon of February 9, 1953, with George Reeves and Phyllis Coates reprising their roles. The cast was expanded to include Jack Larson as Jimmy Olsen, John Hamilton as Perry White, and Robert Shayne as Inspector Henderson. Although Larson has claimed that the character of Jimmy Olsen, cub reporter, originated on the series and was later added to the comics, the fact is that the character had appeared earlier in the Superman comic book. Larson is a capable actor, but his hangdog look and earnest delivery are nerve-wracking. Hamilton is fine as a blustering, unpleasant Perry White, and Shayne is competent (if bland, as ever) as Henderson. None of these actors ever received much more than $350 (if that much) per episode—and no residuals!

Reeves and Coates were not thrilled to be doing the series. "We both felt we'd hit the bottom of the barrel," Coates later told interviewer Roy Kinnard. She and Reeves were not romantically involved, but they were good friends, and she saw how miserable he was with the way his career had turned out. From *Gone With the Wind* to *Superman and the Mole Men*—and then television! Both Coates and Reeves would drown their sorrows with a few drinks on and off the set. Among other things, Coates hated having

to memorize twenty-four pages of dialogue a day. She quit the series after the first season despite offers of better money from the producer. She later wound up in *I Was a Teenage Frankenstein* in 1957 and other quickie horror films. She was replaced by Noel Neill (in the series' second season and thereafter), who continued to deliver her putdowns of Clark with a certain amount of affection.

Lee Sholem, who directed *Superman and the Mole Men*, also directed many of the television episodes. In *Filmfax*, he explained how some of the effects were done on TV. "The takeoffs were all done on wires, two wires on each side with his cape covering them. We also had a springboard below camera level. He would take a run, then take off right over the lens. You didn't need wires for that stunt. Plus, George was a good athlete, in good shape. When you'd take him out of the window, boy, he'd dive through! Of course, he had his mats on the other side. George would rehearse a couple of times and then he'd go at it. But sometimes, you can't help it. As good as George was physically, and the stunt men, too, they had their problems during some of the fight scenes."

Reeves switched from the takeoffs with pulleys, leather belts, and wires to the springboard, nonwire system after he almost had a bad accident when the wires broke. Although he only fell on his fanny, his injuries could have

Above: Clark and Lois examine a corpse in *Superman and the Mole Men*.

been severe. According to Larson, a furious Reeves picked himself up and screamed, "That's the end of the wires! Peter Pan can fly by wires, but my Superman is not going to fly by wires anymore!"

To show Superman in flight, a simple illusion and some matte work sufficed. Reeves would lie down on a glass (invisible) table, and stretch out his arms and legs as if he were flying. He would be superimposed over plane or helicopter views of Hollywood standing in for Metropolis. The results were never particularly convincing. Usually Reeves would simply be a static figure in front of blurred, racing skies or clouds, but sometimes he would go so far as to move his head (peering downward in search of something, for instance) and regular backgrounds such as houses and trees, or the city, would be used. One show features a surprisingly effective shot showing Superman flying *through* the clouds, and there is a splendid takeoff in "The Mind Machine" in which Reeves, standing *between* Lois and an extra, is pulled vertically off the ground and out of the frame without visible wires. (Reeves's accident would write finis to quick but effective shots such as this.)

The episodes in the first season, when Robert Maxwell[6] and Bernard Luber were producers, have a somewhat "harder" edge to them than later ones. "The Human Bomb" deals with a criminal who bets that he can "control" Superman for thirty minutes. He wires himself with dynamite, handcuffs himself to Lois Lane, then orders Superman to stay put while a bank is robbed. There is an exciting climax showing Jimmy struggling with the criminal on a ledge high over the city.

Lee Sholem recalled one incident when Reeves was supposed to crash through a door as Superman. The specially rigged door was made of balsa wood and should have been easy to knock down—that is, if someone had remembered to remove the two-by-fours that were supporting it. The prop man forgot—and George was knocked cold. What with Kirk Alyn at one point fainting from stress in the Superman serial and George Reeves knocking himself unconscious on the TV show, it must be assumed that the Man of Steel is not an easy guy to play.

"The Mind Machine," or hypnotherapy transmitter, either can cure nerve disorders or fry the brains of anyone within twenty-five miles. A scientist-inventor wants to use it for the first purpose; a crime boss for the second. The mobster wants to wipe out people long distance who are testifying against him in court. (It is never explained how the machine is able to tune in on people so far away, and even capture their pictures on an attached video monitor without use of cameras or television waves.) The absurd, but above-average, episode has more suspense and action than usual: Superman first saves a runaway school bus,

[6]Maxwell and Whitney Ellsworth used the pseudonym Richard Fielding to write the screenplay for *Superman and the Mole Men*. Together and separately, they would also use the pen name to write several episodes of the Superman TV series.

Above : George Reeves superimposed over Los Angeles in *The Adventures of Superman* TV series.

Top left: George Reeves catapulted out of a window for his TV series.

then a plane with an unconscious pilot, in economical but clever fashion. Reeves is shown "pulling" the slowed-down bus from behind, as well as lifting up the plane—a mock-up—on his back

Writer Ben Peter Freeman was responsible for two of the most interesting episodes in the series, both from the first season. In "The Stolen Costume" a crook and his moll (Veda Ann Borg) figure out Superman's secret identity when a dying robber, shot by the police, tells them he found the hero's costume in a secret closet in Clark Kent's apartment. In rather shortsighted fashion, the two reprobates try to blow up Kent instead of blackmailing him or doing something a little more grandiose. When Kent confronts them (it's rather disconcerting watching *Clark* smashing through a door instead of Superman), they are unrepentant, and he is forced to take them to a cabin on an icy mountaintop until he can figure out what to do with them. Although he promises to return with some food, they don't believe him and begin to climb down the mountain, with the vivid Veda Ann wearing high heels! She slips, crashes on top of her heavyset friend, and the two fall screaming to their deaths. One has to wonder if Superman was hoping that would happen.

"Mystery in Wax" is a weird little tale in which a Madame Selena crafts wax statues of men who a "voice" tells her will die within six months. The latest statue to be unveiled is of Perry White, who dutifully "commits suicide" by jumping off a pier. All of the other victims have jumped off the same pier, their bodies never being recovered, but nobody gets suspicious until Perry takes a dive. Not believing that her boss has killed himself, Lois Lane pays a call on Madame Selena at her waxworks—and winds up in a cage in the sinister woman's private museum, along with White and all the other "dead" men. The villainous sculptress's husband wore a mask of each victim and feigned each suicide. Madame Selena revels in the power that people's fear of her death-figures gives her. While the proceedings get pretty silly, and Myra McKinney's performance borders on the campy, the episode's macabre premise makes it memorable.

Whitney Ellsworth produced the series for the next five seasons. DC Comics was objecting to the body count, dark story lines, and violent mayhem[7] of the first-season episodes, and wanted a kinder and gentler approach. Kinder and gentler gradually turned into dopier. Lois Lane (Noel Neill) would be mistaken for the reincarnation of an Egyptian queen ("The Tomb of Zaharan") or Jimmy would "invent" an antigravity formula while trying to make a new kind of cake in a mixing bowl ("Whatever Goes Up"). The third from the last episode (a bored and tired George Reeves would direct all three) featured a donkey named Carmelita with psychic powers. Real thrills were in short supply.

Reeves tried to rectify this with the penultimate episode, "The Perils of Superman," which was a throwback to old movie serials. The criminal in this episode is himself inspired by cliff-hangers, and puts Clark, Lois, Perry, and Jimmy in doom traps just to get revenge on Superman. Perry is tied to a log with the obligatory approaching buzzsaw, Lois is tied to train tracks, Jimmy has his car brakes and wheels sabotaged on a mountain road, and Clark is suspended on chains over a pool of acid. When it came to direction, however, Reeves was no William Witney, and the aforementioned episodes are not as well handled as in the average cliff-hanger. The one exception is Jimmy's runaway car ride, which is fairly hair-raising thanks to some fine second-unit work, including shots of cliff edges speeding by and the like.

---

[7]That would hardly be the case today; DC has made a lot of money with "darker" Batman stories and much more graphic comic books.

Opposite: Many fans consider George Reeves the one and only Superman. He thought the TV series was "the bottom of the barrel."

Although "The Perils of Superman" is not a bad episode, one has to wonder why Superman didn't just grab the bad guy, rip off the lead mask concealing his identity, and round up his henchmen, instead of just standing there taking the villain's threats. Lois does her usual taunting of Clark, snickering that he's probably run off and hidden, but he actually acts pretty bravely throughout—he offers to let himself be captured so that the police can follow him, and sneers contemptuously at the crooks as he dangles over acid.

That is one of the nicest things about Reeves's portrayal of Superman. His Clark Kent doesn't seem all that "mild-mannered," and certainly never acts like the nerd Christopher Reeve was to make of him (not to mention Gerard Christopher in TV's *Superboy*) years later.

The final episode of Superman in 1957, "All That Glitters," is very typical of the combination of silly humor and lighthearted premises to which the show had sunk. A professor invents a machine that literally can make gold. Unfortunately, he needs $10,000 worth of plutonium to make $5,000 worth of gold with his device. Before this revelation, Jimmy is hit on the head and dreams that the professor also has made some pills that can give people superpowers. (The best scene shows a mouse that has been fed the pill pulling a huge cabinet behind it.) Lois and Jimmy gain superhuman abilities, fight some crooks—and then Jimmy wakes up. *The Adventures of Superman* ended not with a bang but a whimper.

Perhaps the same is true of George Reeves. Although many claim that he was keeping quite busy professionally after the TV series was canceled in 1957, it could not have been the kind of career that he had envisioned for himself. Jack Larson recalled to critic Gregory J. M. Catsos that at the preview screening in 1953 of *From Here to Eternity*, in which George had a good part, the audience screamed "Superman!" whenever he appeared, which led to most of his footage being scrapped before the picture was officially released. If that sort of thing was happening the *first* year the TV show was aired on ABC, one can only imagine what would have happened several years later when Reeves as Superman was entrenched in the minds of the American public. George knew the odds were against his ever getting a decent role in a serious "A" production.

For many years Reeves was rumored to have been the "kept boy" of the wife of a high-powered MGM executive (which may not have helped his chances in Hollywood). This woman was extremely jealous of him and kept a firm grip on her Superboy. Whether Reeves no longer needed her money (she bought him his house in Benedict Canyon) or simply fell out of love with her, he broke off the affair in 1959 and took up with Lenore Lemmon from New York.

On June 15, 1959, Reeves and Lemmon were entertaining several guests at his house when he excused himself and went up to his bedroom. He had been drinking heavily and may have been arguing with some of the guests. Two shots were fired. At two o'clock the following morning George Reeves died of a gunshot wound to the head.

For years, the legend has been that Reeves committed suicide; that he fancied himself as really being Superman and jumped out of a window to his death. The real truth may be much more sinister.

Reeves's mother did not believe her son had killed himself, and she hired a private detective to prove it.

Reportedly, the investigator was able to discount the suicide theory because of the angle of the bullet and the two bullet holes in the wall. Lemmon later said that she had accidentally fired the gun twice on an earlier occasion, but a Luger, the death gun, is not a repeating pistol. Lenore Lemmon and the executive's wife got into a struggle over the will. Reeves left everything to his dumped "mistress," although Lemmon claimed that he had told others she was to be the beneficiary. The executive's wife claimed that George left most of everything to her because they shared an interest in similar charities. One can only imagine what her husband thought.

There are several theories as to what happened that night. Did Reeves get into a struggle with the guest or guests he argued with, and did the gun really go off accidentally? Was Reeves surprised in his room by a burglar who shot him? (Five thousand dollars was reported stolen from the house, but Lemmon later claimed it was actually $4,000 in traveler's checks for their honeymoon and apparently had not been taken after all.)

Actor Gig Young always felt that Reeves had been murdered by a hitman because of all his indiscretions over the years with certain ladies.

Others still contend that his death was suicide. Even though the *Superman* series was going back into production after a two-year hiatus, Jack Larson sensed that George was despondent. Another season of *Superman* had not been what Reeves had hoped for. Producer Whitney Ellsworth, however, feels that George killed himself out of booze-and-dope confusion. He had been in an automobile accident a couple of weeks before his death and suffered a concussion. The combination of painkillers and alcohol, and the head injury itself, led Reeves to make the terrible decision to end his life. He was engaged to be married to Lenore Lemmon, and his career was hardly over, but he just wasn't thinking straight.

The irony is that Reeves was more successful than he ever realized. He is still remembered three decades later when other actors who starred in "A" productions during the same period are totally forgotten. And his fans remain devoted.

Perhaps too devoted. There is a somewhat fanatical cult surrounding *The Adventures of Superman* which refuses to see the program's shortcomings or the value of any of the Superman vehicles which came after. The TV show had only a mild sense of wonder and never examined Superman's character or even his abilities (in any startling fashion). Even by the standards of the fifties, the effects were rarely worth raving about. Although the series was filmed in color by the third season, the scripts remained as colorless and unmagical as before. Superman was usually pitted against the most bland and mundane of villains. Where were the outrageous, larger-than-life antagonists of the comic books? The cosmic plots and deadly weapons? Why were there no costumed superfoes? Compared to the stories in *Superman* and *Action* comics, the TV shows were as dull as dishwater. This wasn't really Superman as a comics fan knew him, but only a pallid imitation.

The steadfast devotees of the TV series are fond of taking futile potshots at the Christopher Reeve movies of the seventies and eighties. Although those films certainly have their own shortcomings, they are in every way superior to the forties serials and fifties television program, and they are much more faithful to the spirit of the comic books.

Speaking of the comic books, they were still going strong in the fifties and sixties. Many of the stories relied heavily on gimmicks and were often about attempts to discover Superman's identity by Lois or some villain. Covers usually featured Superman or one of his supporting cast acting in a highly unexpected manner—Jimmy felling Superman with Kryptonite, Lois marrying some other man, even Superman threatening to kill someone— with the inside story revealing that the cover scene (if depicted inside at all) was actually a game, a joke, or a covert action, or the result of magic or red Kryptonite (which always affected Superman strangely). Some stories were out-and-out "imaginary" and labeled as such, a chance to explore the mythos out of continuity, which was fun for everybody. The covers were ludicrous come-ons, and the stories were contrived beyond belief, yet they were also oddly charming and undeniably amusing. These types of stories continued into the seventies but became a little more complicated.

Stories in Jimmy Olsen's own comic book were interesting and clever at their best, silly at their worst. Jimmy was always trying to impress Lois's snooty sister, Lucy Lane, and was often being transformed into some grotesquerie by a magic spell or alien potion. In her magazine, Lois Lane spent most of her time plotting against her love rival, an adult Lana Lang, who moved to Metropolis to snare Superman, or dreaming up ways either to prove that Clark and Superman were one and the same, or to trick Superman into marrying her. A smart reporter Lois may have been; a women's libber she was not.

In one story (*Lois Lane* #63), Lois, needing to contact Superman in a hurry, stupidly jumps out of a window to attract his attention, figuring since he's never once failed to save her life he will certainly show up to rescue her this time as well. Superman observes this, but wisely arranges to save her life by "accident," so that she will never try such a moronic stunt again. (A similar incident occurred years later in the film *Superman II*.) Stories in

Lois Lane often reached ridiculous heights: "The Irresistible Lois Lane" in #29 (November 1961) has Lois kissing a variety of super-heroes, all in a convoluted effort to get Superman some red Kryptonite crystals he desperately needs and which are secreted in her lipstick.

Left: Bob Holiday switches from Superman to Clark Kent in the Broadway musical *It's a Bird, It's a Plane, It's Superman!*

Right: Bob Holiday flies over the citizens of Metropolis.

There were more plans for a subsequent television series based on the exploits of the Man of Steel in the sixties, but none of them reached fruition. Whitney Ellsworth, who had produced all but the first season of *The Adventures of Superman*, made a pilot for *The Adventures of Superboy* in 1960 that never aired. When the musical comedy *It's a Bird, It's a Plane, It's Superman!* became a Broadway hit, there was talk of putting its star, Bob Holiday, in a new Superman TV series. It also never happened.

The Broadway show was a whimsical venture with pleasant tunes by Lee Adams and Charles Strouse. ("You've Got Possibilities," sung by Linda Lavin, became a standard.) The story line pits Superman against a comical crack—and cracked—scientist, Dr. Abner Sedgwick, well played by Michael O'Sullivan. Lois Lane was portrayed by Patricia Marand, and as *Daily Planet* columnist Max Mencken, Jack Cassidy stole the show doing his "The Woman for the Man" number. The show was produced and directed by Hal Prince and got mostly respectful notices. (It later was restaged for television.) The book was written by David Newman and Robert Benton, two of the four screenwriters for the *Superman* theatrical movie in 1978.

In the seventies, Superman comic books needed a shot in the arm, and they got it. Stories delved into the Man of Steel's psychological problems, particularly his special loneliness in being virtually the only survivor of the planet Krypton. Other stories dealt with the bizarre consequences of his not dreaming, as he doesn't require sleep. Kryptonite was (temporarily) eliminated as a threat when all of it was made harmless. New villains were introduced, like the dynamic Terra-Man, an earthling raised by extraterrestrials and privy to their superscience. And an answer was finally provided to a nagging question that had been bothering Superman fans for quite some time.

Over the years, everyone had wondered how Superman could possibly fool anyone with his Clark Kent "disguise," in which he puts on glasses and smooths back the nagging lock of hair that curls down over his forehead, and also effects a slightly different voice and posture. *Lois Lane* #63 (1966) featured a cover in which Superman marches out of the *Daily Planet* stock room saying, "I'll tell you why I'll *never* marry *you*, Lana, or *you*, Lois! Who wants a wife so *stupid*, she doesn't realize *I'm Superman* when I take off my Clark Kent glasses!" Headlined as "the story we have never dared publish before," it was all, as usual, a crock. It turned out to be a joke played on the two women by a special agent disguised as Superman, and took up all of two panels in the story inside.

However, a terrific story in *Superman* #330 (December 1978) by Martin Pasko, based on a concept by Al Schroeder III, dealt with this problem in a serious, realistic, and rather brilliant fashion. Earlier stories had already revealed that Superman was capable of superhypnotism. The lenses in his Clark Kent glasses were fashioned from the same Plexiglas as the window in his rocket, so that they wouldn't melt if ever he had to use his X-ray vision while posing as Clark. Some

Above: *Superman* #330 finally presented an explanation for how Clark/Superman had fooled the world for all those years. Copyright © 1978 by DC Comics.

property of the lenses intensified his hypnotic powers so that without even realizing it, Superman had been making people see *not* Superman wearing glasses, but the image of Clark that Superman had always tried to project—frailer, balding, ordinary looking. There was enough of a resemblance to evoke some suspicion, but not enough to make the "two" men look that much alike. Subsequent stories, however, have conveniently "forgotten" Pasko's tale, and the whole issue of the disguise is simply never mentioned, with the readers having to suspend disbelief once again. It's the same way in the movies and on the television shows.

In an age of comic "relevancy," Lois Lane's magazine briefly became a platform for preaching racial equality and black rights. Although well-intentioned, the stories, such as "I Am Curious, Black" in #106 (November 1970), in which Lois becomes a black person for a short period of time, were silly, unrealistic, and utterly simplistic. When Lois (as her own white self) confronts an angry black activist in the ghetto in one story, she so wins the woman over that in the next panel the militant woman is hugging Lois to her bosom and calling her "sister." If only racial and other problems could be solved so easily in the real world!

In the late seventies, producers Alexander and Ilya Salkind decided to base a major motion picture on the Superman comic. Guy Hamilton, who had guided some of the James Bond features, had originally been set to direct, but he backed out and was replaced by Richard (*The Omen*) Donner. Donner claimed that the massive screenplay he was first handed would have meant "the demise of Superman," that it was a parody of a parody and had such ridiculous scenes as Superman flying down after bald-headed Luthor only to have Telly Savalas of *Kojak* whip around and say "Who loves ya, baby?" Mario Puzo's screenplay was worked over by additional writers David and Leslie Newman, and Robert Benton. Donner could never understand how DC Comics—which had *total* control—could have approved the result. He brought in uncredited writer Tom Mankiewicz and the two of them went through the screenplay and whipped it into more filmable condition. A number of actors were considered for the title role—Robert Redford, Warren Beatty, Bruce Jenner—but when they either turned it down or were rejected for various reasons, the decision was made to go with a comparative unknown from the stage, Christopher Reeve. Since they had chosen to go with a younger actor, Reeve was perfect—all he needed to do was fatten himself up a bit; reportedly, he was awfully skinny at his audition.

Different devices were used to make Superman appear to be flying. Hydraulic arms, stage cranes, and assorted cables and wires were employed to hoist actor Reeve up in front of special screens, upon which the moving background would be projected, or later matted in in a technique called a "blue backing process."[8] Stuntmen were

[8]In this process, the screen behind the actor is blank while he is being filmed. The background is added later, and if done carelessly, will leave a bluish-green outline around the actor, spoiling or lessening the impact of the composite shot.

Above: Christopher Reeve poses in front of the Manhattan skyline.

suspended from three-hundred-foot cranes behind a miniature of the Golden Gate Bridge, but these shots were later rejected, as were shots of costumed sky divers. Night shots of stuntmen flying from cranes were used, however. The standard back projection method (an image is beamed from behind onto a translucent screen, before which an actor stands—or "flies") was rejected. Instead a new front projection process was utilized (the background image is projected from in front of the screen) employing an extremely mobile and much lighter combination camera and projector. The actor's movements were limited, but the camera/projector could create an illusion of flight by zooming in and out and moving around to a greater extent than usual. Although drawing some criticism from the persnickety, the results generally were excellent.

Blocks of styrofoam ice were used to recreate the crystalline world of Krypton and the Fortress of Solitude. The plains of Alberta, Canada, stood in for the wheat fields of Kansas. Luthor's underground headquarters in New York's Grand Central Station actually was built in Pinewood Studios in England.

The basic plot of *Superman* covers all the essentials in the Superman mythos: the explosion of Krypton; the missile carrying baby Kal-El; Ma and Pa Kent; the *Daily Planet*, Lois and Jimmy (Margot Kidder and Marc McClure)—and, of course, Lex Luthor (Gene Hackman). Luthor's plan is to blow up California's coastline with missiles and create his own shoreline. He gets Superman to "drop in" on his headquarters by threatening to destroy Metropolis, then traps him with Kryptonite. Luthor has a second missile which is arbitrarily, but conveniently, aimed at Hackensack, New Jersey, where the mother of his moll, Eve Teschmacher (Valerie Perrine), lives. Naturally, Eve switches sides to save dear old mom, and Superman is soon free to save Hackensack, as well as California and the world.

Along the way the viewer is treated to a number of highlights, such as the Kents' discovery of baby Kal-El and the wonderful scene in which the child lifts a vehicle off of Pa Kent (Glenn Ford) when the jack fails. Jonathan Kent's death after having a heart-to-heart talk with Clark is moving, and indeed all the scenes in Smallville have a

Above: Superman goes into action.

41

sweep and majesty to them thanks to Geoffrey Unsworth's stunning photography—sunlit plains, smoky grasslands, awesome vistas—and John Williams's poignant musical score. In fact, Williams's sweeping score gives the film a depth and sensitivity it otherwise might not have had. There are also a lot of thrilling, well-executed action scenes (the helicopter accident; Superman flying after the missiles), and an excellent montage in which Superman corners a cat burglar on a skyscraper, stops some thieves escaping in a boat, retrieves a young girl's cat from a tree, and replaces a lightning-shattered engine under the wing of a plane—all in a night's work.

The most romantic sequence in the film occurs when Superman takes Lois Lane on a flight over Metropolis and through the clouds. She reacts like a schoolgirl in the presence of a god. Reeve/Superman "flies" well, using his arms and legs as rudders, but the Man of Steel doesn't show much common sense when he rescues Lois from the helicopter that dangles from the roof of a skyscraper. When he catches the falling reporter in his arms, he isn't moving at the same downward speed as she is; in real life, every bone in her body would have been broken.

The ending has one of Luthor's missiles hitting the San Andreas fault and causing a massive earthquake, which is harrowingly presented: Superman prevents a tottering bus from falling from a suspension bridge, uses his own body to replace the broken track so that a streamliner can pass safely, stops Jimmy Olsen from tumbling off the edge of a dam, and halts an imminent flood by employing some well-placed boulders. All of this is presented with dramatic flair and eye-popping special effects.

The earthquake sequence generated some controversy in that Lois Lane is "killed" when her car falls into a chasm and is swallowed up, but Superman goes back in time (by circling the globe repeatedly at tremendous speed) and saves her. We have to assume that Superman did not simply let hundreds of people he had saved from floods and bridges die so that he could rescue Lois, but somehow managed to squeeze in one more incredible act with all the others—although the editing never makes this clear. Superman also defies the edict of his father Jor-El (Marlon Brando) against "changing history" to a certain extent. But the big question is: How did Superman even know he was capable of breaking the time barrier? This ability is never referred to previously (although Superman crossed the barrier frequently in the comic books).

There are other questionable moments in the movie. A probable holdover from the original too-many-cooks-spoil-the-broth script, the bumbling shenanigans of Luthor,

Top: Superman takes Lois Lane (Margot Kidder) for a famous ride through the clouds.

Above: The 400th "anniversary" issue of *Superman*. Copyright © 1984 DC Comics.

Eve Teschmacher, and, particularly, Lex's nitwit assistant Otis (Ned Beatty), really lower the tone of the whole picture. Having Lex Luthor portrayed as a comical villain—like something out of the *Batman* TV show of the sixties—is a major deficit. As critic Steven Dimeo put it: "To place the villains in a parody and still try to make Superman a believable mortal reduces our hero to his enemy's subterranean level." Camping up Luthor and company is really inappropriate and unnecessary. The picture would have been much stronger with less cartoony antagonists; even the comic books had stronger opponents (and Luthor himself was rarely if ever portrayed as if he were a slumming stand-up comic).

Another flaw is that neither Superman nor Clark are ever portrayed as three-dimensional characters, except perhaps when young Clark (Jeff East) shows a very real resentment over the treatment accorded him by the other kids and his inability to *show* them his abilities. Even the most outlandish fantasy characters can still be flesh-and-blood human beings at heart, if they are written that way. When Clark shows up in Metropolis years later, his undignified "dufus" routine seems rather odd. He never acted like that at eighteen, and surely his father wouldn't have wanted it that way, so why need he bother playing the nerd?

Christopher Reeve, however, is able to pull it off. A limited actor, Reeve has sex appeal that undoubtedly adds to the appeal of the film and character for certain viewers. As Clark he is "cute" and charming; as Superman he combines a boyish sweetness with an authoritative—but not boorishly macho—masculinity. Reeve subsequently has tried for more serious roles with varying degrees of success, but one suspects that his Superman will remain his greatest achievement. Not a bad legacy—although *George* Reeves would probably not have agreed. Reeve is certainly more effective in his part than the eternally overrated Marlon Brando as Jor-El, giving another of his patented brooding and monotonous performances. Margot Kidder is fine as the brash but likable Lois Lane, and Marc McClure is the best Jimmy Olsen of all: not too old, not too dopey, but just right. Jackie Cooper's Perry White may not erase the memory of the TV series' John Hamilton, but this veteran actor gives his usual polished performance.

For the most part, the effects are superior. In addition to the aforementioned sequences, there is an excellent bit with young Clark racing with a train that utilizes some standard fast motion but is quite effective and clever. And the shot of Superman in a fiery underground lifting a massive plate so that he can seal the San Andreas fault is worthy of note. The more effects-based (and biased) critics found fault with some parts, however. "In some scenes, though, the traveling mattes and process photography behind twenty-six-year-old Christopher Reeve lack the same kind of resolution as his own body. No matter how rigid he keeps himself, the background grounds us then only to the reality of the movie theater seats," wrote Steven Dimeo. "And much too often we can distinguish the miniature models in long shots."

How serious—and damaging—are these special effects "flaws" in *Superman*? Not very. The average moviegoer wouldn't even be aware of them, and even the more knowledgeable critics, including this writer, may concede that whatever *comparative* sloppiness exists in *Superman* does little to detract from its value as grand entertainment. There is hardly a multimillion-dollar special effects epic (including the overrated *Star Wars* series) that doesn't have some flaws which are apparent to the trained eye. In *Superman,* these negligible defects don't add up to much when stacked against such generally expert special effects work and powerful images. The film's greatest flaw may actually be its anti-intellectual quality; otherwise, it is quite a magical and wonderful movie fantasy, one that seems to be improving with age. It is ironic that its inspiration was a derivative comic book figure dreamed up out of spit and chewing gum by two modestly talented juveniles.

The film brought out some interesting reactions from the critics. Most agreed with Rex Reed (who has a cameo as himself in the film): "*Superman* is both the perfect fairy tale for grown-ups and an exciting, rollicking-enough cinematic blockbuster to bring out the child in every age group." He conceded that "anyone who goes to *Superman* expecting Eugene O'Neill is a fool for starters."

Vincent Canby of the *New York Times* wrote, "There isn't a thought in the film's head that would be out of place on a box of Wheaties." Surprisingly, he preferred the *Batman* TV show-like comedy scenes with Hackman. The critic for *Cineaste* ranted that "Superman is a product of super hype and a massive poverty of imagination. The TV reruns are more interesting."

Granted, there is a contingent of fans and some critics who maintain that the old Superman serials and the television program are superior to the motion pictures of the seventies and eighties. This would make sense if those old serials and TV shows were *good*, but they are only mediocre at best, as any discerning viewer can see. Often the old stuff *is* much better than the new—the 1933 *King Kong* is vastly superior to Dino De Laurentiis's overblown 1976 remake, for instance—but that is not *always* the case. But try telling that to a certain ilk of film buff whose opinions are based more on nostalgia and emotion than on any particular facility for criticism. [9]

On one point these stubborn buffs are correct, however. *Superman* and its three sequels have the same irritating inconsistencies and implausibilities as their serial predecessors, something that's far more intolerable in a megabuck movie than a cheapjack Columbia chapterplay. This is the result of having (as with the serials) so many different writers working on and "improving" each screenplay. When the directors, producers, and actors add their own two cents, it's a wonder anything coherent comes out of it at all. "Big" movies tend to get away from their creators.

Superman shows some influence from the old serials, particularly when Otis is followed into the subway by a pursuing agent and disappears into a "wall" that leads into Luthor's headquarters. When the agent tries to follow, the wall pushes outward and knocks him to the tracks and into the path of an oncoming train. The underground "labyrinth," as well as the pursuer's rather gruesome death, are very similar to the stuff of cliff-hangers. The humor of Otis's manner and appearance, followed by a grisly murder, make for an odd juxtaposition.

[9]The more extreme of these buffs seem to spend all their time going from one convention to another, have no knowledge of or interest in the world beyond old movies, and indeed will ignore attending to personal hygiene if it means they will miss a certain obscure and terrible feature.

Above: Kirk Alyn and Noel Neill, the first Superman and Lois Lane, had cameos in *Superman* in 1978.

Superman won a special Oscar for Visual Effects—which it deserved, but Richard Donner was not happy that it received so few nominations. Geoffrey Unsworth's superb cinematography was ignored, as was the production design by John Barry. "They put up pictures like *California Suite*—duplications of the Beverly Hills Hotel," raged Donner. *"Big deal!"*

With the large box-office grosses of *Superman*, a sequel was inevitable. Donner had already shot much of it ("eighty percent," he claims) while filming the first installment. (At some point it was decided to turn the very long screenplay into two pictures.) In spite of his contributions to the sequel, Donner's services were dispensed with by the Salkinds, and he was replaced by Guy Hamilton (whom Donner had replaced initially). By the time the sequel was finished, however, the director of record was Richard Lester.

The sets were very elaborate for *Superman II*. The Fortress of Solitude was completely rebuilt for the sequel, although parts of it were actually a matte painting[10] and did not exist on the set. A miniature New York skyline was built in Pinewood Studios with hundreds of tiny cars on long treadmills standing in for streets. Every car model had working headlights. The base of Niagara Falls was recreated on a studio backlot for the scene when Lois jumps into the water to see if Clark will switch to Superman and save her. (A stuntwoman was used for long shots; Margot Kidder appeared in close-ups in calmer water.)

Most spectacular of all was a $10 million life-size recreation of Manhattan's Times Square area, built at Pinewood. This set required 5,500 tons of sand, cement, and tar; a half million feet of scaffolding; 250,000 feet of timber; 6,000 cubic yards of concrete; 10,000 square feet of glass; and 6,600 sheets of plywood. Photographs taken from every possible angle were employed to create 42nd Street and environs down to the smallest detail. A painted backdrop was used at the end of the street, and two small identical models of the area also were constructed. The set and models were employed in *Superman II*'s most memorable sequence: the Times Square battle between Superman and the three Kryptonian villains.

The script was turned into a storyboard containing thousands of drawings, each showing where the people in the shot would be, in which direction they'd be going, and approximately how long each shot would last. When the movie was completed, the editor had over two million feet of film to play around with.

Superman II employed the same front projection process as its predecessor, so that the projected background and actors would move together "in a coordinated manner" to make it look authentic. The "flying crew" would make sure this was happening by consulting video cameras during filming. The compositing of all the elements in a flying or any other special effects sequence was a painstaking frame-by-frame process.

Occasionally the oldest and simplest methods were used: wires. These figured in the climax when Superman throws around the suddenly powerless supervillains. Terence Stamp wasn't crazy about it: he felt it was undeniably dangerous, particularly if one's mind wandered. The peril had its upside, however. "Danger adds to my presence," he said.

---

[10]"Matte" paintings of clouds, skylines, rooftops, etc., are usually painted directly onto a pane of glass which is then positioned in front of the camera in such a way that there is created a perfect illusion (a mountain behind the set, for instance).

In *Superman II*, an explosion frees Stamp and his evil Kryptonian cohorts, seen briefly at the beginning of *Superman,* from the Phantom Zone wherein they are imprisoned. Possessing the same powers of Superman under a yellow sun, they begin a reign of terror and domination. Superman isn't around to stop them because he has revealed his identity to Lois and given up his powers for her. When he learns of what is happening to his adopted planet, he regains his abilities, takes on the villains, and manages to triumph at the last minute. He then erases the knowledge of his secret identity from Lois's mind with hypnotism.

The screenplay certainly sets up a provocative situation—but one that's also hopelessly contrived, as if solely to show Superman why he must never put his personal feelings ahead of the world's well-being and give up his powers. It makes no sense that he should relinquish them in the first place; his motives are specious at best and are never even examined. In the comic books, Superman was always afraid to reveal his secret identity because he reasoned villains would probably strike back at his loved ones (Jimmy and Lois were always being attacked and kidnapped anyway!), but a powerless Superman could hardly be of use if any vengeance-minded punk came gunning for Clark or Lois. It's such a monumental decision, and it happens so quickly and *casually.* What's worse, Superman learns from Jor-El's spirit that once he uses this (convenient) machine in his fortress to remove his powers, he can *never regain them.* So what happens? He makes a cold, desperate trek as Clark back to the fortress and somehow has them restored. We never learn how or why.

Other problems with *Superman II* are the tiresome comedy relief (more Lex Luthor, of course) and the deliberate pacing. Some of Geoffrey Unsworth's brilliant cinematography, filmed when *Superman* was made, remains, but Robert Paynter's contributions (over two-thirds, reportedly) are not up to his predecessor's level. In many cases, the images are striking not because of the way they're photographed but simply because of the elements within them. *Superman II* lacks the sweep, scope, and beauty of the original, and like the original, substitutes crashing explosive action for depth and inventiveness. Still, it's an extremely entertaining picture and has many standout sequences.

Among them is the Eiffel Tower segment in which Lois clings to the bottom of a descending elevator cage that has a bomb attached to it. After rescuing her, Superman flies the cage off its shaft and hurls it and the bomb into the sun. The whole thrilling sequence is expertly realized. On a quieter level, the scene when the President of the United States (E. G. Marshall in a bad hairpiece) surrenders to the sinister General Zod (Terence Stamp) from Krypton is very effective. "Oh God," says Marshall, kneeling before the general. "*Zod,*" the general corrects him.

The three supervillains are perhaps the best things about *Superman II.* Zod is a callous, condescending, deceptively blasé and evil pseudointellectual with a Napoleon complex. His lady, Ursa (Sarah Douglas), is perhaps even more vicious and cruel, walking about like a sexy, black-leather lizard looking for little bugs on which to

Above: Super-bitch Ursa (Sarah Douglas) discusses with Zod (Terence Stamp) what to do with Lois Lane (Margot Kidder) in *Superman II.*

nibble. Stamp and Douglas are both excellent in their roles, never overplaying, never descending into camp. Hulking Jack O'Halloran as Non has no dialogue, but projects the same kind of brutish presence as Richard Kiel.

Superman II really comes to life during the climactic battle in New York City, which successfully captures the awe and magic of similar scenes as they are done in the comic books. *Cinefantastique* felt this sequence was "quite simply, the finest cinematic transliteration yet of the 'anything's possible' spirit of the comics." It's a breathtaking combination of thrills and movie wizardry, in which manhole covers, buses, huge signs, and cars are employed as weapons. While it could have used tighter editing in spots, it remains the greatest sustained special effects sequence in the series.

In the battle, Superman tries to stop the villains, protect himself, and watch out for concerned citizens of Metropolis who are in the way—all at the same time. Superman kicks Zod into a neon sign several blocks away. Ursa hurls a deadly manhole cover. Innocent citizens are threatened by tons of falling debris. Ursa and Non lift up a bus full of screaming people. Eventually the dastardly supercriminals use their combined superbreaths to create a tremendous wind that sweeps cars and people down the street as if they were no more than twigs. Superman seemingly deserts the city, but he has a trick up his sleeve.

This amazing and meticulous battle was put together by combining a variety of process and live-action shots on the full-size set with shots taken on the miniature one. For instance, the bus was on a chain that was attached to a

crane that pulled it and the bus upward before settling an inch or so. Sarah Douglas held the bus up tight instead of relaxing, and hurt her muscles. She explained to director Lester that for a few seconds you really did feel as if you had superstrength.

Bottom right: Superman faces off against General Zod in *Superman II*.

Bottom left: Superman gets the better of General Zod.

Top right: Returning the Stars and Stripes to the White House in *Superman II*.

When the bus was thrown and overturned, quick cuts of the model bus on the miniature street would be spliced into the action. The small cars and buildings were extremely detailed and realistic. For the windstorm scene, huge

fans and talented stunt people were brought in to make an extremely memorable—and amusing—sequence. Although the film was carefully storyboarded, once the effect and stunts were figured out, Lester ad-libbed some of the gags and actions right on the set.

Superman finally overcomes Zod and company by feigning defeat and putting himself back into the molecule chamber that will strip him of his powers. Zod and Luthor don't realize that Superman has switched things around so that only those *outside* the chamber would be affected. Zod and Non are easily defeated when stripped of their powers, and Lois delivers a very satisfying knockout punch to the jaw of superbitch Ursa.

Of course, Superman realizes that he can never again leave the world unprotected—not even for Lois. (Why a serious relationship between the two of them would preclude his having powers is never explained.) "Don't tell me I'll meet someone," Lois cries. "You're a hard act to follow. When it comes to you, I'm selfish and I'm jealous of the whole world." Not only does Lois lose a boyfriend—or any memory of what they shared together—but she never even gets to find out what it's like to make love to a Man of Steel, as Superman is devoid of his powers when they go to bed in his fortress midway through the picture.

Superman II not only got good reviews, but many critics preferred it to *Superman* and found it more fun. The *New York Times* noted: "*Superman II* works because it's 'about' the dreams of superdom we all have, but more probably because it's about good humor and, often, wit." The *Daily News* critic liked the picture but wrote that it lacked "the original film's structured lyricism and becomes more of an episodic James Bond orgy of mindless destruction." It was suggested that enough was enough and Hollywood should "leave the budget bankrolls to more challenging movie ideas."

Instead, Hollywood came up with *Superman III* (1983), which costars Richard Pryor and is essentially a comedy-thriller with no more depth than an old serial, but with a lot more flair, genuine humor, and newfangled movie magic. Despite its undeniable silliness, *Superman III* does manage to capture some of the "superhuman majesty" of the character.

The comic tone is set during the opening credits, "a long sidewalk sequence of people and things bumping and falling in a train of domino calamities," as one critic put it. The picture was directed by Richard Lester, who helmed parts of *Superman II*, and written by David and Leslie Newman, who provided much of the (ill-advised) comedy relief in *Superman*.

Above: The superb comic book style super-battle from *Superman II*.

48

The springboard of the plot is Gus Gorman (Pryor), a computer wizard who concocts a brilliant plan to steal millions from his boss, Ross Webster (Robert Vaughn). Instead of prosecuting Gorman, Webster decides to use

his employee's special talents on certain illegal and nefarious schemes of his own. First, Gorman takes over a Vulcan weather satellite to destroy the Colombian coffee crop. When Superman intervenes, Gorman creates artificial Kryptonite which turns the Man of Steel into an evil bastard. (He does such things as straightening the Leaning Tower of Pisa.) In return for disposing of the "good" Superman in this fashion, Gorman gets Webster to build him a giant supercomputer which a "reformed" Superman must battle in the climax.

Amusing running gags abound: there's a vendor who keeps switching his statues of the Tower of Pisa, only to have Superman show up and either straighten the tower or push it back into its original leaning position; and there's a couple who win a *Daily Planet* contest tour only to wind up in Colombia, where Pryor's computer-activated hurricane is running riot.

The picture is chock-full of amazing stunts, sequences, and effects. Superman uses his freeze-breath to ice up an entire lake so that he can carry it to the site of a chemical fire and let it melt to douse the flames. (Although one has to wonder why he simply didn't use his freeze-breath on the fire itself, as well as on the beakers of deadly liquid that, he's warned by workers, must not get too hot.) An excellent sequence shows the temporarily evil Superman "symbolically" regaining his right mind and decent disposition by battling his alter ego Clark in a junkyard. The location, editing, music, and fine effects work add to the sequence's fun. Superman uses his heat vision to drop a huge magnet on Clark and stuffs him in a compactor. Clark on the other hand, throws a bunch of tires over and around his alter ego. "Good" Clark eventually wins this obviously psychological battle.

The climax is pretty exciting. The supercomputer draws power from the country's electric supply and turns Webster's evil sister Vera (Annie Ross) into a metal-woman hybrid, its drone. Superman eventually defeats the computer by using acid on it. There is more marvelous effects work in this lengthy and elaborate battle, including missiles and power webs. The computer itself is a multilevel monstrosity with derricklike towers, a huge second-story control room, and lots of consoles and cables.

Bottom: Superman needs a break from his battle with the super-computer in *Superman III*.

Top: Superman gives Richard Pryor a lift in *Superman III*.

This time out, Reeve seems to play Clark too broadly. (Of course, "Clark" *is* just a role that the Man of Steel assumes.) Robert Vaughn as the smooth, wealthy Webster gives his lines just the right delivery, and is amusing and authoritative without ever overdoing it. Annie Ross is a formidable Vera, and Pamela Stephenson makes a delectable Lorelei Ambrosia. It is never explained why Lorelei pretends to be dumber than she is, but it is implied that she and Superman share a night of passion when he's in his evil mode. "That wasn't me," he tells her later. (This equation of sexuality with "evil" seems to be pervasive in American society.)

Superman III is more Pryor's picture than Reeve's or even Superman's, and serves primarily as a showcase for this gifted actor-comedian's impersonations and general shtick. Ironically, Pryor's most sensational scene—when he inadvertently skis right off the artificial slope on Webster's roof and manages to survive a scary and funny fall

from a skyscraper—is due more to a stuntman's genius than to Pryor's.

Margot Kidder's Lois Lane is reduced to a walk-on in *Superman III*.[11] Clark goes back to Smallville and rekindles his romance with childhood sweetheart Lana Lang (well played by the talented Annette O'Toole), who is now a single mother with a young son. Superman saves the boy from being run over by a threshing machine, but nothing much ever comes of his new relationship with Lana. Although she becomes Perry White's secretary at the end of *Superman III*, she is nowhere to be found in *Superman IV*.

Superman III is a perfectly acceptable piece of entertaining, eye-dazzling fluff, but most critics found it to be barely mediocre. "This entry lacks the stylish lensing that characterized the first two Superman pics," wrote *Variety*. Rex Reed was blunter: "Of all the summer trash we're drawing in, *Superman III* is the stupidest and trashiest. Superman has run out of diesel and is now flying on cheap muscatel... the sections of the film never blend into any cohesive entity." *Cinefantastique* found the film "just plain silly.... a supercomputer which can analyze and reproduce an alien substance, turn a human into a robot, and toss about the galaxy's strongest man, but can't defend itself against an axe attack?" What might be more offensive is that because Gus helps Superman at the very end of the film, he gets off without any jail sentence or prosecution! (Perhaps the *Superman* films are more realistic than we imagine.)

[11]In the November/December 1982 issue, *Cinefantastique* reported that Kidder was paid $200,000 for two brief scenes by the producers, the Salkinds, because Richard Pryor was her boyfriend at the time.

Above: Preparing to stop a runaway train in *Superman IV*.

Superman IV: The Quest for Peace opened four years later (1987). In this, a summit crisis develops, scaring schoolkids—and everyone else—with the threat of nuclear destruction. One young boy, Jeremy, sends a letter to Superman in which he asks the Man of Steel to do something about the problem, and our hero addresses the United Nations on world peace (in a scene which is as oddly awe inspiring as it is amusing), announcing that he plans to rid the universe of all nuclear weaponry—which he then proceeds to do. (His flinging all of these missiles, which he has gathered together into an enormous net, into the sun, is a highlight of the picture.)

Naturally, many of the world's less savory leaders object to this strenuously and appeal to Lex Luthor to do something about Superman. Lex's solution is to create his own superpowered being, Nuclear Man (Mark Pillow), to take on the Man of Steel. The "science" involved in this process is bizarre, to say the least. Luthor combines a piece of protoplasm, grown from a strand of Superman's hair, with a metallic piece of "uniform" (which a computer will somehow "grow" into a complete outfit) and sends this into the sun, which spits out a fully clothed Nuclear Man!

Nuclear Man and Superman square off in an exciting battle that is sort of a miniature version of the Times Square fight in *Superman II*—lots of flair, action, and fun. At one point, Nuclear Man steals the Statue of Liberty from its base and drops it onto Manhattan—but luckily Superman catches it. A sequence in which Nuclear Man turns his powers on the cops and a SWAT team and then smashes up through the *Daily Planet* building, is fine, although a battle between the two superhumans on the moon is a little disappointing. (You can almost see the platform on which the actors are standing when they're supposed to be in Outer Space.)

The effects in this film came in for a critical drubbing, even by those who are generally quite uninformed about such matters. The main difference is that the visual effects supervisor, Harrison Ellenshaw, didn't have access to the front projection equipment used in the first three films because the Salkinds were not the producers of *Superman IV*.[12] He had to resort to the more standard bluebacking process. (Flying miniature figures were also employed.) As *Cinefantastique* noted, "there are, however, more forward motion shots of [Superman] flying up past the camera now, a move that's hard to do with front projection."

Another highlight of the film is a reprise from the first picture of Superman's romantic flight through the sky with Lois Lane (who returns as the love interest), done here entirely with forty-four blue-screen shots. Ellenshaw

[12]Cannon owners/producers Menachem Golan and Yoram Globus bought the sequel rights from the Salkinds. Warner Bros. released the picture, but it was a Cannon Group production. The director was Sidney J. Furie.

Above: Superman assures a young boy that he will do his best to save the world from itself.

recalled: "That sequence was a monster. Doing it blue-screen, we had to time and correct Reeve's costume to balance the blue in his suit. Lois flew in a pink dress, so any little variation in color would cause one thing to go out of balance with the other."

Focusing on some of the less successful effects work, the critics seemed completely blind to some of the stunning shots in the film, such as when Nuclear Man crosses his arms and floats down backward into the middle

of a volcano crater. The aforementioned New York battle scenes are effective, and Superman's flight with Lois is simply breathtaking. Some critics get so caught up in the minutiae of effects that they fail to see the larger, or aesthetic, image. This writer is as effects-knowledgeable as the next one, but finds those in *Superman IV* more than adequate in creating a quite magical fantasy experience.

There are nice scenes in the picture that have nothing to do with effects, such as when Clark visits the Kent farm, which he has decided as a gesture of love and loyalty to his late father, he will sell only to a legitimate farmer and not to a developer. A subplot involving the takeover of the *Daily Planet* by a Rupert Murdoch type (Sam Wanamaker) and his daughter Lacy (Mariel Hemingway) engenders an amusing double date between Lacy and Clark and Lois and Superman which really keeps the Man of Steel hopping in an effort to be *two* people in the same place at the same time.

The script also has its share of dopey moments, such as when Superman saves a runaway train on which not one passenger thinks of pulling the emergency cord. Lacy manages to be able to *breathe* in outer space when Nuclear Man kidnaps her, and it is hard to imagine that Superman could *rebuild* the shattered Great Wall of China by using his X-ray vision—or any other kind of heretofore unknown and overly convenient special "vision" power. Sloppy continuity indicates that scenes might have been cut from the film before release. It's never made clear, for instance, exactly *why* Nuclear Man wants to kidnap Lacy, or *how* Superman knows that's who his opponent is after when he shows up at the newspaper. And Nuclear Man registers no shock or surprise at Superman's apparent return from the dead after the former had assumed he had disposed of his enemy for good.

There's nothing wrong with the production values and other aspects of the film, however. Production designer John Graysmark's top-notch work is highlighted by, among other elements, Luthor's stylish skyscraper headquarters; and Alexander Courage's adaptations of John Williams's themes are wonderful. The music during the battle between Superman and his nuclear adversary is particularly good. Margot Kidder really scores as Lois

Above: Mariel Hemingway stands up to Nuclear Man (Mark Pillow) in *Superman IV*

in this entry, and it must be noted that Gene Hackman's performance as the unfortunately comical Luthor is undeniably fine and amusing. Although Mark Pillow has no dialogue as Nuclear Man, his facial expressions and body language get across the impact, strength, and fury of the character most vividly. Jon Cryer is very good as Luthor's nephew, a punk valley boy who is also played for laughs, and Sam Wanamaker is as professional as ever as David Warfield. Mariel Hemingway makes a very sophisticated and sexy Lacy Warfield, proof that a talented actress can make something out of *any* part.

The film ends with Superman dropping the defeated Nuclear Man into a reactor, depositing Luthor back in prison (and Cryer in a reformatory), and deciding to let mankind keep the peace for themselves—if they can. He has apparently had enough of playing God.

The critics had had enough of Superman. In New York, *Superman IV* did not receive *one single* favorable review out of eight. (Of course, it had no local press screening, which didn't help.) There was the usual carping over the special effects, although one critic did suggest that "there's life in the old boy yet." Oddly, many didn't think the film was funny enough, despite Hackman and Cryer. Those who hated such camp stuff as the 1966 *Batman* now seemed dissatisfied because the Superman series wasn't more like it!

For all its flaws and its less epic quality, *Superman IV* is still a well-made and highly entertaining motion picture, a cinematic visualization of the kind of science-dumb but colorful stories that could have been found in the Superman comic about a decade before, when Luthor was into technology and opponents similar to Nuclear Man were very common. The film works as a simple and simpleminded (in spite of its antinuclear message) fantasy, for which no apology is required.

Some felt they were owed more than an apology, however: writers Barry Taff and Kenneth Stoller initiated a lawsuit when they felt Christopher Reeve had appropriated their story idea for *Superman IV*.[13] In their treatment, which was sent to and read by Reeve, were several major plot points (including the basic nuclear disarmament premise) that later turned up in the movie. Reeve was then said to have had a meeting with producer Menachem Golan in which he allegedly told Golan "his" idea for *Superman IV*. When these various elements that were to be part of *Superman IV* became known throughout the film community, many assumed Taff and Stoller had sold their treatment to Golan's Cannon Films. Such was not the case, however.

Taff tried unsuccessfully to get an injunction that would prevent the film's release. When he and Stoller finally saw the script for the picture in 1986, they sued for $45 million in damages. The question became whether Reeve had simply and only borrowed an "idea." But weren't even ideas valuable enough to be copyrighted in Hollywood? Taff made the following statement: "It's ironic that the man who portrays the character and image of the most powerful being in the universe who stands for truth, justice, and the American way, resorts to theft and plagiarism in his attempt at creative effort."

Apparently a Los Angeles judge didn't think Taff and Stoller's claims had enough validity: he dismissed the lawsuit on October 23, 1990.

---

[13]Reeve was credited with the story of *Superman IV*, along with coscreenwriters Lawrence Konner and Mark Rosenthal.

Meanwhile the world is still awaiting—although perhaps not with bated breath—the next Superman feature. First it was announced that Albert Pyun would direct a new sequel for Cannon in 1988. He said at the time, "We're going for a much more realistic, much richer-looking vision of Superman. It'll be something you can get really involved in, not just effects and in-jokes." Instead, Pyun worked on a new Captain America feature, while Cannon Films suggested that Christopher Reeve would write, direct, and star in *Superman V*. Then it was said that Reeve would direct a brand-new actor in *The New Superman*, as he felt he was too old for the role (although he's not as old as George Reeves was). Time will tell if any new Superman movies will materialize.

The Superman comic book sold well enough throughout the seventies and early eighties, but it never got anyone excited; most people just bought it to complete their collections. The Number One Super-Hero was outclassed by countless others. Superman plodded along with only the occasional exciting moment—rehauls for the major villains Luthor and Braniac in the forty-fifth anniversary issue of *Action* (#544), for instance—until decreasing sales prompted DC to do a complete overhaul of the Man of Steel himself, in a miniseries by John Byrne entitled, appropriately enough, *The Man of Steel*.

DC meant business—this was going to be a major revision and updating of the character—and signaled this by publishing a two-part farewell to the "old" Superman in *Superman* #423 (September 1986), the last issue, and *Action* #583 (September 1986). This was an excellent "imaginary" story pitting Superman against virtually all of his major and minor villains of the last few decades, with a guest cast of practically every supporting player. Set in 1997, the entertaining and suspenseful story by Alan Moore asks the question "Whatever Happened to the Man of Tomorrow?" and has a framing sequence in which a reporter calls on Lois Lane Elliot and her husband Jordan to ask her about the inexplicable disappearance and presumed death of Superman years earlier.

The ultimate villain in this is that fifth-dimensional imp, Mr. Mxyzptlk, who, it turns out, does not actually look like the jockey-size vaudevillian with the bowler hat we've all come to know and love, but is really a large red demonic figure glowing with malevolent energy. Because Superman, having vowed never to take a life, is forced to kill Mr. M, he exposes himself to gold Kryptonite, loses his powers, and becomes a mortal man in a conclusion that is not only silly but the story's one negative note. Moore has Superman happily married to Lois in his new identity of Jordan Elliot, bouncing his baby boy on his lap, and reveling in his normal, dull, utterly prosaic existence. After being able to soar through the heavens? Ridiculous!

Writer-artist John Byrne had already developed quite a fan following by working on such Marvel Comics series as *Fantastic Four, Alpha Flight,* and the *Uncanny X-Men* (artist only) when his *Man of Steel* miniseries was released. It streamlined the character, concept, and mythos, dropping the deadwood and more inane aspects of the past nearly fifty years. Just as Clark would no longer pretend to be a wimp, conversely Superman was made less invincible (he needed to breathe air while in space, for instance). Byrne worked with writer Marv Wolfman in creating this "new" Superman. The miniseries and subsequent new *Superman* comic was met with mixed reactions, but was generally approved of by the fans.

Opposite: Planting the American Flag on the moon in *Superman IV*.

Superman's archenemy Lex Luthor was also revamped. Instead of a crazed scientist with zany weapons and costumes, Luthor became a portly financier who hides a criminal personality behind the facade of a respectable businessman. He is obsessed with destroying Superman, who knows the truth about him. In one continued story, Luthor engineers a hostile takeover of a research laboratory. That episode prompted a New York *Daily News* story in which securities research analysts and others commented on the basic veracity of the tale (*Superman #31*, May 1989). Byrne also brought in one of the most interesting new members of Superman's supporting cast, Captain Maggie Sawyer, a brave police officer who happens to be a lesbian. This particular aspect of her character has been handled subtly and  sympathetically, with Superman taking Maggie's side after learning that, due to her sexual orientation, her ex-husband won a custody battle for their daughter, in *Superman #15*. (One suspects it will be a long time before Superman movies or TV shows deal with such controversial material, if ever—more proof that comic books can be more mature than their media counterparts.)

Another provocative story appeared in *Action #592–593*, with Superman at the mercy of a character named Sleez, who takes away the Man of Steel's will and costars him in a porn movie with the beauteous superheroine, Big Barda. Fortunately (or unfortunately, as the case may be), Barda's husband, Mr. Miracle, arrives to break things up before she and Superman can do anything more than kiss on the bed in the just-the-essentials set. (Perhaps only a writer for an independent comics company or for a comic strictly geared for "mature" readers could have done this titillating but disappointing plot line raunchy justice. Although there have been indications that Superman is not a virgin, he remains a bit of a stiff in all ways but one.)

After a couple of years, Byrne left Luthor to return to Marvel Comics, with the result being a slight dip in quality in the series. In its current state, *Superman* is interesting and collectible, but not really "special." Despite some fine stories and excellent artwork, some of yesteryear's silliness seems to be creeping back in. Still, there have been interesting developments, such as the engagement of Clark and Lois (which was actually reported with a big headline on page three of the *New York Post* in October 1990), and the apparent suicide of Lex Luthor, although one imagines he'll be back. Superman also has *finally* told Lois Lane that he and Clark Kent are one and the same person. Dan Jurgens, Roger Stern, and Jerry Ordway (who also contributes some top-notch artwork) are among the current chroniclers of Superman.

Superboy, a separate comic depicting the adventures of Superman as a youth, began in 1949. These early adventures presented Clark Kent as a decent young fellow with a double identity problem, as well as a snooping girlfriend, Lana Lang, who was always trying to uncover his secret identity. The most interesting Superboy stories had him visiting the Legion of Super-Heroes in the far-flung future, where he became just one out of a

Above: John Byrne's first issue of the "new" *Superman*, a valuable collectible. Copyright © 1987 DC Comics, Inc.

whole organization of teens with superpowers. Eventually this group became so popular that the title of Superboy's magazine was changed to *Superboy and the Legion of Super-Heroes.* The Legion eventually got its own magazine, which is running to this day in an altered format. Superboy's magazine was discontinued, and he became relegated to occasional guest-star status, particularly in tricky time-travel stories in which he meets up with his own adult self.

The last of these occasions was the direct result of the aforementioned *Crisis on Infinite Earths* maxiseries. To

explain away the inconsistency in Superman's background[14] and create one definitive Superman, it was decided to eliminate Superboy from continuity altogether. A four-part story in 1987[15] revealed that "Superboy" was not and had never been the real Superman's boyhood self, but rather someone from an "alternate time loop" created by the Legion's arch-foe, the Time Trapper. The story ended movingly with this bogus Superboy dying in the arms of his longtime buddy Mon-El. Since the "destruction" of Superboy was retroactive, recent Legion stories have eliminated all references to him in their origin and other past tales, substituting another heroic figure, Lar Gand.

Ironically, DC Comics had just finished "killing off" their long-lived Superboy when a syndicated television series featuring the Lad of Steel debuted in 1988 to the surprise of everyone. This was produced by Alexander and Ilya Salkind, who had sold film rights to Cannon Films, but retained the television rights to Superman. (It may or may not be argued that "Superboy" is a different character.) The show did not have an auspicious debut ("the dull story could easily have been from the old 1950s *Superman* series," wrote one critic), but it gradually gathered up speed and admirers.

The first actor to play Superboy was John Haymes Newton, who gave the part a sexy, appealing insolence (this Superboy is no Boy Scout, he seemed to be saying), but due to a salary dispute, he was replaced at the start of the second season by Gerard Christopher, who has similar male model looks and makes a convincing Boy of Steel, but who oddly chooses (or was directed) to play Clark—now in college—in a regressively and exaggerated, nerdy fashion. (Apparently no one has shown Gerard the comic books.) Nevertheless, his youthful Clark is likable, as is Stacy Haiduk's Lana Lang.

Although the series comes dangerously close to descending into pure camp in many episodes, generally the program has much more color and flair than the old Superman series. *Superboy* doesn't shy away from presenting real comic book-style stories, and the often costumed villains have special powers or come from outer space—they are never the prosaic thugs of George Reeves's series. Some of the stories are played fairly straight or have clever plot lines. Even the campier ones have their amusing moments, although many are mediocre ("The Yellow Peri") or downright ludicrous ("Bizarro"). Michael Callan turned in a good performance in his first appearance as

[14]Remember: the Earth-1 Superman started out as Superboy, while the Earth-2 Superman never *was* a Superboy.

[15]*Legion of Super-Heroes* #37–38, *Action* #591 and *Superman* (new series) #8.

Above: Classic issue of *Superboy* from the sixties. Copyright © 1969 National Periodical Publications, Inc.

Metallo, and Kevin Bernhardt makes a very striking and intense Byron, vampiric son of Dracula. The actors do the best they can with generally overripe melodramatic dialogue straight out of a comic book.

The third season of the show began with a clever spoof of the Sally Jessy Raphael program. Host Judy is doing a show on "bizarre" relationships, but out in space Bizzaro overhears her, misunderstands what she's saying, and crashes into the studio crying that he wants love. This leads to a young Lex Luthor (effectively if obnoxiously portrayed by Sherman Howard) building not only "The Bride of Bizarro" (in a sequence reminiscent of *Bride of Frankenstein*) but a whole squadron of exploding Luthor duplicates. A more serious episode in which a bigfoot-type monster turns out to be a disfigured former nuclear worker had a message about the immorality in illegally dumping irradiated water into rivers. An alternate reality story line had Superboy following Luthor into another dimension where Luthor is considered a hero and Superboy the villain (in some rather contrived developments), then entering yet another dimension where Superboy is an evil dictator and Lex Luthor and Lana Lang are freedom fighters trying to destroy him. The story was just the kind of thing that used to appear in Superman comic books.

The special effects in *Superboy* are miles beyond the old serials and 1950s Superman TV series, and are almost as good as the special effects in the Superman movies, if much more limited. Many of these effects are videotaped and then blended into the live action, giving them that certain look of immediacy that only tape can provide. The flying and falling scenes are convincing, and the aforementioned alternate dimension episode featured seamless "double" shots and a striking sequence showing Superboy and Luthor flying between dimensions. The effects have become more elaborate with the third season.

Superboy employs some honest-to-goodness comics writers to work on scripts, so it has that real comic book flavor that the old Superman series was lacking. It is still distressingly juvenile, with one-dimensional characters and far too many contrivances (hence it is comic bookish in both the good and bad sense of the term), but many younger viewers undoubtedly have fallen in love with it. It does deserve high marks for at least attempting to be the TV equivalent of a comic book series.

Not surprisingly, DC Comics started up a new *Superboy* series once the show had become a success. Wisely, it was decided to leave the series strictly outside of normal DC continuity to avoid confusion with their other Superman magazines. It appears to be geared for preteen readers and is of little interest to anyone who is not a fan of the series.

Supergirl first appeared in *Action* #252 (May 1959) and soon became a fixture in the Superman line of comics. She took over the lead spot in *Adventure* comics for quite a few issues and then graduated to her own series. In spite of her longevity, Supergirl never emerged as a major figure in the DC canon, certainly not saleswise.

Above: The latest *Superboy* comic is based on the TV series and is outside of DC continuity. This is the collector's item first issue. Copyright © 1990 DC Comics, Inc.

Opposite: *Superboy*, the TV series, with John Haymes Newton.

Supergirl's origin is as follows: When Krypton blew up, a large chunk of it, containing Argo City, flew away intact. This chunk turns into deadly Kryptonite, which eventually kills all of the inhabitants, except little Kara,  whose scientist father Zor-El sends her off to Earth—and Superman—in a rocket. (Sound familiar?) She takes the identity of Linda Lee and enters the Midvale Orphanage, secretly doing good deeds until Superman feels it's time the world knows of her existence. Otto Binder wrote the story, which was illustrated by Al Plastino. Later stories revealed that Kara's parents were still alive, and the usual alterations and adjustments to continuity were made.

Supergirl's career was essentially undistinguished but for two or three occasions. Artist-writer Mike Sekowsky took over her strip in *Adventure* for several issues in the early seventies, and almost managed to give her the same shot in the arm he would give *Wonder Woman*. In these engaging stories, Supergirl faces a variety of female adversaries, including Nasty, Lex Luthor's niece; the nefarious Black Flame; and the diabolical and sadistic Starfire, who manages to strip Supergirl of much of her power for long stretches and even hires a handsome hoodlum to break Supergirl's heart.

Supergirl's demise in *Crisis on Infinite Earths* #7 (October 1985), while helping to save the universe, was extremely effective and poignant due to Marv Wolfman's sensitive scripting and George Perez's powerful artwork. Perhaps the true tragedy of Supergirl, however, is that her character never quite realized her potential. Although a recent story in *Superman* featured a bogus Supergirl from an alternate universe, as of this writing the character is dead and buried. The lackluster box office of the *Supergirl* movie would indicate that this situation will not change.

Alexander and Illya Salkind brought out *Supergirl* in 1984, hoping to match the success of their Superman features while offering the audience a pretty blonde respite from the hunky Man of Steel. It not only made less money, it also was positively (and unfairly) savaged by the critics. "Superschlock," decreed the *New York Post*, while the *Village Voice*'s mixed review read, in part: "A very funny, bad movie, more entertaining for adults than kids. The effects are particularly awful, stuck in the globular aesthetics of '60s light shows." But Kathleen Carroll of the *Daily News* thought *Supergirl* was "lively, escapist fun—especially if you enjoy seeing a woman do a Superman's job."

Carroll's opinion was the more reasoned. It was easy to carp on the mindlessness and silliness of *Supergirl*, but the movie was not meant to be anything other than some frothy fun. As usual, the effects were hardly as bad as the critics suggested. Knocking the special effects work supposedly proved they were more knowledgeable than and superior to the craftsmen who worked on the picture. Some of the effects in *Supergirl* are actually quite good.

The plot has Kara traveling to Earth from Argo City when its power source, a kind of glowing sphere, is unaccountably lost. (In the film, as in the later stories, Argo City is fully populated.) As in the story of her origin,

Opposite: Gerard Christopher, the second Boy of Steel on TV.

Above: A special collector's item anniversary issue of *Adventure Comics* starring Supergirl. Copyright © 1970 National Periodical Publications.

Kara goes to Midvale as Linda Lee, but becomes a student at a girl's school, with Lois Lane's sister as her roommate. Her cousin, Superman, is off in space on a mission, so she must find the power sphere herself. Unfortunately, it has come into the possession of an evil sorceress, Selena (Faye Dunaway), who operates from out of an abandoned amusement park and has a likable sidekick named Bianca (Brenda Vacarro). Selena uses the power sphere to create a mountain with a castle headquarters and to attempt to set herself up as dictator of the planet. Naturally, Supergirl foils her plans, but not without quite a few imaginative struggles.

Dunaway is fond of sending demonic beings after her opponent. First is an invisible destructive "shadow" that tears up trees and fences as it approaches the building Supergirl is in and that partially materializes as a huge, ugly, patchy-skinned creature. At the climax, Selena calls forth a humongous beast with great clawed hands, a ridged, bony face, and enormous fangs. This monstrosity twists and pulls both psychically and physically on Supergirl, but she eventually defeats it.

As Supergirl, Helen Slater is perfect. She possesses an ethereal, otherworldly loveliness, a "foreign" quality, and acts the part very well and believably, with innocence, naïveté, and strength. Madame Selena, on the other hand, is a rather ludicrous villainess, and Dunaway's performance doesn't help at all. Unlike Gene Hackman's

Luthor, Dunaway's Selena isn't funny—but she certainly isn't "serious," cmeither. Her performance reminded Rex Reed of "outtakes from *Mommie, Dearest.*" Brenda Vaccaro is much better as Bianca; she has the proper light touch and comedic delivery. Hart Bochner's Ethan seems too grubby and subliterate to be a worthy boyfriend of Supergirl's, or lust object of Selena's, in spite of his good looks. Maureen Teefy does a very nice job in her brief scenes as Lucy Lane, and Peter O'Toole as Zoltar, the founder of Argo City, does the most with his short but important sequences.

Like a 1950s comic book, the movie never seems part of any real world, and never explains the origin of Argo City or how it fits into the Superman mythos. There is some dreadful expository dialogue in the opening scenes, and the Argo City set is rather ugly and messy, not at all aesthetically striking. It never makes sense that Supergirl would bother checking into college and establishing a fake I.D. when time is of the essence in getting the power source back to Argo City. When did she have the time to fashion a costume modeled after her cousin's? Where did she get the Earth-style clothes that she wears in Midvale? And so on.

Supergirl is not a terrible picture, it's just that it has no real knockout sequences or dramatic impact, despite many exciting moments and the fact that it's consistently entertaining. The Salkinds made a mistake in choosing Jeannot Szwarc, a man who has virtually no visual sense or style at all, to direct *Supergirl*. He did nothing for *Bug, Jaws II,* or *Somewhere in Time,* and he certainly does nothing for the Young Lady of Steel. Yet, unfortunately, there have been far worse pictures than *Supergirl.*

Opposite: Helen Slater poses as *Supergirl*.

Above: Selena (Faye Dunaway, center) and Bianca (Brenda Vaccaro) are about to have an encounter with Supergirl.

CHAPTER TWO
GOTHAM'S
CRUSADER:
THE BATMAN

BDESPITE MAJOR DIFFERENCES BETWEEN THE TWO CHARACTERS,

atman has something in common with Superman: loneliness and a sense of abandonment. Superman is the last survivor of his home planet; Batman is the last survivor of his family. Through circumstances beyond their control, both found their solitary fates due to cataclysmic events. Superman luckily had Ma and Pa Kent to guide him and shape his values as a youngster. By the time Bruce Wayne lost his wealthy parents, he was old enough to have learned valuable lessons from them and to develop a sense of morality that he occasionally bends, but never dismisses.

Batman started out as a "dark" figure. The *film noir*ish ambiance of the 1989 *Batman* feature was not a "new" look but a return to an old one. He did not have a younger partner when he first appeared in 1939 (*Detective Comics #27*), and his antagonists—such as the vampiric Monk in *Detective* #31–32—were occasionally on the heavily grotesque side. On rare occasions he would use a gun, like the pulp magazine heroes after whom he was modeled.

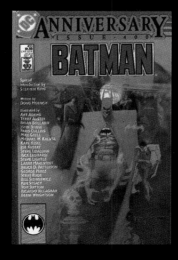

Bob Kane was working at DC Comics for several months when his editor, knowing that Kane wanted to make more money, asked him to come up with another hero who could be as popular as Superman. What Kane came up with was a combination of several of influences: the masked Zorro character with his dual identity; a batlike flying machine designed by Leonardo da Vinci (of all people!); and the sinister cloaked villain of the 1926 film adaptation of Mary Roberts Rinehart's *The Bat*. Zorro's foppish alter ego, the blasé count, was the model for Bruce Wayne.

Writer Bill Finger then was asked to put in his two cents, and he helped redesign the costume. Finger wrote the early stories and cites the pulp characters the Phantom, the Shadow, and even Doc Savage as influences,[1] as well as 1930s Warner Bros. gangster movies. Gardner Fox, a prolific comics writer, also did many of the early stories, and Jerry Robinson did much of the artwork, along with Kane. Gardner Fox introduced Bat-devices such as the Batarang, and was the first to put Batman into the seemingly inescapable death traps that soon became series trademarks. Robinson created the Joker, Batman's number one archenemy.

The two-page origin story in *Detective* #33 was crude but effective. Over the years, there have been minor alterations and refinements, but the basics remain unchanged: Dr. Thomas Wayne is walking home from a movie with his wife and young son, when they are accosted by a stickup man named Joe Chill. When the Waynes resist, Chill guns down the parents. Years later it is learned that Chill was actually hired by a vengeful mob boss to murder Thomas Wayne. Bruce then vows to bring his parents' killer—and all criminals—to justice. From then on Bruce Wayne becomes just a role Batman uses in his never-ending war on crime, as he dedicates himself to helping others in ways that the police cannot.

In the early stories, the Caped Crusader was known as *The* Batman. (The use of the article was briefly revived in the seventies.) He was a loner, a nocturnal creature, and the police weren't certain what to make of him. One of his most interesting foes was Two-Face, the tragic district attorney Harvey Dent, whose left side was horribly disfigured by acid, forcing him into the role of a master criminal who decides to do right or wrong with the toss of a similarly scarred coin. Then there was the Catwoman, who first wore a catlike headpiece before switching to the more conventional and attractive purple mask with ears.

Batman's young partner, Robin, was introduced in 1940. It was reasoned that he was a character with whom the typical youthful reader of *Detective* could identify. Batman also was awarded his own quarterly magazine. Although the introduction of Robin undeniably added to the longevity of the strip, it was also the beginning of the end for the dark, sinister Batman. From then on, the stories took on a lighter tone, for the most part, as if The Batman were afraid to envelop his younger charge in anything *too* nasty. Nevertheless, the boy took plenty of risks.

Dick Grayson was part of the Flying Graysons circus act when his parents were murdered in a deliberate "accident." Bruce Wayne not only helps the boy get the goods on his parents' murderer, but makes Dick his ward and Batman's brightly costumed partner. It might be wondered why any adult would ever subject a *youth* to the constant parade of danger endured by the Dynamic Duo, but one accepts the dubious partnership in the same way one accepts that detective Fenton Hardy would subject his teenage sons to continued peril in the Hardy Boys series.

There has always been speculation about other motives for Batman's having a youthful partner. Hints of a sexual relationship between the two would appear unfounded, as there has never been anything in the comics to indicate

[1]Many people believe that Kane and Finger were also inspired by the pulp magazine character The Black Bat, who was similar to Batman, but *The Black Bat* first appeared simultaneously with *Detective* #27. It was just a strange coincidence.

such activity. Besides, any sexual relationship between Batman and Robin would make Bruce Wayne less a homosexual than a pederast. Batman could still be a hero if he were gay, but not if he were a child molester. Recent stories have indicated that Batman keeps taking on boy partners (the first Robin has grown up; the second has died) out of simple loneliness, a need to be close to someone who shares and understands his mission and can be a surrogate son. This somewhat specious explanation seems drummed up to avoid any taint of homosexual speculation. The real reason: Robin is apparently still needed for (some) reader identification. As long as Robin is a minor, a gay angle just wouldn't work.

In 1943, Columbia Pictures released the first of two Batman serials. Unlike other serial adaptations of comic book characters, the cliff-hanger actually added some things to the comic book mythos. The "Bat's Cave"

underground headquarters debuted in the serial (directed by Lambert Hillyer) and became the Batcave of the comics. The secret entrance through a grandfather's clock was likewise introduced in Columbia's *Batman*. Although Alfred the butler had already been introduced in the comic by the time the serial was released, he was redesigned to look more like the actor who portrayed him in the chapterplay.

The story line has Batman and Robin battling saboteurs on the home front. The main villain is the Japanese Dr.

Above: Batman is pensive in his "Bat's Cave" while Robin watches in *Batman*.

Daka, (J. Carrol Naish), a weak-tea Fu Manchu type who operates out of a headquarters hidden below a chamber of horrors depicting Japanese atrocities. Naish is clearly having fun playing Dr. Daka—he basically does an imitation of Chinese Charlie Chan—but with his slicked-back black hair, mustache, and lipstick, he looks like a cartoon Oriental. At one point, another character assumes that Dr. Daka is merely an actor in the horror chamber. "Your accent is a little off, but your makeup is perfect," he says, in what has to be an in-joke.

Dr. Daka recruits Caucasions into his group of "dishonored men" known as the League of the New Order (of Hirohito). Most of these wronged men and ex-convicts are disenchanted enough with America to betray their country, but those who aren't are forcibly submitted to the doctor's brain machine (it looks like a glorified hair dryer with wires), which turns them into zombies. Batman and Robin get involved when this happens to the uncle of Bruce Wayne's love interest, Linda Page.

Through fifteen chapters, the cold-blooded Dr. Daka tries to dispose of his enemies and finalize his evil plans, but Batman and Robin are always there to thwart him. When Daka's men put a bomb on a trestle to destroy a cargo train, he later cackles with childlike enthusiasm: "Was the train wrecked? How many were killed?" He talks to his pet alligators as if they were dogs, and when he runs out of food for them, he positively giggles at the thought of ordering one of his zombies to jump into the pit and be their dinner. (He's interrupted before he can do this.)

We first see The Batman (as most characters refer to him in the serial) sitting in his darkened Bat's Cave at a big desk, brooding, shadows of bats flickering behind him and overhead. Batman's relationship with Robin is more like that of two brothers than of guardian and ward. Robin thinks that the senior partner should drop the bored playboy façade. Commissioner Gordon doesn't appear in the serial; he's replaced by a likable, portly Irish cop, Captain Arnold.

The casting of Batman and Robin is excellent. Although Lewis Wilson has slight British pronunciations and a

Above: A publicity shot of the stars of *Batman*.

somewhat chunky body, he is very good and quite convincing as both Bruce and the Caped Crusader. He gives an extremely smooth portrayal of Bruce Wayne, and really shows what he can do in chapter nine when he disguises himself as "Chuck White," an illiterate pugilist who is as far removed from Wayne—and Wilson—as possible. Another talented actor, Douglas Croft, plays Robin. Croft was the Ronald Reagan character as a boy in *Kings Row* and was doing a serial after several "A" productions proved not to be a step upward for him. Nevertheless, Croft makes a spunky, boyish, *believable* Robin, and has an absolutely unruly mop of wild curly hair that fits his tough but cherubic personality.

William Austin is perfectly cast as Alfred the butler. As in the comics, Alfred works (halfheartedly) with Batman and Robin on occasion, sometimes in disguise. Most of the screenplay's welcome comedy relief centers on this character. During a frantic battle in chapter three, Alfred gets to the phone and shouts: "Get me Scotland Yard— Get me the police—*Get me anybody!*" He winds up shooting up the whole place in his hysteria and nearly kills the Dynamic Duo along with the crooks.

The script follows the comics fairly closely, which at the time were still relatively "earthbound," although Batman's leaving a black "bat-mark" on the forehead of captured foes was a device that was neither a carryover from the comics nor adapted into them later. There are no crazy props or zany-costumed villains—unless one wants to include Daka and his smoking jacket—and no origin is provided. Some of the cliff-hangers concocted for the serial are pretty feeble, particularly the ones for the first two chapters. First, Batman falls from a roof (the process shot showing him waving and wiggling wildly as he falls past windows is hilarious) but lands anticlimactically on a handy scaffold. Then, he falls from a suddenly-sparking wire across which he's carrying Linda, but the miraculous "save" consists of nothing more than the rope secured to his person holding and preventing the two from hitting the ground. Other cliff-hangers employ the "missing information" gambit: in one case, Batman turns out not to be under the falling, fiery piece of ceiling after all; in another, we learn the following week that he escaped the inevitable blast by going through a convenient trapdoor before the cabin could explode.

Some cliff-hanger "solutions" depend on the character's having a propensity for survival that borders on Superman-like invulnerability. Two mechanic-zombies are sent in the place of the real pilots to steal a special plane while Batman is aboard. When it subsequently is shot down by the authorities (a clever combination of a real plane

Above: Poster art for *Batman*, the serial.

69

and a toy model, and stock footage of soldiers firing heavy-duty guns), Batman simply survives with hardly a scratch. In chapter eleven, there's a vivid accident scene in which Daka's thugs drive a massive truck into a cab in which Batman (disguised as Chuck White) is riding. Although the car is *mashed,* our hero is admitted to the hospital for only a few minor injuries and is almost immediately released!

One or two of the cliff-hangers are more effective, however. At the end of chapter three, Batman tries to retrieve a bomb from a railroad trestle while battling Daka's henchmen but is knocked out before he can do so.

Despite the obvious back projection, the sight of the oncoming train rushing toward Batman's unconscious body is rather thrilling. Another hair-raiser shows Batman thrown down an elevator shaft while a freight car slowly descends. Chapter thirteen has a great pair of concurrent cliff-hangers: Linda is put under the mind device and about to be "zombie-ized" while Batman and Robin fall into a pit outside Daka's headquarters, the closing walls of which are punctuated with a multitude of spikes. The final cliff-hanger, in which we assume Batman has been captured, placed in a box, and dumped into Daka's alligator pit, features some permissible "cheating." (Guess who's not really in the box?)

It all ends happily—except for Dr. Daka. When an associate hands him the day's take for his Chamber of Horrors, Daka says with prescience, "If I was in this for profit, I'd say this was a very bad day." Bad day, indeed. Daka is not only hog-tied by Robin, but, while trying to escape later, falls into his own alligator pit and is heard from no more.

Batman is an entertaining and amusing serial with more than its share of delightfully dopey moments. Daka can see through the miniature cameras he has placed in his zombie's heads, for instance, but how is he able to see on his TV screen the very zombies who are supposedly *projecting* the image? At one point, he orders a zombie to "leave the roof." The zombie takes it literally and jumps off the side of the building!

In an early chapter, Linda Page is kidnapped when responding to a bogus message supposedly from her missing Uncle Martin. Yet she stupidly goes off alone again to "meet Uncle Martin" when she later gets another (bogus) message from him. In chapter five, Dr. Daka receives a shipment from Japan containing a messenger who is in suspended animation. The man revives, delivers his message, and dies. Surely there are easier ways of passing messages than sending boxes of frozen delivery boys across the ocean in submarines. The dumbest moment occurs in chapter fourteen, when Daka's men see Robin getting into Bruce Wayne's car and follow it, hoping to

Above: Batman and Robin have Dr. Daka (J. Carrol Naish) cornered.

70

corner him. Batman and Robin change into Bruce and Dick in the backseat, and when the hoods catch up to them, Bruce gets out and "fools" them while Dick hides. It seems incredible that the two could ever hope to keep their identities a secret when they use the *same car* whether in their guises as Wayne and Grayson or Batman and Robin—and Alfred is the chauffeur in either case!

When the serial was released on videocassette by Goodtimes, changes were made in the narration, apparently to make it less offensive to Japanese–Americans. When the Japanese section of town is shown in the opening chapter, the narrator originally described it as resembling a ghost town because the inhabitants had been rounded up and put in internment camps, with anti-Japanese slurs and references to wise government decisions added for good measure. The new narration, substituting "hoodlums" for Japanese, is hardly an improvement, as it makes it seem as if the entire Japanese–American community consists of nothing but criminals.

Writing in *Cinefantastique,* David Scapperotti noted: "The revisions aren't surprising when you consider that Columbia is now owned by Japan's Sony Corporation. It appears that some of Daka's operatives escaped Batman's justice and were rewarded with positions in the new George Orwell department at Columbia. No doubt we can expect to see David Lean's *Bridge on the River Kwai* reissued as the story of a joyous Anglo–Japanese cooperative construction job interrupted by imperialistic American terrorists." Perhaps rather than worrying about the feelings of modern-day Japanese–Americans, Columbia/Sony just doesn't want to remind anyone of past history. However, even the "revised" *Batman* serial makes it pretty clear who was fighting who during World War II.

In 1949, Columbia pictures came out with a second Batman serial, entitled *Batman and Robin,* directed by Spencer Bennet of the Superman serials. The first chapter gets right into the action with the montage of a rampant crime wave. One of the thefts is of a machine with which "any moving vehicle can be brought under control and guided to wherever the operator desires." (The demonstration with a toy train and truck isn't very convincing, however.) The machine requires diamonds to run, and a mysterious masked and cloaked villain named the Wizard appears to mastermind an operation to steal some. The Wizard's headquarters can apparently be reached only by taking a submarine on automatic pilot from a hidden grotto to an underground cavern.

Vicki Vale is the nominal love interest in this story, and her brother Jimmy has gotten in with the wrong crowd—the Wizard's gang. He causes a lot of mischief as Batman and Robin try to foil the nefarious plots of the Wizard—and generally succeed. A late development has the Wizard using a device meant to neutralize the stolen machine

Above: Batman is captured by Dr. Daka.

71

to create a beam that can turn him invisible. This was borrowed from the 1941 *Dick Tracy vs. Crime Inc.* chapterplay with its invisible villain, the Ghost.

The serial manages to workup a lot of suspense over the true identity of the Wizard. Is it Professor Hammil (William Fawcett), who goes around in a wheelchair in public, but actually has a device that "energizes" him and allows him to walk? Is it radio announcer Barry Brown (Rick Vallin), who predicts the Wizard's crimes even before they happen? (Our bright heroes consider him a major suspect, but never wonder why he would draw attention to himself that way.) Or could it be that private detective who's always in the way? There are a couple of clever twists before the secret is disclosed, but the sharper viewers should figure out the ending before Batman does. When the Wizard's right hand is injured in a battle, all three main suspects show up with wounds in that same spot. Batman eventually uses infrared light to unmask the Wizard, just as Dick Tracy did to uncover the Ghost. The screenwriters took a cue from Agatha Christie when they concocted the surprise conclusion.

Batman and Robin is an engaging serial, but it has little of the atmosphere of the early comic stories. Everything seems to happen in broad daylight, with Batman rarely if ever engaging in nocturnal activity. Batman and Robin themselves are grim, humorless, and businesslike in their various guises, but this just makes them more dull than "dark." They drive a rather ordinary looking dark convertible in their wanderings. Robert Lowery, a Victor Mature look-alike who appeared in a variety of "B" movies, makes a passable Bruce Wayne/Batman. John Duncan, who plays Dick Grayson/Robin, is not a kid but a short young man in his early twenties. He has the stocky build and flattened features of a pugilist and is hardly the boyish scamp of the comic books.

Jane Adams, as the photographer Vicki Vale, is interchangeable with a hundred other serial heroines, calling on Bruce Wayne for inexplicable reasons, as the plot demands. Veteran actor Lyle Talbot, who was Lex Luthor in *Atom Man vs. Superman*, plays Commissioner Gordon. Talbot is bland and lacking in authority and does his acting with his belly.

Besides having a mediocre musical score, *Batman and Robin* is cursed with some truly lame cliff-hangers. At the end of chapter two, Batman is fighting a hood atop a train (with the obligatory back projection) as it races toward a tunnel. But Batman never seems to be in any danger. As the following chapter shows, all he has to do is either duck or move to one side. Chapter three has him falling over a cliff—more of a hill actually—and simply landing on a tree, not far below. In chapters five and six, Batman and Vicki escape from water which has flaming gasoline on it merely by climbing up to the dock on a ladder—not really an ingenious "escape." When Batman is left unconscious, surrounded by fire, at the end of chapter eight, he simply gets up and steps through some cartons in the following episode. Only on rare occasions does he use any special devices or have to show some ingenuity. He employs breathing tubes and an acetylene torch to get out of a CO_2 trap in chapters six and seven.

The one decent cliff-hanger occurs at the end of chapter ten, in which Batman falls from a very high window only to *thump* hard on the ground behind a truck. There can be no denying that he fell this time and hit the sidewalk. How could he have survived? Of course, he didn't survive. Because it wasn't Batman in the costume but

Opposite: Batman attempts to defuse a dangerous device.

New Adventures of
BATMAN AND ROBIN
Chapter 1
**BATMAN
TAKES OVER**
A COLUMBIA SERIAL

Copyright 1949 National Comics Publications, Inc.

Jimmy Vale, trying to make up for his past wrongs by decoying the villains away from an unconscious Caped Crusader. Like the final cliff-hanger in the first Batman serial, this withholds information from the audience but is undeniably effective.

Batman and Robin has its share of inane moments, too. When Vicki is captured by the crooks and manages to repair a phone so she can call for help, she doesn't dial the police with her location, but instead contacts Alfred. This would have made sense if she knew Batman's secret identity, but what does she expect the unheroic Bruce Wayne—or his butler—to do? In an earlier sequence when Batman is confronted by three hoodlums, he dives for the two unarmed men instead of the guy with the gun! Smart thinking, Batman; this is one guy who has luck on his side.

Meanwhile, the comic books were going strong throughout the fifties and sixties, with the Dynamic Duo's antagonists becoming more and more bizarre, the *noir* atmosphere replaced by colorful gadgetry and outlandish story lines. One of the most memorable opponents was "The Gorilla Boss of Gotham City," a mob chief who has his brain transplanted into the head of a gorilla that is inexplicably as large as King Kong. The climax has the Gorilla Boss carrying what he thinks is Batman to the top of a tall tower with the object of giving his adversary very little of the tender loving care Kong gave his beloved Fay Wray.

The supporting cast in Batman began expanding, while old stalwarts such as Alfred became the stars of their own stories. "The Secret of Batman's Butler," in which Alfred mistakenly believes that he has betrayed his employer, exhibits the real charm and appeal of the character, while showing how he became Batman's assistant and confidant. Other members of the "Bat-family" soon showed up, including a beauteous Batwoman ("wealthy heiress Kathy Kane"), a Bat-Girl[2] (Kathy's niece, Betty); Ace, the Bat-Hound (who could put on his own mask since it was attached to a special stand); and even Bat-Mite, a mischievous imp in the tradition of Superman's Mr. Mxyzptlk who wore his own miniature Batman outfit.

These characters all began interacting in the overcrowded Batman comic. "Batwoman's Publicity Agent" turned out to be Bat-Mite, working with Bat-Hound, to win Batwoman's love in a silly but amusing adventure. "Prisoners of Three Worlds," a book-length epic in Batman #153 (February 1963) featured Batman, Robin, Batwoman, and Bat-Girl (no Bat-Hound or Bat-Mite?)—and their energy duplicates—in a story that spanned two dimensions and involved aliens, monsters, ray guns—and love (the girls for the boys, at least). It was a fun story, but a far cry from the original vision of Bob Kane and Bill Finger.

The relationship between Batman and Robin and fellow superstar Superman also was cemented. They appeared together in *World's Finest* Comics and guest starred in each other's magazines. "The New Team of Superman and Robin" came about when Batman supposedly breaks his leg and is incapacitated for awhile. He

[2]These new characters would work out for a few days or weeks and somehow develop the same kind of skill and athletic ability that Batman and Robin had honed after years of practice.

Opposite top: Two new stars for the second Batman serial.

Opposite bottom: A lobby card for *Batman and Robin*.

wonders if Robin will find it dull working with him when his stint with the Man of Steel ends. It turns out that Superman only told Batman his leg was broken, and put it in a cast for him, because he knew a poison Batman had inhaled would slowly kill him unless he got some rest. Superman knew the only way to keep duty-bound Batman resting was to lie to him about his leg. Besides being well illustrated, the story demonstrates the warm friendship between the Man of Steel and the Caped Crusader, as well as between Batman and his ward.

The stories of this period with their Bat-gimmicks, assorted doom traps, corny but colorfully costumed villains, and a large assortment of characters, were full of sweetness and innocence, but they wouldn't play in our more

sophisticated era. Some critics might feel that today's children are missing out on this kind of good-natured frivolity, but there still are plenty of comics and stories geared toward the youngsters. And other comics provide that childlike sense of wonder for preteens while also satisfying the more demanding tastes of older readers.

By the sixties, the stories in Batman comics were almost as looney as those that would soon appear on the Batman TV show—only they were played straight. A story in *Batman* #147 (May 1962), entitled "Batman Becomes Bat-Baby," in which the Caped Crusader is turned into a two-year-old by a sinister ray, illustrates how ingenious Batman can be under decidedly unusual circumstances. Determined not to be deterred by his size (his mind remains the same), Batman takes advantage of his new status to round up the crooks and turn himself back to normal. What could have been a ludicrous camp story is actually quite engrossing. On the other hand, "The New Crimes of the Mad Hatter," published sometime later, is a silly trifle that greatly resembles the kind of stories that would air a couple of years later on television's *Batman* series in both style and situations.

The *Batman* TV show was broadcast on ABC in prime time from January 12, 1966, until March 14, 1968. For the initial two seasons, there were two interlocking episodes per week, the first ending in a cliff-hanger. The original idea to do a serious version of the Dynamic Duo was abandoned when executive producer William Dozier pushed for a parody format, figuring that was the only way it could work. Kids who were fans of the Batman comic book were appalled that their older brothers and sisters and parents were laughing (often derisively) instead of taking the whole thing seriously.

Batman did its best to be a (slightly condescending) television version of a comic book. All the conventions were there (and ripe for satire): the overuse of adjectives in every sentence ("*stately* Wayne Manor," for instance); the corny, overstated narration; the off-kilter angles of comic panels (in which some comic books of the time indulged, but certainly not all); and the highly dramatic and unlikely poses that heroes, in particular, would assume (the human body just doesn't work that way). It was all there, and for a time it was amusing. After awhile, however, the joke was wearing pretty thin.

Adam West was chosen to play Bruce Wayne and Batman, and proved a deft comedian. West never strained for a laugh; he would let the dialogue and situations do it for him. His Bruce Wayne was smooth and urbane but kind of

Above: *Batman* #147. "Batman Becomes Bat-Baby" was actually a pretty good story (but it wouldn't play today). Copyright © 1962 National Periodical Publications.

stupid. His splendid comic Batman was surprisingly efficient and always melodramatic. Newcomer Burt Ward was also perfect as Dick Grayson and Robin, bristling with boyish enthusiasm and a need to prove himself to his "father," trying to do the right thing but sometimes failing, bowing to the superior wisdom of his surrogate parent (and vaguely resenting it).

Neil Hamilton as Commissioner Gordon had a superb deadpan delivery, and there was good support from Stafford Repp as Chief O'Hara and Alan Napier as a highly sophisticated, occasionally bemused Alfred. These were all good actors giving their all to a lot of silliness, and somehow it worked. As Aunt Harriet, Madge Blake, with her slow, hesitant delivery, became irritating after awhile, however.

The production values in the show were terrific. There were elaborate sets and death traps, and a great-looking Batmobile. *Batman* became an "in" show, and major stars were anxious to appear as guest villains. But not everyone was satisfied—Batman cocreator Bob Kane was extremely annoyed with the parody treatment. After

what was being done to the character in the comic books (compared to the early stories), it might seem odd that Kane would object to the television version, but the comics still respected Batman, whereas the TV show clearly didn't.

Stanley Ralph Ross was one of the writers for *Batman*. He would include dirty words in foreign languages in his scripts, wondering if anyone would catch on. Although he later claimed that he invented the romance between Catwoman and Batman for the television series, Catwoman had had a "thing" for Batman for years in the comic books before the TV show ever aired. Ross first realized how popular the show had become when a live report about a space mission cut into the show and there was an outcry because fans missed a few Bat-minutes.

The first two episodes featured the menace of the Riddler (played with maniacal glee by Frank Gorshin), who plants an exploding cake in the Moldavia exhibit at the Gotham City World's Fair. Any claim to seriousness the episode might have had went out the window when Batman enters a disco in search of a suspect and starts to dance the "Batusi." Jill St. John guest starred as a gun moll who stupidly falls into the Batcave's reactor. Most interesting is the way in which the Riddler sets up

Top: Burt Ward (Robin) and Adam West (Batman) in the camp *Batman* TV series of the sixties.

Bottom: Robin goes into action on the *Batman* TV show.

Batman and Robin so he can sue them for false arrest. "What is it no man wants to have yet no man wants to lose?" he riddles. Answer: a lawsuit. It was not an auspicious show debut otherwise. Although these episodes hold the attention in a dopey way, they are not very good or even particularly funny.

Much of the limited fun of the series was provided by the guest stars. Zelda the Great perfectly fit Anne Baxter's dramatic, breathless way of overplaying. She also must be commended for putting fussy Aunt Harriet in "a straitjacket over a flaming pool of oil." When an associate invents an impossible "doom-trap," Zelda decides to lure Batman into it so *he* can figure out an escape. The most amusing scene has Batman encountering a jewelry store clerk who says, "Seeing you in the flesh is...faintly...faint-making." Batman is so stiff and naïve that he assumes the woman is frightened of him instead of attracted to him.

Other memorable villains include the delightful Vincent Price as Egghead, who kidnaps Bruce and other millionaires and insists that the Indians still own Gotham, and Victor Buono as the flamboyant King Tut, a great conception for a fat Bat-foe. (In the Egghead episode, Bruce claims: "At age eleven I was junior marble champ of Gotham City." Dick can only shake his head and reply, "Even then.") Cesar Romero really scored as a laugh-a-minute Joker, but Walter Slezak as Clock King was a good actor in a dull villain.

By far the best guest villain—in one of the best episodes—was Tallulah Bankhead as the Black Widow. Bankhead may sound like Mr. Magoo, but she's terrific as a classy bankrobbing crook. Veteran character actor Grady Sutton is an extra bonus as a stammering bank clerk who has to sit under a special Bat-device like a hair-curling machine to see if he's been "mesmerized." The episode features some clever dialogue and amusing situations. Once the novelty of seeing Bankhead in the series wears off, however, the second episode becomes fairly routine and merely silly. It does have a funny bit when the Black Widow disguises herself as Robin, but speaks in her *own* voice to a policeman, along with Tallulah's patented "dahlings."

There were some clever moments along the way. The "Rats Like Cheese" episode, with George Sanders as Mr. Freeze, has an inventive climax in which Freeze can flood any fraction of the room with either extreme cold or a more bearable temperature. (Different colors denote the way the room is "divided.") Freeze starts reducing the size of the warm part of the room until Batman and Robin are trapped in a warm cube in a room of deadly frigidity. The Ma Parker episode with Shelley Winters as the leader of a gun-totin' brood has an interesting premise. Parker has slowly planted henchmen as guards in the Gotham State Penitentiary, and when she herself is imprisoned there, they take over the place and use it as a base of operations. The script plays well and actually has some suspense and surprises. Ma's rocket-powered wheelchair is a plus.

In each episode, Batman and Robin would appear to be climbing a wall but were actually stooping over the floor with the camera tilted sideways. Out of a trapdoor—the "window" in the wall—would pop a surprise big name for a cameo. By far the most memorable appeared in the otherwise mediocre two-part episode in which Batman meets the Green Hornet (Van Williams). No less than Edward G. Robinson plays a painter who decries Andy Warhol-style "pop art" and says, "Canned tomato soup is to eat, not to frame and hang on a wall."

The final two episodes of the series in 1968 illustrated *Batman* at its best and its worst. A bit of inspired lunacy was provided by the penultimate show, in which Ida Lupino plays Dr. Cassandra. While robbing "Spiffany's" on "fashionable Fifteenth Avenue" of its "Mope" diamond, Cassandra turns her "Alvino Ray Gun" on Batman, Robin, and Batgirl. "I feel like I'm getting flat," says Batgirl. The gun reduces the trio to one-dimensional cutouts. Learning of their deplorable condition, Chief O'Hara stands in Commissioner Gordon's office and announces "Any minute they'll be coming through that door"—and the cutouts are slid beneath the door! The commissioner has them *mailed* to Alfred, who puts the trio in a "three-dimensional Bat-restorer." "Arch criminals only—all others keep out!" reads a sign over a wing in Gotham Prison. Ida Lupino is a very good as Dr. Cassandra, and the humorous script is quite inventive.

The last show, guest starring Zsa Zsa Gabor as Minerva, is another story, however. One problem is that although Gabor is in turn imperious and sexy, she fails to get across the humor of her lines, and isn't even convincing as she grapples with Batgirl. It was a disappointing finish for the Caped Crusader and company.

Looking back, *Batman* did have more than its share of fun, but can be taken only in small doses. Watching too many of the series' often mind-numbingly stupid episodes in succession can really rot the brain. Nevertheless, there are still fans of the series who swear by it.

An unanticipated side effect of the popularity of *Batman* was the reemergence of innuendo in regard to the sexuality of the Caped Crusader and Boy Wonder. Most of this was of a snide nature, such as when Nanette Fabray, asked on a game show to complete the sentence "Batman and Robin are..." remarked "fags." A DC Comics editor, writing in an introduction to a hardbound collection of Batman stories, blamed the gay community for casting aspersions on Batman's manhood. Considering that the jokes and allegations making the rounds were neither good-natured nor approving but mean-spirited and entirely homophobic, it was unlikely that gays were responsible. In any case, the name "Bruce" suddenly became suspect, the moniker of choice for all "limp-wristed" characters in films and sitcoms of the period.

To counteract this, Batgirl was introduced in the third season of the series. She had first appeared shortly before that in *Detective* #359 (January 1967) and was an entirely different character from the original Bat-Girl. This Batgirl (unhyphenated) was Barbara Gordon, the librarian-daughter of the commissioner. On television she was played with spritely confidence by the shapely starlet Yvonne Craig. Her addition, however, did not save the show from eventual cancellation.

But first, there was the *Batman* movie in 1966, an all-original theatrical feature directed by Leslie H. Martinson and starring the regular cast of the *Batman* TV series. William Dozier again served as producer, and frequent Bat-writer Lorenzo Semple, Jr., fashioned the screenplay. Batgirl did not appear, although she went on to become a continuing character in the comic books.

Above: *Detective* #359 introduced the new (second) Batgirl, Barbara Gordon. Copyright © 1967 National Periodical Publications.

The plot has four major Bat-villains banding together to kidnap a commodore who has invented a "total dehydrator," which can extract every bit of moisture from the human body. Catwoman pretends to be Kitka, a Russian journalist, in order to date then kidnap Bruce Wayne as part of a plot to kill Batman. Wayne comes close to falling in love with her. When they're "captured" and taken to the Penguin's preatomic submarine, that romantic fool Wayne tells Kitka something along the lines of "I fear we have nothing to look forward to but death"—the eternal optimist.

The villains attack the "United Security Council" and use the dehydrator to kidnap the council members by reducing them to piles of ashes. Naturally, Batman and Robin get the ashes back but really screw up when it comes to supervising the rehydrating of the council members (using an elaborate faucet-pipe arrangement that leads water to a tube hanging over each seat at the council table). Although the Dynamic Duo have done their best to separate the ashes of each council member and place them on each chair, when the men are returned to "normal," their minds are all mixed up.

Frank Gorshin, Cesar Romero, and Burgess Meredith repeated their roles as Riddler, Joker, and Penguin, respectively. The Catwoman was played by Lee Meriwether. Although Meriwether is not as appropriate for the role as Julie Newmar—or the best, most catlike Catwoman, Eartha Kitt—she turns in a surprisingly good performance. By this time, The Riddler's riddles were more inane than clever: "What sits in a tree, weighs six ounces, and is very dangerous?" Answer: "A sparrow with a machine gun."

Each villain seems to be having a ball, and the actors certainly play well together; at times they reach a certain height of comic lunacy. These particular Bat-foes all have their own crazy noises and verbalizations: purring, snorting, chuckling, giggling—what a cacophony when they all do it together! They are like asylum inmates psychotically trapped in a never-ending Halloween party.

The movie has some good gags in it: When Batman sinks into the ocean on a Bat-ladder (while Robin maneuvers in a copter overhead), a rubber shark is grabbing onto his leg as he's finally pulled back up; the Penguin's submarine has a duck's flipper at the end of it. Perhaps the funniest sustained bit has Batman frantically looking for a place to dispose of a cannonball-size bomb with a flickering fuse. "Some days you just can't get rid of a bomb," he mutters.

One of the death traps is rather suspensefully handled. Batman is magnetized to a buoy as torpedoes speed toward him. When the batteries on his antitorpedo polarity device run down, a brave porpoise sacrifices itself to save him and Robin and is blown up in their stead.

Although the picture has the usual good photography, production values, and settings, there's no denying that what works satisfactorily in small doses on the TV screen becomes quite tiresome after nearly two hours in the theater. By the time the Penguin has gained entrance to the Batcave through subterfuge, the movie is too much like the TV show and the fun has petered out.

Opposite top: The four villains surround Bruce Wayne (Adam West) in the *Batman* theatrical feature.

Opposite bottom: The inmates have taken over the asylum: *Batman* 1966.

Most of the critics agreed, although the reviews were kinder than expected. Kathleen Carroll of the New York *Daily News* gave *Batman* a surprising three stars, loved the "perfectly zany" situations, and had some nice words for West and Ward, too. "Their formality makes the clever pop dialogue funny." Archer Winston of the *Post*, on the other hand, called it "a compendium of everything Bat-awful that can be Bat-imagined." Batman was now an American joke, but his reign as a funster would soon be over.

Adam West over the years has received virtually no royalties. He later told interviewer Jim Neibaur: "I signed my contract just after the Screen Actors Guild had made new contracts which called for residuals through only six runs, and that, of course, has trickled down to nothing. I have a percentage of the merchandising, which, I'm told, has gone over three billion dollars, but it has been very difficult to collect." Stanley Ralph Ross thinks that West has no cause to worry. "Adam is wealthy. He married a rich woman."

In 1986, West sued an ad agency responsible for a small chain-store commercial with actors dressed as Batman and Robin along with other Bat-paraphernalia. West wanted $900,000 in damages for invasion of privacy, unfair competition, and unauthorized use of an endorsement. In January 1990, he lost the lawsuit because DC Comics had given the agency permission to use the Batman character. West also got some publicity when he campaigned to get the title role in a more serious *Batman* movie planned for release in the early eighties. (Even if it had been a comical treatment, West was a little long in the tooth at the time.) "I think I should have at least some sort of a part," he said. In the late eighties, he again tried to win the role that went to Michael Keaton in *Batman* (1989), but the producers were so afraid of being tainted by "camp" that they didn't even offer West a cameo.

Because of the popularity of the TV show, the comic book went through a camp phase in the sixties that is now considered the most forgettable of the Batman's career. By the seventies, saner heads had prevailed and Batman was almost back to being the grim avenger of the night that he once was. There have been many memorable stories—along with surprising developments—during the past two decades. And Batman became more aware of the world around him—the real world.

In the late sixties and early seventies, a bizarre rumor was spread that Paul McCartney of The Beatles had been killed and replaced with a double. Allegedly there were clues to this in song lyrics and album covers; John Lennon could be heard saying "I Buried Paul" if one song was played backwards. In *Batman* #222 (June 1970), "Dead... Till Proven Alive," Batman discovered that *three* members of "The Twists" band had been killed, but the surviving one started a rumor about his own death to keep anyone from suspecting the truth. (The band was making too much money as a foursome to stop now, so he hired three look-alikes and continued.) It was a great story idea, if wildly contrived and implausible.

Although it's been said that the "grim" Batman did not return until Frank Miller did his *The Dark Knight Returns* comic book miniseries in the mid-eighties, the stories were actually becoming much darker and more serious long

Above: The 400th "anniversary" issue of *Batman* was a real collector's item. Copyright © 1986 DC Comics, Inc.

before that, particularly with the help of writers like Denny O'Neil and artists such as Neal Adams (whose rich, deep, detailed, and dramatic work makes him one of the finest comics illustrators ever). These two crafted many fine tales over the years, such as "A Vow From the Grave" (*Detective* #410, April 1971) in which jealousy among a stranded circus sideshow troupe leads to murder, and "Night of the Reaper" (*Batman* #237, December 1971) in which a concentration camp survivor stalks his Nazi tormentor during Halloween festivities.

"Night of the Stalker" in *Detective* #439 (February–March 1974), written by Steve Englehart and illustrated by Vin and Sal Amendola (who also plotted) and Dick Giordano, has become a Batman classic. In it, Batman sees a boy's parents gunned down just as his had been years before and stalks their murderers up mountains and through forests. Of course he can't bring the boy's parents back, and the moving conclusion shows him sobbing with agonizing memories of being orphaned in such a brutal fashion. This is the key to Batman's character: The sudden, unexpected violence that changed his whole life is something that he simply will not abide. His entire career has been a struggle to bring to justice those who would murder so callously and senselessly. In that context, it is easy to see why so many felt the *Batman* TV parody to be an insulting trivialization of the character.

But while such Batman stories were demonstrating a new maturity, there still was a certain amount of inspired wackiness, much of it the creation of that macabre archfoe, The Joker. The Joker, created by Jerry Robinson, first appeared in *Batman* #1 (1940). The Crown Prince of Crime was inspired in part by the title character in the film adaptation of Victor Hugo's *The Man Who Laughs* and his grotesque, disfigured grin. Over the years, the Joker transformed from a bizarre hoodlum to a deadly psychopath to a comical figure and back again. He briefly had his own book in the seventies, and it was comic in every sense of the word.

Two especially memorable Joker stories appeared in the seventies. "The Joker's Five-Way Revenge" was featured in *Batman* #251 (September 1973) and was another Denny O'Neil/Neal Adams collaboration. Killing off members of his gang who he thinks have betrayed him, the Joker leads Batman on a merry chase through Gotham. The climax has Batman pushed into a tank with a hungry shark. Not only are his hands tied behind him, but he has to save a man in a wheelchair who has been thrown in as well. The story is fine and the artwork excellent.

Detective #475–476 (February–April 1978) offered one of the most famous two-part Joker stories ever published. "The Laughing Fish" and "Sign of the Joker" have the Crown Prince poisoning the waters so that all the fish develop the same trademark Joker grin—complete with white face and red "lips." Naturally he applies for a copyright on his "Joker-fish" so that he can "get a cut of every fish sale in America." When the authorities balk, the Joker begins to ingeniously murder everyone in his way despite Batman's best efforts to stop him. Although it sounds like the sort of thing that appeared on the television series, the clever story is played straight and illustrates the Joker's oddly logical derangement. The fish look like him, so why shouldn't he own them? He'll simply keep on killing every copyright officer until he finds one who agrees with him. (These murder scenes are suspenseful, eerie, and ultimately horrifying, with the victims keeling over, wearing the Joker's disfiguring grin.) The story was written by Steven Englehart and drawn by Marshall Rogers.

Meanwhile—in a development that can only happen in comic books—Robin was growing older while Batman stayed the same. Dick Grayson went to college, dropped out, joined the *New Teen Titans* (a very popular comic

featuring the exploits of a team of youthful super-heroes) and changed his name to Nightwing, with a new costume to match. After several years of near estrangement—Batman resented Robin's not needing him, and Robin resented Batman's resentment—they again have become friends, of a sort.

A new Robin, Jason Todd, was introduced in a story that began in *Batman* #358 (April 1983) and wound up four issues later in *Detective* #526 (May 1983).[3] This exciting tale by Gerry Conway pits Batman against the savage, embittered hoodlum, Killer Croc, who has the strength and skin of a crocodile. Before the story is concluded, Croc murders husband and wife circus performers named Todd, and their son Jason (unaware of their deaths) participates in his capture, just as Grayson did with his own parents' murderer years ago. The story ends with Jason taking over the role of Boy Wonder from Dick Grayson.

Inexplicably, DC Comics later gave a brand-new origin to Jason/Robin that virtually made him a completely different character. Here, Jason is a modern-day Oliver Twist whom Batman rescues from a life of crime.[4] Although the story occurred after the *Crisis on Infinite Earths*, in which DC streamlined its "universe," no good reason was ever given for making the switch. Jason himself was written out of continuity for good when readers voted 5,343 to 5,271 to kill him off. Although DC Comics got a lot of publicity mileage out of Robin's death at the Joker's hands in *Batman* #438 (1988), it wasn't the "real" Robin, Dick Grayson. As of this writing, Batman has taken yet a third Boy Wonder as a partner, making the death of Jason seem rather pointless in retrospect. This character's introduction was contrived and "comic bookish" in the worst sense of the word.

In 1986, DC Comics published a four-part miniseries written and penciled by Frank Miller, who had done some excellent work on Marvel's *Daredevil* and other series. *The Dark Knight Returns* takes place many years in the future, when Batman has retired and become a heavy drinker. Robin is dead, and the city is overrun by creeps called "mutants" who look like white skinheads but talk and act more like the black inner-city street gangs. Superman, a supporting character, is in the service of the government and spends most of his time fighting enemy soldiers. When Batman comes out of retirement to battle the renewed menace of the Joker, as well as the mutants, a pop psychologist suggests that Batman *causes* crime since the maladjusted—who "are victims of Batman's psychosis" (sexual repression)—must react to him and become his opposite.

[3]The other issues in the four-part story were *Batman* #359 and *Detective* #525.

[4]*Batman* #408 (July 1987).

Top: A collector's mini-series told of *The Untold Legend of the Batman*. Copyright © 1980 by DC Comics, Inc.

Bottom: Book Three of Frank Miller's trendy *Dark Knight* series. Copyright © 1986 DC Comics, Inc.

Miller fashioned a graphic novel that is not black and white, but complex, absorbing, and occasionally powerful (and also too unpleasant to be that enjoyable to read). His satiric targets include everything from Dr. Ruth Westheimer and the writers' strike, to psychobabble, Ronald Reagan, and nuclear war. There are many horrifying and effective vignettes showing life in Gotham City under siege and the pervasive influence of television and the media. (There are perhaps too *many* scenes of the TV news, however, making the story overly choppy.) Superimposed over this cold and only slightly exaggerated reality, the fantasy figures of Batman and a new female Robin seem almost trivial and fantastic. Furthermore, Miller's storytelling is off—it works against the impact of the saga with its too-abrupt segues, obtuse, confusing art (sometimes you can't tell what you're looking at), and the trendy but distancing and off-putting style. His work is almost always cinematic but often needlessly muddled.

The ridiculous ending of *The Dark Knight Returns* has Batman allying himself with some of the mutants, a bunch of teenage psychopaths who he imagines will make good candidates to carry on in his place! *The Dark Knight Returns* is clearly the product of a thinking mind, but not necessarily a mature one.

Naturally, the miniseries was overpraised. For one thing, some much-maligned comics fans, feeling over-compensatory and defensive, had to insist that *The Dark Knight Returns* was not just a darn good Batman story, but a work of genius. And while many comics fans are well-read, literate people, there are others, particularly teenagers, who look at nothing but comics and simply didn't know that the themes in *The Dark Knight Returns* already had been dealt with in honest-to-goodness literature. Still, Miller deserves credit for at least trying to do something (very) different and quite thought-provoking with the formula, albeit clumsily. The ambitious, literate, if not entirely successful *Dark Knight Returns* is certainly miles away from "Batwoman's Publicity Agent" (for better or worse).

A more satisfying Batman graphic novel was Alan Moore and Brian Bolland's *The Killing Joke*, published in 1988, in which an origin for the Joker was finally provided. Here, the Joker was once just a third-rate stand-up comic hardly able to feed himself or his pregnant wife. After she dies in a tragic accident, the bewildered widower is pressured into guiding a gang of thieves through a chemical plant where he used to work. Batman mistakenly believes that he's the leader of the gang and what follows is the famous plunge into deadly chemicals that turns the Joker into a disfigured and dangerously unstable menace. Although the DC editors have said *The Killing Joke* is only *one* possible origin for the Joker, the results of his shooting and crippling Batgirl have carried over into regular continuity.

In 1984, it was announced by producers Mike Uslan (a former Batman comic writer) and Ben Melnicker (who with Uslan had produced *Swamp Thing*, another DC hero), that a new, serious treatment of Batman would soon be making its way to the screen. Tom Mankiewicz, the script doctor for the first Superman feature, was drafted to do the screenplay. The Joker would be the major antagonist, with perhaps an appearance by another foe for added flavor. The creators took the project seriously and were concerned with such details as the exact date on the giant penny that always appeared as a souvenir trophy in the Batcave in older stories. "The film must be about the creature of the night and capture the spirit of what Batman was originally about and what the comic, by and large, has reverted to in the last couple of years," Uslan said. Robin would turn up only at the very end.

Despite the interest of such directors as Joe Dante and Ivan Reitman, the project—and Mankiewicz's script—never got off the ground. Tim Burton, who eventually directed the 1989 *Batman* film, later said he felt that the first Batman·script was too much like *Superman* or even the Batman TV show. He also had trouble with the story structure, which "followed Wayne through childhood to his genesis as a crimefighter. . . . there was absolutely no exploration or acknowledgment of the character's psychological structure."

A few years later, the Batman project was on the move again, under the auspices of producers Jon Peters and Peter Guber, with Melniker and Uslan as executive producers. Sam Hamm was brought in to contribute an original script. He said, "*Superman* set the model for how to do a super-hero movie by opening up with the big, spectacular origin sequence. It struck me that Batman was a different kind of character and couldn't be treated quite the same way because, while being rather exaggerated, grand, and operatic, Batman deals with material that is within the province of possibility. You really don't have to explain why a man can fly or why bullets bounce off his chest."

The whole origin/costume question was an irritant to director Burton. "He dresses like this for theatrical effect. We had to find a psychological basis for his dress code. You can't just do, 'Well, I'm avenging the death of my parents—Oh! a bat's flown in through the window. Yes, that's it. I'll become a Batman!' That's all stupid comic book stuff. . . . He dresses up as a bat because he wants to have an amazing visual impact. It all gets away from the fact he's just being a simple vigilante, something I have always loathed about the character. He's creating an opera wherever he goes to provoke a strong, larger-than-life reaction."

Hamm's script was tampered with by the studio; there were rewrites by Charles McKeown and Warren Skaaren. "It's typical studio thinking that when a big, expensive picture is going into production, they start getting itchy about any of the more idiosyncratic material in the script," said Hamm. The black humor was left intact, but Bruce Wayne was no longer dark, tormented, and psychologically mixed up. A larger-than-life hero, Hamm noted, can't be "plagued with doubts about the validity of what he's doing."

As in Mankiewicz's script, Robin appeared only toward the end. Burton decided to drop the character just before filming began. He was gratified to see that DC Comics had killed him off at about that time, and Warner Communications didn't need to be persuaded that Robin didn't matter. Charles McKeown added an inspired plot point: that the Joker was the murderer of Bruce Wayne's parents, as opposed to Joe Chill in the comic books.

Several actors were considered for the role of Batman, including Mel Gibson, Pierce Brosnan, Charlie Sheen, and even Bill Murray. The one finally chosen seemed no more appropriate than Murray: Michael Keaton. Immediately a storm of protest went up in comics shops across the nation. If comedian Keaton played Batman, the movie would turn out to be just another joke, it was reasoned. Patrons in comic book stores were asked to sign petitions, and there was even talk of a boycott. (Months later many of these same people were doing free advertising for Warner Bros. by walking around wearing Batman T-shirts.)

Bob Kane had been championing Jack Nicholson for the Joker early on. He took a still of Nicholson from *The*

Opposite top: Batman (Michael Keaton) rescues Vicki Vale (Kim Basinger) in *Batman* '89.

Opposite bottom: Batman poses with his streamlined Batmobile.

Shining and drew green hair and red lips over it—voila! *That* was the Joker. Everyone seemed to agree. Nicholson demanded script changes (and a huge take of the potential profits) before signing to do the film, but Hamm claimed that they were mostly just substitutions of one punch line for another.

Jack Palance was brought in to play the gang boss, Grissom. "[He] was the only person who could possibly portray Nicholson's boss," said director Burton. "He is one of the few living actors who had the emotional weight and authority to counterpoint Nicholson's strong character." Casting veteran British actor Michael Gough as the butler, Alfred, was truly inspired. Sean Young was originally set to play Vicki Vale but was replaced by lush-mouthed Kim Basinger. A relatively unknown comic, Robert Wuhl, was signed to play the part of a new character Alexander Knox, a reporter. Pat Hingle's turn as Commissioner Gordon, and Billy Dee Williams's as Harvey Dent (who becomes Two-Face in the comics) amounted to little more than cameos.

Armed with a budget of about $40 million, Burton and crew went to work. One of the most important elements was the scenic design, handled by Anton Furst, who fashioned a Gotham City that is full of opposing styles of architecture from different decades. Said Burton, "Gotham City is basically New York[5] caricatured with a mix of styles squashed together—an island of big, tall cartoon buildings textured with extreme designs." Furst was given $5.5 million to construct the extra-sturdy sets on the backlot of Pinewood Studios—a *Superman* set that had been built there had been blown away and the ones for *Batman* had to last for possible sequels. Furst could afford to build only one main street, so he added alleyways and bridges to increase the perspective and opportunities for camera angles. Most buildings were erected to a height of forty feet, with the cathedral that figures in the climax built to fifty feet.

Nick Dudman created the makeup for the film. Six prosthetic devices were applied to Nicholson's face to help turn him into the Joker, including a tip of the nose, a chin, two upper lips, and two lower lips with cheeks attached. After early tests revealed that the white makeup simply washed out next to the bright colors (hair and lips) under somber lighting, Dudman shadowed the makeup so that it would work.

Tim Burton had not directed many pictures by the time he was given the assignment on *Batman*. His best-known was a quirky, special effects-laden comedy called *Beetlejuice* that also starred Michael Keaton. Sam Hamm was also a relative newcomer; he and Burton were odd choices to put together such an important (i.e., expensive) theatrical feature.

The promotion for the film began in early 1989 and intensified as summer approached. There were all the aforementioned T-shirts littering the landscape. The new, stylized Bat-logo—which some people mistook for an open mouth with a couple of teeth in it—was plastered on subway walls, construction sites, kiosks, and bus stops. Preview reels were unveiled at comics conventions and in movie theaters. The year of the bat was beginning.

Was *Batman* worth all the hoopla? Yes and no. The picture is certainly entertaining and visually impressive, but Burton's direction lacks confidence, and the pacing borders on the tedious. Burton is rarely able to craft very credible or exciting battle scenes (with the exception of the climax). The movie lacks a strong, cohesive plot and is

---

[5]New York had always been the inspiration for Gotham City and, in fact, was referred to as the location of early Batman adventures.

Above: Jack Nicholson as the malevolent Joker.

devoid of suspense and intensity. There is very little depth in Sam Hamm's screenplay—or what's left of it—and the characters remain underdeveloped. Perhaps the problem is that *Batman* is just too "big" a movie and, despite its claims to *film noir*, simply too bright and colorful—too "pretty"—for the character.

A major flaw of the movie is the flashback showing the murder of Bruce Wayne's parents as the boy watches in horror. The scene is supposed to explain Batman's motivation, his obsession, the very purpose of his existence, but Burton doesn't give it the powerful emphasis it requires. He almost tosses it away. This is not great moviemaking by any means.

Although Michael Keaton isn't as bad in the title role as many expected—he has a refreshing, charming quality and is not unbelievable—he's generally much too laid back. He never gets across the intense, haunted man that Batman is under the surface (regardless of whether Batman is in or out of costume). This lack of intensity is particularly apparent when he's literally facing the man who murdered his parents—and knows it—at the climax. Earlier, when he asks the Joker, "Do you want to get crazy?" it doesn't quite work because Keaton fails to come

across as someone who's holding in over-powering emotions or restraining a demon.

Conversely, Jack Nicholson as the Joker is a little too over-the-top. The main problem is that he's funny when he should be terrifying, particularly as "the world's first fully functioning homicidal artist." Nicholson has to be held responsible for coming up with his own ill-advised gag lines. Many of them are hilarious, but they vitiate the character's menace and perversity. This is a Joker who is scary only in deed, not word—or presence. Jack Palance, who is, as usual, wonderful as Grissom, would have made a better, more frightening Joker, being naturally sinister-looking and intense enough for a score of actors. The Joker is more Nicholson's stunt than a well-thought-out performance.

The story takes place early in Batman's career, when the police aren't sure whether he's friend or foe. Jack Napier

Above: Michael Keaton in his impressively padded Batman outfit.

(Nicholson) wants to snatch the Gotham rackets from Grissom and is fooling with Grissom's sweetie (Jerry Hall). A cop on Grissom's payroll makes sure that Napier falls into a vat of noxious chemicals, and shortly thereafter, the Joker is born. He defaces artwork in the Gotham museum, and contaminates toiletries so that using a certain combination of them will lead to death—complete with the trademark Joker grin (Burton even botches this). He also plans to release poisonous gas into a crowd of merrymakers during a parade. The final confrontation between Batman and Joker—with Vicki caught in the middle—takes place high atop Gotham Cathedral.

The picture does have several worthwhile moments, such as when the Joker turns a recalcitrant associate into a

crispy corpse with a device secreted in his palm. (One might wonder where he got the device; Napier didn't seem like an electronics genius before.) There's a thrilling ride to and through the Batcave. The aforementioned parade sequence, with Gotham citizens greedily grabbing for money thrown by the Joker while balloons release the gas, features some spectacular shots of the city seen from the sleek, beautifully designed Batplane overhead. (The Batmobile is also a looker.) The superb climax in the cathedral is exciting, hair-raising, and well executed—although it doesn't make sense that Vicki wouldn't at least *try* to get away from the Joker.

The battle between Batman, the Joker, and the Joker's goons in the cathedral bell tower is topped by what follows, when Napier tries to send Batman and Vicki, desperately holding onto the edge of the roof, hurtling to their deaths on the sidewalk below. The Joker's demise—he tries to get away in a helicopter but Batman sends out

a wire that snags him to a gargoyle—is a masterstroke, and a fitting finish for the monster. The gargoyle snaps off the side of the building and the Joker plummets to the ground, pulled down by the heavy ornament's weight.

Despite its $40 million budget, *Batman* has some of those same stupid moments that always have plagued super-hero movies. When Bruce and Vicki have dinner together, why would he have placed her at one end of the long table and himself far, far away at the other? How did the Joker's goons—the ones who attack Batman, not the ones

Top: The Joker parboils a screaming victim.   Bottom: Batman descends into the action like a winged bird of prey.

who arrive with the helicopter—know to lie in wait at the top of the cathedral when the Joker himself couldn't have been sure that that's where he'd wind up? And while it's understandable that Vicki would figure out Batman's secret identity, when she comes to Bruce later in the story, it's merely to discuss their days-old romance and not the fact that he's Batman! In addition, many have criticized the film for failing to include a scene of revelation or

disclosure. We just see Alfred ushering Vicki into the Batcave as if it were an everyday occurrence. Just as hard to swallow is that one shot from the Joker's pistol could down the Batplane.

Not only does the film have these comic-book inconsistencies, but some sequences border on the *Batman* TV show, in particular when the Joker and his gang bounce into an art museum carrying a ghetto blaster that spews forth some dreadful "music" by rock star Prince. The scenes showing unshaven and pockmarked TV anchor people who are afraid to use possibly contaminated makeup also seemed questionable, but on subsequent viewings, they seem less amusing than disturbing.

Anton Furst's scenic design is undeniably stunning, but sometimes *too* stylish when it needs to be gritty. Nevertheless the sets are great: a Gotham City that seems like a garish hybrid of the 1930s (complete with period

Top: Batman confronts his archenemy, The Joker.

Bottom: The climax of *Batman* on the belltower of Gotham Cathedral.

92

clothes and hats) and 1990s; a remarkable, huge Batcave set; Grissom's virile office and his moll's beautiful apartment. Photography and special effects are generally first-rate. A real plus is Danny Elfman's Wagnerian musical score, which gives many sequences an added note of impact and intensity. "This is a darkly ruminative, deeply probing musical genre masterpiece," raved Noah Andre Trudeau.

Batman garnered generally respectful, occasionally guarded, and sometimes overstated reviews from the media. It was the top-grossing picture of 1989, earning over $240 million. However *Premiere* reported that it was not quite as big a hit on videocassette, with an estimated one-third of the fifteen million copies ordered (at the price of $24.98) not selling.

Batman II is in preproduction as this book goes to press. Sam Hamm has again written the script. Tim Burton will direct and Michael Keaton will star. Various reports have Jack Nicholson coming back as the Joker (even though he was killed off in the original). As it stands, the villains will be the Penguin (the brains) and the Catwoman (the muscle), with a lot of sexual interplay between the latter character and Batman. (In her revised comics origin, the Catwoman is an ex-hooker.) The Penguin will be played by Danny DeVito, and Michelle Pfeiffer will be the Catwoman.

Batman is still going strong in the comics. DC unveiled the new series *Legends of the Dark Knight* in 1989. Superman and Batman, who were good friends in the old days but in new continuity have a guarded relationship, teamed up in a three-part *World's Finest* and may be coming to a new understanding. Batman stories are generally dark and grim and bloody—horror stories—with the occasional flight of fancy, depending on who's writing the script. Will the introduction of a new Robin add some (dreaded) sunshine and light to the Dark Knight's life?

Let's hope not.

Batman works best in the shadows.

Top: In the late eighties, DC Comics unveiled a brand new Batman series: *Legends of the Dark Knight*. Copyright © 1989 DC Comics, Inc.

Bottom: Batman made the cover of N.Y.'s "hometown" paper. Illustration by Jerry Ordway. Copyright © 1989 DC Comics.

CHAPTER THREE
CAPTAIN AMERICA: CONSCIENCE OF THE COUNTRY

One of the most successful of all the super-heroes was born of conflagration and conflict, a product of commercial exploitation and propaganda that eventually outgrew its *raison d'être* and achieved a glorious comeback—a comeback that outstripped his original adventures and took on substance and dimension in the bargain.

The United States was very close to entering the European struggle in early 1941 when cocreators Joe Simon and Jack Kirby decided the time was right for a patriot hero, a variation on Superman that would embody the nation's values, as well as the strength and heroism of its fighting men. With the American flag as the basis for his costume and a face that was, ironically, pure Aryan as well as American, Captain America was born!

Captain America initially appeared on the newsstands in the first issue of Timely Comics' *Captain America* (April 1941). Steve Rogers was a skinny youth who is transformed into a fighting avenger by a superserum, and is meant to be the first of a corps of superpowered agents who will tackle fifth columnists and saboteurs. Rogers became a private in the army, and soon teamed up with camp mascot, "Bucky" Barnes, his boy partner. "Cap" was essentially one-dimensional by necessity: he was a device, a symbol of America's courage and the personification of its fighting strength. The cover of issue #1 had Cap socking Hitler himself in the jaw while goose-steppers stood about firing guns helplessly.

The character soon engendered a rash of red, white, and blue imitations. Although Cap was not the first patriotic hero—Quality's Uncle Sam and MLJ's Shield came first—he was the most successful and longest lasting of them all. Joe Simon's stories were punchy and vivid, while Jack Kirby's artwork, heavily influenced by films, revolutionized the industry, for it was stylish, fluid, beautifully composed, and packed with frenzied action and movement from start to finish. (Kirby introduced his specialty, the knockout full-page panel in CA #4,[1] and elaborate double-page spreads in issue #6) Cap fought a grotesque succession of German and Japanese villains and monsters (bizarrely distorted by Kirby's pencils) for several years, successfully adapting the old pulp formula to the comics medium. Over the years, other writers and artists on Captain America adventures included Stan Lee, Manly Wade Wellman (stories), and Syd

[1]The full-page panel in "Ivan the Terrible," a mediocre dream story, is of Bucky and Cap being carried on the shoulders of grateful subjects.

Above: *Fantasy Masterpieces* #5 presented more reprints of classic Captain America stories from the forties. Copyright © 1966 by Zenith Books (Marvel Comics).

Shores and Al Avison (art).

Cap's colorful adversaries included The Hunchback of Hollywood; The Butterfly; Dr. Grimm; The Fang, Arch Fiend of the Orient; and the Ringmaster, an early incarnation of the villain who would return in modified form to plague the Hulk, Spider-Man, and other Marvel heroes in later years. Certain of these early stories are standouts: "The Gruesome Secret of the Dragon of Doom" (CA #5) features a Japanese underwater vessel disguised as a monstrous serpent, as well as a full-page Kirby schematic of the inner workings of this incredible machine. Bucky's reaction when he thinks Cap has sacrificed his life to save Pearl Harbor—and when he realizes that his father surrogate is still alive—is touching, and establishes the warm, platonic bond that was later to be cruelly severed and cause Cap such emotional distress in the sixties.

"Death Loads the Bases" in issue #7 has Cap and Bucky investigating when several ballplayers are murdered during games. They come up against the Toad, a sinister masked villain who wears a black, batlike outfit, in a story that is presented as an action-mystery. There are several possible suspects for the secret identity of the Toad; his eventual unmasking provides a bit of a surprise.

Kirby's artwork reached a peak in *Captain America #10* with "The Phantom Hound of Cardiff Moor." This derivative of *The Hound of the Baskervilles* is suspenseful and clever in its own right, but Kirby's artwork is the selling point. By this time, Kirby had already experimented with very irregular panel borders—wavy lines, serrated circles, lightning bolts, jigsaw puzzle-like designs—but his two-page splash in "Phantom Hound" is particularly effective, combining a collage of the cast's faces on one side, Cap versus a jumping animal in the middle, a serrated circle of the hound (background) and a victim's leg (foreground) on the right, and the actual opening panels of the story at the bottom. Surely it influenced Jim Steranko and other artists years later. Cap has to battle not only a vicious dog, but also a creepy villain who dresses up like one (a truly grotesque costume) and actually commits the murders for which the dog is blamed.

It's interesting to note that in one story, "Killers of the Bund," Steve (Cap) Rogers notes that he's "found German-American people to be very nice." The same concession was rarely accorded Japanese-Americans in comics during World War II.

Although Captain America is very popular today, contemporary comics readers may find it hard to believe that he was once a household name. His enormous appeal carried the character past the end of World War II, when most other patriotic heroes bit the dust, and he began fighting "ordinary" criminals with horrific modus operandi. Bucky was replaced with Golden Girl—an unsuccessful sales ploy—but in late 1949 the battle was finally over: *Captain America* became *Captain America's Weird Tales* (for one issue), then dropped Cap altogether one issue later.

The 1943 *Captain America* Republic serial seemed to have little to do with the comic book. Captain America's secret identity wasn't Steve Rogers, but Grant Gardner, a district attorney, who carried a gun rather than the famous CA shield and wore a modified uniform with a big star on both the chest and the back and a striped midriff. The weird villains were replaced by the obligatory mad doctor and his thuggish henchmen. In spite of this, *Captain America* is one of the better movie serials of the period.

An ad for the *Captain America* serial.

Dick Purcell was cast in the lead role of Cap and Gardner. Purcell plays the one-dimensional hero as a pleasant and amiable fellow who can be tough when he has to be. Dressed as Cap, however, Purcell comes off as pudgy, fat-faced and quite ludicrous—until you get used to him.

Lorna Gray is good as his feisty and unflappable assistant Gail Richards, a spunky gal who gets involved in quite a bit of the action and is always grabbing for the pistol in her purse but rarely managing to get it out in time. Gail is aware of her boss's secret identity and is his confidante, but we never discover how or why she learned, or was told, this information, and, in fact, there's no origin story of any kind. Lionel Atwill plays the evil Dr. Maldor, who reveals (to the audience at least) in the opening chapter that he is the diabolical archfoe, The Scarab. Atwill's underplaying makes him that much more menacing.

The Scarab is a hypnotist who poisons victims and orders them to kill themselves. The poison, which is derived from orchids,[2] leaves purple blotches on their faces and makes them more susceptible to the Scarab's commands—like driving a car over a cliff or jumping out of a high window. The Scarab then gets his hands on a "Dynamic Vibrator" which uses light and sound waves to make things disintegrate. As the opening chapter reaches its cliff-hanger, Captain America is caught in the total collapse of a "dynamically vibrated" skyscraper. He's able to leap from a window and onto the next building before he can be crushed, however.

Next, the dastardly Scarab sets his sights on Professor Dodge, inventor of an Electronic Fire Bolt. The Scarab also has his men pump "nitrogas" into the Techni-Gas Oil Plant—causing an explosion—and has a henchman eliminate the member of a Mayan expedition who discredited him by firing a blowgun "under the D.A.'s very nose." He reacts to this murder (as Dr. Maldor) by calling it "a shocking exhibition of barbarism." The most interesting story element involves a device which can restore life to plants and animals in conjunction with a special serum. Maldor has Dodge bring one of his hoods back to life, but nothing particularly inventive comes out of this subplot.

Before the fifteen-chapter serial concludes, Gardner actually asks Maldor to testify against one of the Scarab's men. Maldor works overtime to keep the D.A. from suspecting his identity, but definitely comes to the conclusion

[2]If we are to judge by popular fiction, the orchid has to be the deadliest flower in history.

Above: Dick Purcell (Captain America) prepares to go into action.

that Gardner and Captain America are the same. The final segment has Cap and Maldor battling while Gail is almost enveloped by a mist that will shrivel and mummify her. At the end, the city learns that its district attorney and never-by-the-book masked vigilante are the same person, but a situation that would cause a scandal in real life never seems to raise an eyebrow. Maldor fries in the electric chair for his crimes. (Justice was certainly a lot simpler back then.)

Captain America is fast-paced and entertaining in spite of its prosaic cliff-hangers. The escapes are never very ingenious, and some of them are outright "cheats." One of the better cliff-hangers—and sequences in general—occurs in chapter two. The Scarab's hoods terrorize Professor Dodge—in an attempt to get him to

talk—by overturning the chair to which he's tied in the path of a bulldozer, which sickeningly crushes other chairs and crates as it makes its way toward him. Captain America shows up but is knocked out by one of the villains, and winds up in the same predicament as the professor. (The "thrilling" escape simply has Captain America getting up in time to save them both.)

In chapter three, a bomb planted in Gardner's car will blow up when he reaches a certain speed. Much suspense is generated as Gail and the highway patrol desperately try to contact him and warn him of the danger. In chapter five, the Scarab's men, trying to force Gail to divulge Captain America's identity, place her under a paper cutter that is as large and nasty as a guillotine. Chapter thirteen has Cap forced out of a window with only the curtain he's clinging to between him and certain death. The curtain begins to pop off its rod ring by ring....The tense sequence ends with his falling several stories but landing safely on a laundry truck. Another interesting sequence has the Scarab tying another tight-lipped victim to a low chandelier and using a cat-o'-nine-tails on his back, but this isn't developed as well as it could have been. The problem is that Dr. Maldor is more expedient than sadistic.

Top: Captain America delivers a knock-out punch.

Bottom: Captain America "holds up" a couple of crooks.

The frequent fistfights in the chapterplay are furious, exciting, and athletic, and a lot of villains fall out of windows from great heights. The stuntwork is generally excellent.

As usual, *Captain America* has its dumber aspects. The Scarab's gang has a remote camera that somehow can transmit pictures of the back of the van in which it is located even though the lens is focused only on the road ahead. Captain America supposedly can do what the district attorney can't do—rough up criminals—but he doesn't do anything that, say, Dick Tracy wouldn't do, and his costumed identity seems unnecessary. What's worse, he and Grant Gardner drive around in the same car, hardly a bright thing to do when you've got an identity to protect and a dozen thugs are out to kill you. Still, *Captain America* is superior to other serials which were equally idiotic in spots.

Two decades later, Captain America was reintroduced in *The Avengers* (1963). "Captain America Joins...The Avengers" is a Lee-Kirby classic which posits that the good Captain, having fallen into frigid seas, has been frozen in ice and thereby put into suspended animation, for decades. The Sub-Mariner, back in his villainous phase, comes across some Eskimos who are worshipping a block of ice with a dark figure inside and throws said cube into the sea, where it eventually melts. The floating body is picked up by The Avengers' submarine.

Our first look at the bedraggled Cap lying unconscious in bed, tatters of his normal clothing barely covering the famous uniform underneath, is a superb Jack Kirby drawing. Cap looks like more than a sleeping prince; he looks as if he'd been through the wars—and of course he has been. In short order, he revives and relates how his last memory is of failing to catch onto and defuse a flying bomb to which his younger partner Bucky had been clinging. What happened to Cap we already know. Bucky, of course, was killed when the bomb went off.

Although years have gone by, the ice has kept Cap looking just as young as the day he disappeared. He's also in fine trim (although it's rather ridiculous that he would be able to show off such fancy footwork for The Avengers only moments after coming out of a twenty-year state of suspended animation!). His anachronistic feelings and grief over the lost years are handled rather superficially (though ultimately stories would delve into these matters much more deeply). For instance, twenty-four years later, *The Avengers* #227 has a sensitive scene showing Cap's reaction to finding treasured mementoes of his past life torn up, trashed by a supervillain, the son of the man who killed Bucky.

That man, of course, was Baron Zemo, and it wasn't long before the resuscitated Cap settled accounts with him, although he was to be haunted by the death of his young partner for years to come. One of the highlights of *The Avengers* #4 is the touching moment when Cap mistakes young Rick Jones, former associate of The Hulk (an early member of the team), for the late Bucky. For a brief period, Jones becomes Cap's partner, a stand-in Bucky. Although Bucky is dead, the murderous Baron Zemo is still living, and uses Rick to lure Cap into a trap in the Amazon jungle in issue #15 of *The Avengers* (1965). The ruse backfires, and Baron Zemo only winds up causing his own death.

Cap was a sensation all over again, and soon became the most popular member of The Avengers. When the other founding members all left the team in issue #16, Cap stayed to serve as leader to a flock of new members recruited from the supporting casts of other Marvel Comics. He was given his own feature in the back of *Tales of Suspense*, which first ran new stories of his and Bucky's adventures during World War II (homefront saboteurs and Axis agents like evil hypnotist Sando were the usual villains) before jumping forward to present-day tales. Kirby's layouts, superb compositions, and thrilling action scenes recaptured the glory of the 1940s Cap and then some. Later stories became more contemporary, leading to the very successful revival of Cap's own magazine, which is still being published.

Captain America has undergone many changes over the years. The old Cap was a symbol, a superpatriot, war machine, and propaganda tool—and performed all these functions admirably. The 1960s Cap, entering a more sophisticated era (and without a war to bolster him), had to keep up with the times in personality and outlook. He could remain a symbol, but he also had to be a human being. And if he was a symbol, just *which* America did he represent? Hawks? Doves? Law-and-order freaks or bleeding hearts? Black America or white America?

The America of the sixties and seventies was one of ethnic, political, and sociosexual dissimilarity. Would Cap reflect this, or become just an old war-horse suspended in time? Cap was a handsome, heterosexual, blond, blue-eyed male. Did he represent only others just like him? Or everyone?

In a few short years we had the answer, though it came piecemeal. By the 1980s Captain America/Steve Rogers had a black partner, a Jewish girlfriend, and an old friend who was gay. The point had been made: this Captain America represents the majority of the country in all its diversity. The writers turned what could have been a rockbound conservative into the liberal, compassionate Captain America.

Cap's partner, the Falcon, was introduced in the sixties in a series of stories in *Tales of Suspense*, when America was reexamining its racial attitudes. Ghetto social worker Sam Wilson was an agile black hero with the power of flight and a real live falcon who does his bidding and has a mean pair of claws. Years later, the readers learned that, in grief and pain over personal tragedies in his life, Sam sank into the persona of small-time criminal "Snap" Wilson. Assuming Sam was truly a hoodlum, Cap's archenemy, the Red Skull, took Sam, wiped away Sam's (falsely) evil persona, and made him "good." The plan was to manipulate events so that Cap took Falcon as his new partner. The Falcon would serve as the Skull's deadly backup when the effects of the brainwashing were erased.

Top left: The cover of *Captain America* #337 was deliberately modeled after the cover of *Avengers* #4, which reintroduced the captain to the Marvel Universe in the sixties. Copyright © 1987 by Marvel Entertainment Group, Inc.

Bottom: *Tales of Suspense* #88 featured new stories of Captain America. Copyright © 1966 by Vista Publications, Inc. (Marvel Comics).

Fortunately, Sam Wilson deep down was and always had been a "good guy," and the Skull's efforts were for naught. The Falcon was popular enough to become Cap's official partner for many issues, with his name and likeness being featured on each cover.

Bernadette "Bernie" Rosenthal met Steve Rogers in issue #248 in 1980 in a story crafted by writer Roger Stern and artists John Byrne and Josef Rubinstein. Steve and the pretty Bernadette are immediately taken with

each other; Bernie particularly admires Steve's incredible "presence," although surely his good looks and physique aren't lost on her, either. Eventually Cap (who is a much older man even if he doesn't look it) is charmed by Bernie, although he is disoriented by her contemporary references to a popular culture that is far ahead of his 1940s tastes. The two become lovers, turning to each other for support and comfort when times get rough. The villain of the clever piece is Machinesmith, a once-human computer that can "jump" into any number of robot bodies.

Arnie Roth was introduced in *Captain America* #270 in 1982 by writer J. M. DeMatteis, who brought a previously untapped depth and emotional resonance to Cap's adventures. Arnie had been a childhood pal of Steve Rogers, but remembers only the skinny, gawky, youthful Steve who could never play or fight as hard as he, Arnie, could. Decades later, Steve is still young and handsome, while Arnie is a fat, balding, middle-aged man. Steve's first reaction at seeing his old friend is close to total denial—Arnie represents a past life, and because he has always known the truth about Cap from the early days when his puny friend suddenly developed a completely different and healthier physique, he could compromise Cap's secret identity.

Arnie, who it is revealed is gay, has contacted Steve after all these years because his friend and roommate, Michael, is in trouble. His relationship with Michael is handled with subtlety, sensitivity, and intelligence. (For better or worse, the issue of whether Arnie has ever been attracted to Steve is never examined.) At the beginning of this story, Steve is resisting making a commitment to Bernie for a multitude of reasons. At the end, after saving Michael's life, he is so moved by the closeness between the two men, Arnie and Michael, when they're reunited, that he realizes what he may be missing by rejecting Bernie's offer of love: warmth, companionship, a buffer against life's hardships. The title of this superb story says it all: "Someone Who Cares."

Black partner. Jewish lover. Gay best friend. What would have happened, however, if Captain America hadn't changed with the times? That question was answered in *Captain America* #153–156 in 1972, when a second Captain America—who thinks he's the genuine item—appears out of nowhere (along with a partner who looks just

Top: John Byrne drew Captain America in the eighties. *Captain America* #254 Copyright © 1980 by Marvel Comics Group.

Bottom: Captain America faced his temporary replacement gone insane in *Captain America* #156. Copyright © 1972 by Magazine Management, Inc.; Marvel Comics Group.

like Bucky), attacks the Falcon with racist tirades, and boasts of his determination to wipe out the man, the real Cap, who is "impersonating" *him*.

Steve Englehart was one of Cap's best scripters and proved it with this suspenseful—if rather broadly told—four-part saga, which was written in part to clear up a loose end in Marvel Comics continuity. *The Avengers* #4 had made it clear that Cap had been put into suspended animation at the end of World War II. But how did that explain the Captain America character who appeared in the fifties in a brief revival of the Timely[3] magazine superheroes?

Englehart's answer was that the government had created a new Cap, with a surgically altered face, to act as a symbol during the Korean conflict. When that war ended prematurely, the new Cap's brief career suddenly was over. This didn't stop him from going into battle later, however, along with a young partner who resembled Bucky, when a new Red Skull threatened the world. Unfortunately, something was wrong with the formula that gave the new Cap and Bucky their powers, driving them to a sort of Cold War paranoia. Like superpowered McCarthys, they saw everyone who wasn't a white, pure-blooded American as a Communist. Eventually they had to be restrained.

Having been put in suspended animation until a cure could be found for them, the bogus Cap and his partner have now been released by a man who violently opposed the current political situation. They're nasty pieces of work, full of hatred and Cold War lunacy. The real Captain America and the Falcon have a hard time putting the two phony ones down for the count.[4] The four-part story was one of the most intriguing and entertaining ever published in *Captain America*.

In 1979, two made-for-TV movies loosely based on the comic book were aired. Ex-marine Steve Rogers (played by Reb Brown) now is a drifter and artist who only wants to kick back and stay loose—until circumstances invade this life-style. It seems that his father was the original Captain America, who took a Full Latent Ability Gain (FLAG) hormone which had him working at close to 100 percent of his capacity instead of the usual third. The elder Rogers wanted to become a supervigilante, to go after the criminals that the law couldn't touch. (Strangely, there is no mention of Nazis or other wartime menaces.) He was mockingly christened "Captain America" by his enemies, not because he was merely a flag-waving patriot but because he really believed in American ideals. He was eventually murdered.

[4]Years later, when a black character in *Captain America* took the name Bucky, fans in the South pointed out that "Bucky" was a derogative term for blacks; the character was rapidly rechristened "Battlestar."

[3]Marvel Comics was called Timely in the 1940s and 1950s.

Above: Reb Brown as *Captain America* in the telefilm.

When a friend of his is also murdered, the younger Steve finds himself caught up in events that are out of his league, as well as the target of a power mad industrialist named Brackett (Steve Forrest). He has a severe accident

when pursued by Brackett's henchmen, and is taken to the Government National Security Labs. Although earlier refusing to be injected with the FLAG hormone, which apparently can work only on "Rogers cells," Steve finds now there is no choice: The hormone can save his life. His reaction is more irritation than gratitude. He develops increased strength, agility, and hearing, but he doesn't want to be tested.

Brackett, in the meantime, is still up to no good. Years earlier he had faked the plane-crash "death" of the wife of an associate, Dr. Hadyn, so he could keep her prisoner and force Hadyn's cooperation in a neutron bomb project on which he (Hadyn) was working. Brackett's ultimate goal is to get a billion dollars' worth of gold from the Phoenix International Gold Repository. Naturally Steve becomes a new Captain America and thwarts Brackett's plans. When he goes into action, Rogers wears a very modified red, white, and blue uniform that only hints at the costume in the comics. An epilogue, however, shows him wearing an outfit just like his dad's that is more closely modeled on the one in the *Captain America* comic books.

The TV *Captain America* is rather dull at times and has not one knockout action sequence. A battle in a meat-packing plant, for instance, is just mediocre. A plus is Ronald W. Browne's photography of sweeping vistas and landscapes; there are some great scenery and aerial shots. Don Ingalls's teleplay is merely functional, and Rod Holcomb's direction is strictly by the numbers. Mike Post and Pete Carpenter's music is pleasant, but doesn't add one whit of tension, suspense, or atmosphere to the proceedings and is overly full of minor "patriotic" fervor.

Although no great actor, Reb Brown (Steve/Cap) is amiable and appealing as a man of some sensitivity and strength and is at ease in front of a camera. Steve Forrest makes the most of his role as Brackett. Heather Menzies is the nominal love interest, Wendy Day, a doctor in the lab, and Len Birman is their boss, Dr. Simon Mills.

The second *Captain America* telefilm, subtitled *Death Too Soon*, is also known as *Captain America II*. Apparently Steve Rogers has been busy in the intervening period as the world at large now seems to know of Captain America's existence. Most of the time, however, he prefers to sit on the beach and do sketches,[5] with his lazy cat as a companion. A stunt cyclist as well as a special agent, he has a cycle that's all tricked up with a

[5]Cap (Steve Rogers) actually became an artist in the comic books in the eighties or thereabouts and, at one point, was assigned to draw the "Captain America" comic book.

Above: Reb Brown, without his helmet, smiles for the camera.

parachute and some sort of radar sense. In the opening scene, Cap stops two thieves from stealing a pension check from an old lady and exhibits heightened speed (he can run as fast as a dune buggy) and moderate superstrength. (In a later scene, he throws his cycle over an eight-foot wall, and then jumps up to the top of the wall himself.) He wears a motorcycle visor and helmet instead of a mask. His shield is bulletproof but appears to be made of plastic and is partially transparent. Cap often uses it as a boomerang.

The story pits Cap against a revolutionary known as "Miguel" (Christopher Lee), who has kidnapped a professor who is trying to find a cure for "the disease of aging." Miguel threatens to spread a rapid-aging gas in a major city unless he's paid $1 million. Cap tracks him to Bellville, where the townspeople not only are curiously edgy but also urge our hero to leave. While Miguel's minions try to run Cap out of town and even jail him for a spell, the U.S. government refuses to give in to blackmail, and Portland, Oregon, is sprayed. If he isn't paid, Miguel says, he won't divulge the antidote.

Cap learns the source of Bellville's nervousness and hostility when he discovers that Miguel had sprayed the town by helicopter weeks earlier. To keep them compliant Miguel has given the residents a mild antidote which retards, but does not stop, the aging process. Steve befriends a young mother and her son who tell him everything they know, and Cap is surprised to learn that Miguel's headquarters is an active American penitentiary, where the arch criminal is masquerading as the warden! (Shades of the "Ma Parker" episode on *Batman*.) In their final confrontation, Miguel is hit with the liquid aging spray and dies.

There are a couple of good scenes in the one hundred-minute telefilm. One shows Cap, as Steve Rogers, battling a bunch of bat-armed rowdies. He leaps up to the balcony of a nearby house, then waits until they climb up

after him via more conventional means before jumping back down to the ground and ripping the supports out from under the balcony. The men topple like tenpins. (You'd have to wonder, though, if this wouldn't compromise Cap's secret identity.)

Another good scene has Cap turning his cycle into a hang glider and taking off after Miguel in the air. There is some nice stunt flying, and an effective process shot shows Cap high in the sky and the earth far below. Another scene is thrilling, but suspect: When Cap is caught between two groups of enemy jeeps on a dam, he simply drives his cycle over the side. Although the cleverly edited stunt work is excellent, it is hard to believe that either Cap or his cycle would come through without a scratch.

Top: *Captain America* cruises the highways of America on his motorbike.

Bottom: Steve Rogers (Reb Brown) takes some time out for a little r and r.

Like its predecessor, *Captain America II* is a modest production that makes good use of nice scenery and locations, and features some outstanding photography by Vincent A. Martinelli. The many sweeping shots of highways and countrysides, as well as a shot of a helicopter spraying the reddish antidote over main streets of Portland, are almost better than the telefilm deserves. Ivan Nagy's direction is fairly routine, but Wilton Schiller and Patricia Payne fashioned a workable script that has a clever plot and many nice touches.

Unfortunately, Miguel is a colorless villain as written and played; in his limited appearances Christopher Lee neither gets anything out of nor gives anything to the picture. A deglamorized Lana Wood is better as Miguel's tough assistant, Yolanda, who gets her kicks giving orders to the "troops." Len Birman is back as Cap's boss, this time with Connie Sellecca at his side, but the best work comes from Bill Lucking as a Bellville rowdie and Katherine Justice as the mother who finally tells Cap what's going on in her town.

While *Captain America II* is vastly inferior to the comic book series—and did nothing to thrill the folks at Marvel Comics—it makes an acceptable made-for-TV adventure. With a more dramatic presentation, better direction and music, it might have amounted to a creditable feature. Plans for a regular Captain America TV series never materialized.

Over the past twenty-five-plus years, Captain America has been the protagonist of many interesting comics stories, and has come up against some formidable opponents.

Madame Hydra (later known as Viper) is a psychotic, scar-faced beauty with terrorist and nihilist leanings. After running the evil organization, Hydra, for awhile, she set up her own operations and time and again tried to unleash some dastardly plot against the country or the world. And time and again Cap would stop her. An early battle, the one in which she parted company with Hydra in an explosive fashion, has become a collector's classic: *Captain America* #113 (May 1969). "The Strange Death of Captain America" is a textbook case of how to tell a simple, if plot-heavy story,[6] neatly, concisely, and with great flair and "drama."

Stan Lee's story is excellent, but it is artist Jim Steranko's fluid, exciting, and extremely creative pencils that make this a standout. Steranko employs all the tricks of his trade: full-page or half-page collages showing the past history and girlhood of Madame Hydra, her anguish over the hideously scarred side of her face in otherwise voluptuous trappings; a neatly segmented funeral procession for Cap; and splendid two-page centerfold with the "dead" Captain America assaulting the forces of Hydra in a cemetery where they are entombing the bodies of the Avengers; and a superb pinup of Cap (with Rick Jones dressed as Bucky) standing astride a pile of fallen foes while holding one Hydra member high above his head, the moon and twilight sky outlined behind them. The explosion that allegedly kills off the tormented Madame Hydra is rendered in sharp black and white.

When not using collages—the comic book equivalent of montage—Steranko breaks boundaries, in much the way Jack Kirby did years earlier, by using panels of different sizes in various eye-appealing and cinematic

[6]The Avengers superteam, who guest-star, are also overcome by Madame Hydra, among other developments. Cap's death is, of course, a ruse. In the eighties, the same story probably would have been told over several issues, yet it never seems cramped or "crowded."

combinations. His work has the stylish, irresistible flow and action of the best of the forties work, blended with a unique, personalized contemporary appeal that is distinctly modern, circa 1969. His fine pencil work is expertly embellished by Tom Palmer, and the issue's coloring, particularly in its use of jet blacks, blues, and grays, is excellent. Steranko[7] became one of the most widely imitated artists in the business, and Palmer remains one of the industry's finest embellishers.

Cap's most formidable and enduring enemy, created by Ed Herron, is the Red Skull, who first appeared back in 1945 in the first issue of *Captain America*. In time, in bits and pieces, we learned the Skull's origin. His father tried to drown him as a baby after his mother died in childbirth. The following morning, the father committed suicide. Young Johann Schmidt became a beggar and thief, eking out a desperate living on the streets. A Jewish store owner's daughter became his first homicide victim when she resisted his physical advances.

Years later, he is a bellboy in Berlin when he witnesses an argument between Hitler and his Gestapo chief in a hotel room. "I could teach that bellboy to do a better job than you!" Hitler screams in rage. He winds up taking Schmidt under his wing, instructing him until the protégé who was to become the Skull eventually surpasses Hitler in sheer evil. Parts of this story were told in *Tales of Suspense* #66 and other sixties issues, but J. M. DeMatteis brought it all together in a special origin issue, *Captain America* #298 (1984).

The Skull was brought back into the Captain's silver-age saga in an issue of *Tales of Suspense* and returned many times thereafter to tangle with his red, white, and blue-clad nemesis. Issues #88–91 of *Suspense* (1966) feature a four-part serial in which the Skull lures Cap into danger by making him believe Bucky is still alive. (The lad turns out to be a robot.) The Red Skull seals one square mile of the heart of New York City in a bubble and lifts it off the ground with his powerful machines, threatening to send it hurtling to oblivion unless Cap swears fealty to him. Naturally, Cap must comply, and the Skull even forces him to tell the world he (Cap) now serves his greatest enemy.

Cap brings part of his troubles on himself. Proving that he—and not Superman— is the world's biggest Boy Scout, Cap obediently sits down in an electronic "death chair" *after* the people have been freed simply on the Skull's orders. After all, Cap did give his word that he would obey the Skull. Why he should keep a promise that was exacted through the Skull's threats to murder millions of innocent people never seems to occur to the star-spangled avenger. His strange code of honor would get him into trouble in years to come, even with other, less scrupulous (or less dopey) Marvel heroes, and provide some interesting plot angles.

Perhaps the greatest—and longest—Red Skull-versus-Cap epic began in 1984 in issue #290 and didn't wind up until a year later. This saga introduced the sinister

---

[7]Steranko is also author of the superb two-volume *Steranko History of Comics*.

Above: *Tales of Suspense* #90 featured the villainy of the Red Skull, who also survived into modern times. Copyright © 1967 by Vista Publications, Inc. (Marvel Comics).

Mother Superior, the Red Skull's daughter, who wears an outfit that makes her look like a nun slumming as a cocktail waitress in a tavern in Hell. She has a black gown slit up one side, as well as a black cloak flowing from beneath a wide epaulet; her hair is completely hidden by a very tight skullcap. Her minions are the Sisters of Sin: Dream, Pleasure, Agony, and Death. Amazingly, these rather sexy women (one, however, was a withered old crone) in actuality are little girls whose growth and maturity had been machine-accelerated by the Skull.

The Skull and his daughter pull out all the stops to destroy Steve Rogers once and for all. Before the conflict is over, it embroils virtually all of Steve's closest friends, permanently altering some of them in the process. Pacifist Dave Cox (rather than disapproving of him, Cap understood and admired his own brand of courage) is transformed into a maniacal villain, the Slayer. Arnie Roth is turned into a rouged, mincing marionette, forced by the Skull to accuse Steve of being a "closet queen." Nomad,[8] Steve's latest partner, is bewitched into betraying Rogers; he sneaks a formula into Cap's food and drink that reverses the supersoldier serum and starts turning him old and gray, his actual age. The Falcon and Bernie Rosenthal are captured and imprisoned in the Skull's horrific mansion. And the Skull forces Steve to vividly relive the moment when Bucky Barnes died and he survived to bear the grief and guilt. In issue #300, they battle literally to the death—the Red Skull's death. Yes, Cap's archenemy dies…until fifty issues later, when we learn that crazed geneticist Arnim Zola, who developed a process to "preserve consciousness upon death," used it to transfer the Skull's mind into a clone of Captain America's. His handsome Aryan face doesn't last long, however, when he gets a faceful of murderous mist that decays his flesh and leaves him looking just like…a red skull.[9]

It was only natural that the Red Skull become the centerpiece of a 1989 theatrical film based on Captain America (as of this writing unreleased and deemed by many unreleasable). The screenplay was written by Stephen Tolkin, who admitted he was "no fan of super-hero stories. In and of themselves they don't mean that much to me, although good things have been done in the form." Tolkin therefore deliberately constructed a story in which Steve Rogers wears the Captain America uniform as little as possible—at the very beginning, and at the end. "All the rest of the time, he's wearing jeans and a shirt."

Changes were also made to the Red Skull. Instead of the German Johann Schmidt, the Skull is now the Italian Tadzio De Santis, who was kidnapped in the thirties by the Nazis and experimented on. Cap and the Skull have more of a link than they do in the comics. Both have been injected with the supersoldier formula concocted by the female Italian scientist, Dr. Vasari, who escaped from the Nazis when they experimented on Tadzio without her permission. Once Vasari is in America, Cap's origin proceeds to unfold pretty much the way it does in the comics, with 4-F Steve Rogers volunteering to be tested with her formula. Later developments are also straight from the comic book: Battling the Skull, Cap winds up on a rocket, falls off, and is frozen for twenty years—this time in the Canadian tundra. A boy who witnesses part of the above grows up to become President of the United States and is

---

[8]Nomad, which Cap had once called himself during a period of disillusionment following the Watergate scandal (symbolized by a story line in *Captain America*), was the name taken by the second, 1950s "paranoiac" Bucky once he was cured and free to reenter the world.

[9]Although at times pretentious and undeniably contrived, these Skull/Mother Superior issues are among the best in Cap's long history. Various writers on these and other Skull stories mentioned included Mark Gruenwald, J. M. DeMatteis, Michael Ellis, and Michael Carlin. Artists include Ron Frenz, Steve Leialoha, Paul Neary, Kieron Dwyer, and John Byrne.

rescued by Cap from the Red Skull's clutches.

In the comic books, Captain America fell in love with Peggy Carter during World War II, and then with her younger sister Sharon two decades later (causing understandable complications). In Tolkin's script, Peggy becomes Bernice Stewart (a new version of Bernie Rosenthal?) and her *daughter* is Sharon. Tolkin explained the main thrust of his screenplay. "Basically, my script is the story of somebody from the 1940s coming to the 1980s and relating to a change in values." According to *Amazing Heroes* columnist Andy Mangels, this was the best part of Tolkin's screenplay. "What [is] most fascinating [is] the man-out-of-time aspects of Steve Rogers and the political theories and intrigue bandied about between the players."

According to Mangels, "The Red Skull isn't the operative villain in our world. All governments are corrupt. America's, despite the wonderful principles the country was founded with [sic], remains much too corrupt and much too good at covering it up. It's not surprising that Steve Rogers shows a little leftist leanings in the script; he stands for the principles of what America should be, not what it has turned into in the last two hundred years." This is basically the way Captain America is in the comic books. Tolkin's screenplay shows that the Skull is behind quite a few nefarious schemes, but is only a small part of "the governmental corruption...lurking behind every Pentagon door," as Mangels puts it. Reportedly, not all of the script's political material made it intact into the movie.

The movie was directed by Albert Pyun, who was behind a creditable 1982 effort *The Sword and the Sorcerer*, but whose other projects usually wound up going direct to video. One problem was that Pyun was often called in to fix or finish up other's projects, such as the utterly lamentable and unwatchable remake of *Journey to the Center of the Earth* (begun in 1986, released in 1989). Many films are announced by Pyun, but few ever reach the movie screen.

For Pyun, there was only one actor for the role, Matt Salinger, the son of the reclusive writer J. D. Salinger. Matt had already appeared in the television miniseries *Blood and Orchids* and the telefilm *Deadly Deception*. Although Salinger was afraid of becoming typecast, Pyun, who had known him and his stage work, convinced him that he should take the role. The original plan was to cast a muscle boy in the part—someone like Lundgren or Schwarzenegger—but it was decided that Salinger's six-foot, four-inch frame would fit the bill. A costume was designed for him that was almost an exact duplicate of the one in the comics.

Filming was started in June 1989 in Yugoslavia, with the town of Rovigno standing in for World War II Italy. Redondo

Above: Matt Salinger was chosen to play *Captain America* in the new theatrical feature.

Beach, California, doubled for Steve Roger's hometown. Bad weather—and a low budget—meant that rapid rewrites were in order. A chase sequence that was originally to have employed everything from surfboards and water skis to pedal boats was skinned to the bone: Cap gets away from his pursuers on a bicycle. There was so much rain that the scenes shot in Europe all have a kind of gray look to them, which may work better for the atmosphere.

There was much special effects work, including the launching of a V-1 rocket plane that utilized wires, cranes, and an hydraulic system, as well as a small army of brave stuntmen. Pyun was proud of the sequences involving Captain America's shield, which, he claimed, they were able to get to work "like it does in the comic books." Sometimes it was attached to guide wires; other times, Salinger employed his skill as a Frisbee thrower to toss the shield with surprising accuracy.

Actor Scott Paulin was chosen to play the Red Skull. Of his character, Paulin said, "He spends the whole movie bitter about [his lost childhood]. He's willing to punish the whole world for his emptiness, and at the same time, he's searching for his own childhood. Anyone who has a dark side to himself and has a feeling that it may have come to him in childhood, knows who this character is—of course, in an extraordinarily exaggerated fashion."

Paulin wasn't crazy about spending five hours in a makeup chair each day. Salinger also found his costume quite uncomfortable. The skintight, formfitting outfit was made by Vin Burnham Costumes and Creatures. At least Paulin didn't have to wear his skull face throughout all of the movie (anymore than Salinger had to wear his costume that often); screenwriter Tolkin had decided the Skull would have had plastic surgery on his face by the 1980s. "I don't think people wanted to keep looking at this horrible skull face forever." But Paulin felt that there was still an "artificial" look to him, that he as an actor had to convey great age coupled with great strength (from the supersoldier formula) and that it was quite a challenge.

Ronny Cox was cast as the president, with Kim Dillingham as both Bernice Stewart and her daughter, Sharon. Ned Beatty, Darren McGavin, and Bill Mumy also appear. In the comics, Sharon was a special agent who assisted Cap on many missions (as did Peggy before her); in the film, she is simply a yuppie, possibly meant for contrast.

While comic book fans waited in anticipation for a movie they hoped would be at least as good as *Batman* (1989), and Marvel Comics got busy with publicity on their own end, the release date for the picture kept getting pushed further and further back. Countless projects and merchandising schemes related to the motion picture were promised and advertised, but never materialized. Summer 1990 came and went and there was no *Captain America*. People knew that this was not going to be the kind of multimillion dollar production *Batman* was (not with 21st Century releasing and Albert Pyun directing), but at least they expected *some* kind of "major motion picture." Although Marvel Comics characters had done quite well on television, when it came to movies they seemed to be jinxed. By December, the film had still not been released, and there was a question whether it would even make it to home video.

In his column in Marvel's news magazine, *Marvel Age*, Stan Lee, head honcho, was busy explaining. In a masterstroke of tact and diplomacy, Lee assured his readers that the film was good, but that the producers wanted to make it even better. What was particularly needed was more action. "Director Albert Pyun," Lee wrote, "did it so well and so excitingly that everyone in the audience [at a screening] kept clamoring for more." This is perhaps the first time in movie history that a cast and crew have been called back to the studio—and back to location—to reshoot scenes because the director had done it "so well."

Cinefantastique had also seen the finished product, and its report was not encouraging. "The super-hero movie takes another giant leap *backward*...the one Marvel Comics character whose story could have generated a genuinely meaningful adventure about the American Spirit instead *de*generates into a meaning*less* collection of pitifully produced gun-and-fistfights that makes the 1979 Reb Brown made-for-television version look spectacular in comparison." Reviewer S. C. Dacy complained that Salinger looked exactly the same both before and after being injected with the serum (perhaps the budget wasn't large enough for an additional actor), criticized Paulin's overplaying as the Skull, and complained that Sharon was like a valley girl.

Whatever the eventual fate of *Captain America,* the movie, Captain America the character—who celebrates his fiftieth anniversary in 1991—is going stronger than ever, and will likely be going strong for many years to come.

CHAPTER FOUR
THE (ALMOST)
FORGOTTEN HERO:
CAPTAIN MARVEL

Superman. Batman. Captain America. All are still going strong and, with the exception of Captain America, have been consistently published for decades. Which had the best-selling super-hero comic book in history? The answer is the *comparatively* obscure Captain Marvel, otherwise known as "The Big Red Cheese."

In the thirties and forties, one of the very biggest comic book companies was Fawcett Publications (now defunct). Fawcett was already a major magazine outfit when its management saw how much money there was to be made producing comic books and instructed editor Bill Parker to start a new line. He planned a lead feature consisting of several individually powered characters whose names put together would spell out "Shazam." When his boss thought a single hero would be better, Parker changed the concept and created "Captain Thunder." Charles Clarence Beck, an artist from Minneapolis, was drafted to draw the feature.

It was decided that Captain Thunder would appear in *Whiz Comics*.[1] Not only was this first issue not distributed, it was never even used for copyright registration, as another decision changed the hero's name to Captain Marvel. He made his debut in *Whiz Comics* #2 (February 1940).

Captain Marvel had obvious similarities to Superman right from the first. On the cover of *Whiz* #2, he is seen throwing an automobile just as Superman does on the cover of *Action* #1. His origin is completely different, however: Billy Batson, a young paperboy, is instructed to follow a mysterious figure into a subway, and not being particularly "street smart," he accompanies this fellow on a short trip in a weird-looking subway car to a hidden cavern. There Billy meets the wizened magician Shazam, who has been using the powers of the gods to battle evil for three thousand years. He has chosen Billy as his successor.

When Billy utters the magic word SHAZAM! he acquires the wisdom of *S*olomon, the strength of *H*ercules, the stamina of *A*tlas, the power of *Z*eus, the courage of *A*chilles, and the speed of *M*ercury. He also transforms into a full-grown adult male who resembles Fred MacMurray. Although Billy is basically a sweet kid, his powerful alter ego is menacing, as tough and violent as Superman was in his early appearances. He threatens the mad doctor Sivana that when they meet again, "you will be behind prison walls—or dead!"

The early Captain Marvel stories were simplistic and featured primitive, but nicely composed, artwork by C. C. Beck. When editor Parker left Fawcett, Beck became

Above: *Whiz Comics* #2 introduced Captain Marvel to the world. Copyright 1940 Fawcett Publications. Copyright © 1974 National Periodical Publications, Inc.

[1]Fawcett's founder, Wilfred H. Fawcett, had created the famous *Captain Billy's Whiz-Bang* years before.

Opposite: Captain Marvel suspects something rotten is up.

113

the true guiding hand behind the character he had helped create. (Beck had contributed the costume design as well as the whole look and feel of the strip.) Before long, there was so much demand for new stories—in both *Whiz Comics* and the new *Captain Marvel* book—that additional artists and writers had to be brought in. Jack Kirby drew a few stories. New editor Ed Herron contributed several tales, while the prolific Otto Binder wrote nearly half of every story published featuring Captain Marvel or any of his "family." Eventually a certain formula was established: Captain Marvel's adventures were more gentle and lighthearted than those of Superman, and certainly far less grim and violent than Captain America's often grisly exploits.

Captain Marvel soon had a large supporting cast. There was Captain Marvel, Junior, the crippled Freddy Freeman, who gains magical powers, such as the usual superstrength and the ability to fly, but always remains the same age. He appeared in his own magazine and in *Master Comics* and was superbly drawn by artist Mac Raboy. Billy Batson's twin sister, Mary, could turn into the powerful Mary Marvel when she invoked the word SHAZAM! She appeared in her own title and in *Wow* Magazine.

Three other boys with the name Billy Batson became the Three Lieutenant Marvels. A lovable con artist pretended to be Billy and Mary's uncle and was known as Uncle Marvel in spite of his absence of powers. There

was even a Marvel Bunny, Hoppy, as well as a Freckles Marvel and a Baby Marvel. Some of these were one-shot characters, while others returned to guest-star in stories time and again. Hoppy even got his own comic book.

Captain Marvel acquired quite a rogues' gallery during his lengthy run. Besides his evil archfoe, Dr. Sivana, there were Sivana's daughter, Beautia; Black Adam, Captain Marvel's opposite number; the satanic Ibac; the robotic Mr. Atom; the vicious Captain Nazi; and the Oriental fiend, the Red Crusher. The wildest of all was the unknown, shadowy Mr. Mind, who with his "Monster Society" battled Captain Marvel for twenty-five successive issues and turned out to be nothing more than a tiny, if diabolical, worm from another planet.

Like Superman, Captain Marvel got more and more powerful as the years went by. His stories

Tom Tyler poses dramatically.

also became more cosmic. But whereas Superman's stories, as fantastic as they might be, remained comparatively "down to earth," Captain Marvel's adventures were outlandish and had absolutely no pretense to "reality." At their best they were engaging; at their worst, monumentally silly.

Republic Pictures tried their own approach in 1941 with the serial *The Adventures of Captain Marvel*. Transferring a typical Captain Marvel story into a film would have resulted in a live-action cartoon—in fact, a cartoon would have been more appropriate—so the serial made the character more earthbound and realistic. As played straight by actor Tom Tyler, Captain Marvel is neither charming nor dopey. On the contrary, he's not only efficient, but cold-blooded. When he threatens to throw a man to his death unless he talks, you believe he'll do it. And he does ruthlessly murder several creepy characters during the course of the serial. Tyler and the screenwriters give us a Captain Marvel who's similar to the character as he appeared in the earliest issues of *Whiz Comics*.

Tyler had previously appeared in several "B" Westerns. For the role of alter ego Billy Batson, the producers brought in Frank "Junior" Coghlan, a busy juvenile of the period. Coghlan's Billy is older than in the comic books, appearing to be in his late teens or even early twenties, but has Batson's sweet nature, adolescent looks, and a high, boyish voice. In spite of his own tough-guy antics, Tyler's voice is "cultivated" and also a little high, though not a "sissy" voice like Billy's. Billy Benedict, best known as "Whitey" of the Dead End Kids/Bowery Boys features, has a supporting role but doesn't do much for the first six chapters or so.

The story begins in the Valley of Tombs, where the Malcolm Archaeological expedition (including radio broadcaster Billy Batson) is searching for the lost secrets of the Scorpion Dynasty. Scoffing at native curses, the team enters the tomb and finds a small golden scorpion idol with five quartz lenses. When employed properly, this idol-device can use the energy of the sun to turn base metals into gold and can also cause explosions. Said properties ignite the greed and power lust of one member of the party, who disguises himself as the "Scorpion" to commit evil deeds and obtain the idol for his own purposes.

Top: Tom Tyler has a chat with Gene Autry on the backlot.

Left: Portrait shot of Tyler/Captain Marvel.

An explosion traps Billy in another chamber of the tomb. There the elderly wizard, Shazam, appears to him from "out of the past." Shazam, who guards the secret of the scorpion idol, returned to life when the others invaded the tomb, and now he wants Billy to protect innocents from the curse of the Scorpion. With the magic word SHAZAM! Billy becomes Captain Marvel in a puff of smoke. Although the basic elements are the same, the origin of the character is quite different from the one in *Whiz Comics #2*.

Each member of the party takes one of the five quartz lenses, while Billy holds on to an informative scroll. That night the hooded Scorpion leads a raid on the party; sentries are murdered, the scroll is stolen, and Billy is tied up. To make matters worse, volcanic activity convinces the natives, that the sacred tomb has been desecrated, and they attack en masse. Captain Marvel, who obviously never has sworn *not* to take a life, uses the natives' own machine gun to shoot them in the back as they flee!

The following eleven chapters detail how the malevolent Scorpion connives, murders, and plunders in attempt after attempt to retrieve all five lenses and gain ultimate power. The Scorpion repeatedly tries to kill Captain Marvel and all the rest of the cast, using bombs, machine guns, guillotines, electricity, and the laserlike power of the scorpion idol itself. While the Scorpion succeeds in doing away with most of his fellow scientists, Captain Marvel and his pals come away, of course, unscathed.

The death traps are occasionally inventive. In chapter two, the Scorpion uses a "persuasion" device on a colleague. Tripping a photoelectric beam starts a treadmill that takes an unwary victim down a hallway to a huge guillotine suspended across the corridor. In Captain Marvel's case, the blade merely smashes against his chest. In chapter six, the Scorpion plays the beam of the idol into the mouth of a tunnel where Captain Marvel is located, with the result that our hero is cornered by a flood of molten rock with only a dead end behind him, but a convenient hole in the ceiling of the tunnel allows him to escape. The shots of melting rock and the process work in this sequence are pretty good.

The best cliff-hanger occurs at the end of chapter four. Betty (Louise Currie), a secretary to one of the scientists, is placed unconscious in a car that is then sent hurtling down the several levels of a parking garage until it rolls out across the street and smashes into a building on the other side. Captain Marvel shows up in the following chapter to save the day, but the audience is treated to some well-executed thrills before he does.

Above: Captain Marvel flies into action—an athletic jump from a stuntman.

Betty also figures in another exciting midchapter sequence when she and her car are locked in the back of a big truck, which moments later is abandoned by the Scorpion's men. Driverless, it proceeds to run away down a winding cliff highway, until Captain Marvel comes to the rescue.

On more than one occasion the serial cheats a bit in its cliff-hangers. At the end of chapter three, a time bomb goes off in Billy's plane, and we see the explosion. The beginning of chapter four adds some "missing" information: Billy had changed to Captain Marvel before the bomb went off and of course is uninjured. This moderate example, however, is nothing compared to the elaborate fakery pulled at the end of chapter nine.

The Scorpion is questioning one of the other scientists, Dr. Lang, who is suspended in an iron cage. Where is the lens? the Scorpion wants to know. (That's all he ever wants to know.) Captain Marvel shows up and chases the Scorpion through underground catacombs but the archfoe doubles back and murders Lang, who previously had been forced to tell his secretary Betty to get his lens out of his safe. Now, with his dying breath, he tries to warn her over the phone about the safe's built-in death trap. The chapter ends with Billy and Betty at Lang's safe, followed by a shot of machine guns in the opposite wall firing and presumably riddling them with bullets.

Not so! In chapter ten, we see missing shots of one of the Scorpion's hoods pushing aside Betty and Billy and opening the safe himself. The two not only are saved, but were never even in any danger!

Chapter ten does contain an interesting sequence when the remaining members of the expedition travel by steamer back to the Valley of Tombs in Bangkok and are caught in a typhoon. When the ship hits the rocks, Captain Marvel flies ashore with the end of a rope to rig up a breeches buoy and save the other passengers. While the business with the breeches buoy is fairly dramatic and suspenseful, it would have made much more sense for the captain to simply *fly* the few passengers to safety. This would certainly have been faster and a lot less dangerous. The sequence ends with the breeches buoy breaking and the ship sliding off the rocks. Betty is still on board, but Captain Marvel saves her again.

Other effective sequences include an exciting battle in chapter five in which Captain Marvel is nearly bashed by a falling engine, throws a hoodlum from a roof to his death (in true contemporary "Dirty Harry" style), and pulls up an elevator car containing some crooks by wrapping his hands around the cable. There are some lively fisticuffs between the butler of one scientist and the Scorpion's henchman in chapter six which really tear up the scenery, and a good shot of another gunman falling over the side of a dam in chapter seven. Betty faints at the sight but Captain Marvel prevents her from falling off herself.

The effects in *The Adventures of Captain Marvel* are quite good for the period and hold up well today. The combination of stunts, props, process shots, etc., basically set the mold for all subsequent super-hero films. All of Captain Marvel's powers are illustrated—superstrength, invulnerability (to bullets and other things), flying, athletic abilities. The flying effects are particularly good. There's a great bit in chapter six which first shows Captain Marvel falling past window after window as he jumps down to the sidewalk, and then flying up again.

Although similar processes were used in the *Adventures of Superman* TV series years later, the flying effects in *Captain Marvel* seem much more elaborate. Many of these scenes were actually done by consummate stuntman

Dave Sharpe, standing in for star Tom Tyler. Sometimes he would be filmed diving off a building. Other times he would take a running leap at a special three-foot device that would send the athletic fellow hurtling eighteen feet into the air. Several crew members would stand twenty feet away with a fire net to catch him, although on at least one occasion Sharpe came down right on the edge of the net and bruised his butt.

Effects-man Howard Lydecker also built an over-sized Captain Marvel dummy that was used in some sequences. The dummy was sent down a wire for two-hundred yards over Mulholland Drive and later used to show Captain Marvel flying to the top of the Biltmore Garage building. The dummy is well de-signed and looks quite effective in quick cuts.

"Junior" Coghlan explained to *Filmfax* writer Jan Henderson how the switch was made from Batson to Marvel in the serial: "We had a typical, old-fashioned camera trough with flash powder in it. At the proper time, I'd say 'SHAZAM!' and Pow! the thing would go off. Billy [director William Witney] would yell

Top: A nice composite shot of Captain Marvel soaring through the clouds.

Left: Boo! Hiss! The sinister Scarab wants to kill Billy Batson.

'Cut!' I'd get out, Tom Tyler'd get in, they'd start the camera and repeat the flash. Afterward, the film editors would cut it together, and when the smoke dissolved, Billy Batson would be gone and Captain Marvel would be there. The only problem was, a couple times on location, when the wind was blowing the wrong way, I nearly lost some eyebrows!"

Coghlan also recalled an incident when some crew members forgot to remove several gasoline cans, full of fumes, from a tent that was rigged to burst into flames. When the tent was set on fire, the gasoline blew up and made things much hotter for the hapless actors than ever intended.

Tom Tyler is appropriately heroic and formidable as a determined, if almost mute, Captain Marvel. (One of his longer speeches, in which he merely tells Betty how she can reach him, doesn't occur until halfway through the serial.) Contrasted to the boyishly earnest Coghlan, Tyler practically comes on like a hoodlum, as if he were a butch wish fulfillment of comparatively epicene Billy or the fantasy of some stereotypical comic book fan.

Harry Worth played the Scorpion, although Gerald Mohr's voice came from behind the hood so that the Scorpion's real identity could come as a surprise. To keep the audience guessing, different cast members would wear the Scorpion costume. In spite of the mystery identity angle, though, the Scorpion is a rather dull villain. With so many actors impersonating him and even a dubbed voice, it's no wonder.

Louise Currie offers a mediocre performance as Betty. In chapter nine, Betty suspects that the Scorpion might be Dr. Lang (George Pembroke). But when she gets a call from Dr. Lang, who she thinks may be a ruthless saboteur and murderer, she doesn't even react to his voice except with her usual cheery smile. Even if this bit were filmed out of sequence, it doesn't excuse Currie's perfunctory playing throughout.

The screenplay, concocted by a bevy of writers, has a clever and suspenseful story line although it is not terribly inspired in other respects. No one ever seems the least bit curious about Captain Marvel, his sudden appearance, or his amazing abilities. There are creeping inconsistencies (what with five writers) and loopy moments. In chapter twelve, for instance, the Scorpion captures Billy, Betty, and Whitey, ties them to poles in a cavern, but puts a gag only in Billy's mouth. What's stupid about this is that although the Scorpion knows that Billy Batson and Captain

Above: Rifles are no match for Captain Marvel.

119

Marvel are one and the same, he *doesn't* know that Billy can change into Captain Marvel only by saying SHAZAM! so why would he bother with a gag? Why bother tying Billy at all, for that matter, since the Scorpion knows those ropes won't hold Captain Marvel.

At the end of the twelve-chapter serial, the Scorpion attempts to stir up the natives in the Valley of Tombs to destroy the "infidels" who pursue him. Many of them believe that he is the personification of the scorpion god. Fortunately, he is disintegrated by a disillusioned resurrectionist wielding the scorpion-idol weapon. Captain Marvel throws the weapon into the lava and reverts for all time to Billy Batson, sans any memory of what happened.

If the production values in *The Adventures of Captain Marvel* look superior to other serials, it's because a great deal of stock footage from "A" films was employed to bolster the "B" movie proceedings. The ever-reliable William

Witney delivered on the action sequences, while his codirector John English mostly handled the dialogue scenes. Cy Feuer's musical score can best be described as insipid. Although Frank Coghlan claims that the serial was filmed late in 1939 and in January of 1940—and not released until March of 1941—it's unlikely that filming took place that early. *Whiz Comics #2*, which featured the first appearance of Captain Marvel, went on sale only a couple of months before its February 1940 cover date. When Coghlan talks about buying Christmas presents for the cast—Tom Tyler got a jockstrap because of the tight suit he wore—he must be referring to the Christmas of 1940.

There's a blooper in chapter eleven of the serial, although it's unlikely that it was widely noticed. When Captain Marvel lifts a tree so that Whitey and the others can pass by in their car, on close view at the right, you can see a crewman peeking out, then receding, from around the side of the mountain. It's a very quick and in the distance. It wouldn't have made much sense to bother spending money to reshoot the scene.

Although *The Adventures of Captain Marvel* is considered by many to be one of the best—if not *the* best—of the classic serials, it is neither as good nor (in spite of far superior effects) as entertaining as the first *Superman* serial or the *Captain America* cliff-hanger. Still, it's not without a certain charm and appeal.

Not only was the serial successful, but the comic book was going better than ever. By 1946, each issue of *Captain Marvel* was selling nearly 1.5 million copies. DC Comics, aka National Periodical Publications, the publisher of Superman, was by no means unaware of the competition. Other publishers had come out with knockoffs of the Man of Steel, but none sold as well as the Big Red Cheese. National decided to sue not only

Above: Captain Marvel does the twist with the Scarab. *Ouch!*

Fawcett Publications, but also Republic Pictures, which released the serial. The notable Louis Nizer was National's attorney.

Fawcett was accused of infringement of copyright and unfair competition. Artists, writers, and editors—experts from both companies—were called to the witness stand. Although the judge admitted that it was fairly obvious that copying had taken place, he decided to dismiss the complaint. There was not evidence of unfair competition, or any indication that Fawcett was trying to confuse readers or pass off its character as DC's Man of Steel. Further, National had lost its copyright when Superman newspaper strips were published without the proper notices.

Nizer moved for an appeal, and a new trial began in 1951. The legal costs were enormous, and Fawcett's staff was spending as much time going through old comics trying to prove that superfeats did not begin with Superman as they were working on stories. Finally in 1953, Fawcett decided to discontinue its comics line—not just Captain Marvel, but every character—and settle with DC out of court. Sales were dropping across the board for super-hero characters from every publisher, and Fawcett executives thought the time was right to abandon ship. Why keep publishing and paying huge legal fees when it might not be worth it in the long run? The company's lack of faith in the continuing sales appeal of super-heroes was indicated by its decision to cancel all its comic books, most of which were not the subject of any litigation.

In one way, the big guns at Fawcett were correct. Most super-hero titles did die out due to lack of readership as the fifties progressed. But Superman was not affected. Since Captain Marvel was outselling the Man of Steel, would the former's comic book have lasted, riding out the antisuper-hero trend of the fifties, had the lawsuit been won? Would Captain Marvel today be more famous than the Man of Steel? We'll never know.

We do have the answer to another question, however. Was Captain Marvel just a carbon copy and illegal duplication of Superman? The reply came from the very instigators of the lawsuit, DC Comics: *No.* For if Captain Marvel had been nothing more than a pale imitation, DC would never have bought the rights to the character or begun publishing not only new stories in the 1970s—but reprints of 1940s material (the very stories in litigation!).

Captain Marvel had always been a simple variation on the super he-man, just as Superman himself was a variation on, say, Samson or Hercules, or Doc Savage for that matter. Not only was Billy/Marvel a very different character from Clark Kent/Kal-El, but the whole approach was completely different. DC's lawsuit could be dismissed as one prompted by greed and jealousy, something that only made the lawyers rich, were it not for the

Above: The Scarab's goons corner Billy Batson ("Junior" Coghlan).

121

fact that if Captain Marvel had continued to be published, today *his* might be the household name and Superman the "forgotten" hero.

In April 1966, the comic company M. F. Enterprises came out with a new *Captain Marvel* that had no relation to the original, although he wore a red outfit, as well as blue boots and a black mask. This blond fellow had the amazing ability to split his body literally into several sections—for instance, his fist could fly off the end of his arm and sock in the jaw a villain who would otherwise be out of reach. The book's title was changed to *Captain Marvel Presents the Terrible Five* and died an unlamented death in 1967. In spite of the rather original superpower of the character, he never caught on with the buyers of comics.

Two years later, Marvel Comics decided to adopt the name Captain Marvel—a natural considering the comic company's own name—and in May 1968 brought out the first issue of a brand new *Captain Marvel*. "Marvel's space-born super-hero" was born Mar-Vell, a "son of the Kree empire," which was constantly at war with the Skrull empire. Strategically located, Earth became a battleground between the two far-flung and powerful races. Mar-Vell, wearing a green outfit with a sort of finned headpiece, had to battle not only his enemies, the Skrulls, but also renegade Kree who didn't like Mar-Vell's way. The basic premise could not have been further from that of the original Captain Marvel.

Later, declining sales prompted a new direction and costume for the character. Now decked out in a brilliant red and blue outfit with a bright gold sunburst on his chest, along with a simpler mask replacing the headpiece and

revealing his sleek thatch of silver (on occasion, blond) hair, Mar-Vell battled more traditional earthbound villains as well as aliens.

Mar-Vell has been exiled to Earth because he cannot support the regime of Ronan, an evil Kree who has usurped the rulership of Mar-Vell's planet. As in the original Captain Marvel, but with its own unique twist, Mar-Vell's life and adventures are now bound to a youngster's, in this case the ubiquitous Rick Jones, who had been a companion first to the Hulk, and then to Captain America. By touching his wristbands together, Rick can bring Captain Marvel out of a "negative zone" when an emergency arises. When Mar-Vell walks the earth, Rick must take his place in nowheresville.

This made for an extremely uneasy alliance, with Rick's bitterness over having his life constantly disrupted, having to sit out the real action in the negative zone all the time, tempered only by his sympathy for Mar-Vell's own plight. This uncomfortable arrangement lasted for quite a few issues, and the series had a respectable run.

Above: Marvel Comics' *Captain Marvel* #34 came from outer space. Copyright © 1974 by Marvel Comics Group.

122

Issue #19 (December 1969) features an imaginative story by Roy Thomas, with Gil Kane's and Dan Adkin's usual fluid artwork. "The Mad Master of the Murder Maze" is in some ways a deliberate throwback to the storytelling of the forties, an unusual self-contained little psychodrama set in an apartment building where Rick Jones has found a job. The landlord of this unusual housing project, Cornelius Webb, has built Minos Towers for one reason only: to subject the unsuspecting, carefully chosen tenants to stress and terror, reducing them to animals in a sociological experiment upon which he plans to base his next best-seller. Captain Marvel switches places with Rick in time to stop the madman's plans and ironically reduce him to something not quite of sound mind. Swift-paced, simplistic, economical, and absurd, with no tip of the hat to any particular logic, the entertaining story resembles a Simon-Kirby classic starring, say, Manhunter or Sandman. It also has an interesting subtext: When you cease to think of people as human beings with rights and feelings, you're in danger of becoming dehumanized yourself.

Issue #34 (September 1974), written and drawn by Jim Starlin (with dialogue and inking assists from Steve Englehart and Jack Abel, respectively), who guided many of the later adventures of the good captain, introduced a literally explosive new villain, Nitro, who could blow himself up—causing the expected destruction—only to re-form to do it all over again. Rick and Mar-Vell had their hands full taking care of this adversary in an extremely well-drawn and colored adventure. Starlin was also behind *The Death of Captain Marvel*, the captain's last appearance (aside from flashbacks) in Marvel Comics' very first "graphic novel," an outsize, bound comic book with thicker

paper and larger pages. Mar-Vell battles Death itself, but loses, and virtually everyone he's ever encountered, good or bad, comes to pay his respects as he lies dying.

In 1973, DC began publishing *Shazam!*, a comic book that featured the exploits of the original Captain Marvel, Captain Marvel, Jr., Mary Marvel, and other members of the Marvel Family. Since Marvel Comics had used the name Captain Marvel in the interim for one of their own heroes, who appeared in a magazine of that name, DC had to use the title *Shazam!* for their book.

The premise behind the new stories was intriguing. Billy Batson had been put in suspended animation for twenty years by Dr. Sivana, and now was a grown man who still looked like a kid. Occasionally he would let loose with some youthful angst (but nothing too heavy) over this situation. Once again C. C. Beck was drafted to draw the new stories, which were written by Elliot Maggin and Dennis O'Neil. Each issue would run two new tales and one classic from the forties.

Ironically, the older stories were better drawn and better written than the newer ones, which were generally silly and strictly for the kiddies. The forties tales had a natural charm instead of a forced quality to them and could appeal even to adults as examples of a simpler era in storytelling.

Top: DC Comics' revived the original Captain Marvel in the seventies in *Shazam #3*. Copyright © 1973 by National Periodical Publications, Inc.

Middle: *Shazam #4* appealed primarily to collectors. Copyright © 1973 National Periodical Publications.

Sales for the new series were not spectacular. A "dynamic new look" was unveiled after nearly three years, but it didn't save the book from eventual cancellation. This was in spite of a live-action television adaptation shown every Saturday morning for children, beginning in 1974. The first actor to play Captain Marvel was John Bostwick. He was replaced by John Davey in the second season. There was little attempt to stick *too* closely to the original concept and characters.

In 1975, Captain Marvel was joined by the super-heroine Isis (JoAnna Cameron), a schoolteacher who uses her powers to aid youngsters and battle evil. The combined *Shazam/Isis* hour on CBS became one of the most popular Saturday morning shows ever produced, although more kids tuned in for the second half hour with Isis than the first half hour with Captain Marvel. Isis used an amulet to gain her powers.

In 1982, Marvel Comics introduced yet another Captain Marvel in the pages of *The Amazing Spider-Man* annual #16, written by Roger Stern (with art by John Romita, Jr. *and* Sr.). Monica Rambeau is a lieutenant in the New Orleans Harbor Patrol, and happens to be black. Through a convoluted series of events, Monica winds up using her fists to smash a villain's energy disrupter, capable of destroying whole cities, and absorbs enough power to turn into a living beam of energy—*any* energy. At will, she can transform into light, microwaves, radio waves, X-rays, etc., giving her an incredible array of powers. She joined the Avengers superteam, briefly became its leader, and starred in her own one-shot special, but has yet to receive her own regular series. She remains an interesting character, and one hopes she'll be utilized more frequently in the future.

It was several years before the original Captain Marvel returned to DC comic books. He appeared twice (three issues altogether) in *All-Star Squadron*, a comic book published in the eighties but with stories set during World War II. The Justice Society of America and other heroes, including those from defunct comics companies whose rights DC had bought, joined together during the duration of the war, at Roosevelt's request, to battle the Axis powers. What prevented such heavyweights as Superman, Wonder Woman, and Green Lantern from simply flying into Germany and smashing Hitler was the evil dictator's Spear of Destiny, which could sap the will of heroes vulnerable to magic and turn them into full-fledged super-Nazis! (Hirohito also had a magic talisman that functioned

Above: John Davey as Captain Marvel poses for his Saturday morning television show in the seventies, *Shazam*.

in a similar manner.) Naturally these heroes had to stay away from Germany.

In *All-Star Squadron #36–37* (1984), Captain Marvel, who lives on another Earth in another dimension (Earth-S, for Shazam), is snatched from his world to Earth-2 (the locale of *All-Star Squadron* where golden-age DC heroes live) by a scientist working for Hitler. The transferal apparently makes him split into two separate beings. Not only is he Billy and the Captain, with Billy retaining free will but remaining comparatively helpless, but he's also "Hauptmann Wunder," becoming loyal to Hitler and the Nazi cause—due to the influence of the magical spear. It took the best efforts of the All-Star Squadron—as well as those of Captain Marvel, Jr., and Mary Marvel, who came over from Earth-S to help the Big Red Cheese and who also temporarily turned into Nazis—to foil Hitler's plot and return the Captain to normal and back to his own world and his fight against the Earth-S Hitler.

Roy Thomas fashioned an exciting story that features good banter and characterizations. A highlight is the pounding fistfight in the sky between Superman and Captain Marvel, with Superman remarking, "...you really are just like the 'big red cheese' in the funny books." He then reflects: "But that Captain Marvel's one of the good guys—even if I always figured he was just a knockoff of me." Illustrators for this two-part adventure include Rich Buckler, Richard Howell, and Arvell Jones.

The following year, Thomas reintroduced Mr. Mind and the Monster Society of Evil in *All-Star Squadron #51–54*. This adventure is good-humored (aside from a grim opening—a sailor is murdered in front of his fiancée—which is out of tone with what follows), if quite silly as *All-Star Squadron* stories go. These adventures present Mr. Mind as a benevolent dictator of a worm world who comes to Earth out of boredom as well as to meet his idol, Charlie McCarthy. Finding out that the dummy is, well, just a dummy, with Edgar Bergen doing the actual talking, the disillusioned little worm decides to join the Justice Society—but finds nobody at its headquarters. Feeling dejected, he proceeds to form his own society—one dedicated to evil (to approximate his mood, one supposes) rather than good.

The Monster Society consists of Oom, a shaggy gray gargoyle of great strength and near mindlessness, the bespectacled Mr. Who (every time he said his name, it turned into an Abbott and Costello routine) who could

Above: Captain Marvel takes to the air in *Shazam*.

grow into a giant; Ramulus (formerly Nightshade), a green, goateed fellow in a robe and high collar who could control the growth of plants; and Nyola, a bitchy high priestess of an Aztec god who seems determined to slash Hawkgirl's throat. Played mostly for laughs, the Monster Society of Evil seemed a secondary menace in these issues, some of which were part of the maxiseries *Crisis on Infinite Earths* continuity where All-Star Squadron members were worrying about the sudden disappearance of the entire Justice Society.

Mr. Mind and his group didn't actually appear in issue #52, but Captain Marvel did, as All-Star members Green Lantern, Johnny Quick, and his new bride Liberty Belle wound up on Earth-S where the Captain was fighting off shadow men created by the "crisis." In what is surely an inspired development, Johnny and Liberty wind up spending their wedding night in Billy Batson's bedroom, with Liberty Belle a touch disconcerted by the juvenile trappings of the room. "Captain Marvel he may be, part-time," she remarks, "but he's still a *kid* the rest of the time, obviously."

Captain Marvel and Mr. Mind never meet during this story line, which turns out to take place directly before the original appearances with his first (or more accurately second) Monster Society of Evil. Overthrown by the other members of the group in issue #53, Mr. Mind soars through the gap between universes that Green Lantern and newlyweds Johnny Quick and Liberty Belle have used to cross back to their own earth from Earth-S, and is overjoyed to see a brand new world that he thinks will be easy pickings. (The rest of the Monster Society is trounced by the All-Stars in the following issue.)[2]

While these particular issues are not masterpieces, they are looney and amusing, with Mr. Mind remaining a clever, likable character, although not one who really fits smoothly into today's more serious approach to comics.

DC Comics reintroduced Captain Marvel (just as they reintroduced Superman in the *Man of Steel*), getting back to the basics, in a four-part 1986 miniseries written by Roy and Dann Thomas and entitled *Shazam! The New Beginning*. The series was illustrated by Tom Mandrake. In the fourth and final issue, a defeated Dr. Sivana sits in a dive beside a bottle of tequila, musing that he needs the right gimmick or partner. The final panel of the penultimate page is a closeup of a worm on the bottom of the bottle.

Around the same time, DC issued another miniseries, titled *Legends,* in which the world starts to turn against its super-heroes in a plot engineered by the sinister Darkseid. Darkseid takes the inexperienced Captain Marvel out of the action by making him believe he is responsible for the accidental death of an opponent, something that sensitive young Billy just can't handle. He learns the truth and is back to fighting power by the end of the story, however.

[2]Writer Roy Thomas worked hard to maintain a "retroactive" continuity in his *All-Star Squadron* stories, using special notes on the "letters" pages to explain how each new period All-Star adventure fitted in with the *Justice Society of America* and other stories published decades before in the 1940s. Although, frustratingly, many of these original stories were not readily available for perusal by the contemporary reader, Thomas's efforts are still fascinating and commendable.

Above: *All-Star Squadron* #37 featured an all out battle between Captain Marvel and his old competition, Superman. Copyright © 1984 DC Comics, Inc.

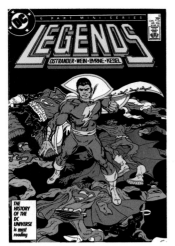

An outgrowth of the *Legends* miniseries was a brand new, lighthearted version of the old Justice League of America, shortened simply to *Justice League*, in which Captain Marvel was teamed with Batman, an alternate Green Lantern (Guy Gardner), the Martian Manhunter, Blue Beetle, and a variety of second-stringers. Marvel was portrayed as childlike in some ways (even in his adult incarnation), manly in others. He's naïve, drinks hot milk, and takes remarks at face value, but he has a sense of humor. Guy refers to him as "Captain Whitebread." He didn't have all that much to do or say until issue #5, and two issues later he was gone from the group and the magazine, never to return.

As of this writing, DC is planning to come out with a new Captain Marvel series, this one written and drawn by John Byrne of *Man of Steel* fame. Time will tell if Byrne can revitalize the character and make him once again a leader in sales and a comic force to reckon with. Probably if superstar artist/writer Byrne can't do it, nobody can. Captain Marvel may remain merely a whispered legend, a symbol of a simpler era and style. Or he may rise triumphant once again.

Top left: The *Legends* mini-series #5, a collectors' special, reintroduced Captain Marvel to the DC Universe in the late eighties. Copyright © 1987 by DC Comics, Inc.

Bottom right: The hot parody comic *Justice League* had Captain Marvel as a member for several issues. This first issue is a real collector's item. Copyright © 1987 by DC Comics, Inc.

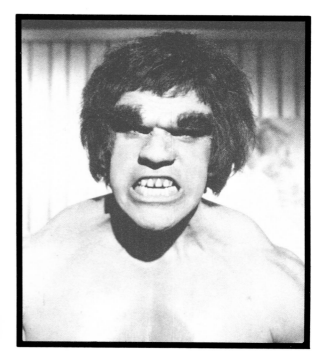

CHAPTER FIVE
OTHER HEROES

SPIDER-MAN

Spider-Man first appeared in *Amazing Fantasy #15* (1962) and has since gone on to become a comic book legend, one of the most popular super-heroes of all time, By 1990, his adventures were chronicled in no less than four separate books: *Amazing Spider-Man* (an outgrowth of *Amazing Fantasy*), *Spectacular Spider-Man*, *Web of Spider-Man*, and the most recent addition, simply *Spider-Man*,[1] which features the stories and very stylish artwork of a relatively new Spider-artist, Todd McFarlane. The web spinner's beginnings were humble, just another "long underwear" character, and although there was something different about him from the start, no one could have suspected just how enormously appealing he would become.

His first adventure showed how nerdy, not-too-popular high school science major Peter Parker was bitten at a special science exhibition by a radioactive spider that has just been caught in the rays of a weird machine (an absurd but certainly unique origin). Suddenly, Parker can climb buildings like an athletic arachnid, and also has the proportionate strength of a spider. He designs a costume for himself complete with wrist devices that shoot out webbing.

But his new power makes him cocky. After appearing on television, Spider-Man can't be bothered nabbing a petty crook being pursued by an officer. As fate would have it, this same crook later burglarizes the home of Peter's aunt and uncle (who have raised Peter) and fatally shoots Uncle Ben. Using his powers, Peter captures the killer but realizes that his own arrogant shirking of duty caused his uncle's death.

This first story by Stan Lee and Steve Ditko is brief and concise, an interesting minidrama that shows that we cannot ignore our responsibility to others, that our loved ones *are* "somebody else" to other people. It also functions as a neat study of loneliness and its effects on young outsiders, in this case the development of a self-promotional (exaggerated, but believable) and callow flamboyancy on the part of Parker, whose real, more subdued, persona is hidden behind his mask.

Later stories deepened Parker's characterization and continued to feature Steve Ditko's excellent artwork, but are noteworthy in a larger sense. These stories, under Stan Lee's guidance, are the hallmark of the Marvel style of added "realism" in comics

---

[1]The first issue of *Spider-Man* became the "best-selling comic book in the past forty years, possibly ever," according to the Associated Press, with sales of over 2.35 million copies. In subsequent issues, Todd McFarlane's artwork seemed a touch cluttered and unappealing and his storytelling skills noticeably lacking.

Above: *Amazing Spider-Man #121* became a collectible due to the death of Spider-Man's girlfriend, Gwen Stacy. Copyright © 1973 by Marvel Comics Group.

and show how Lee and his associates brought about a new wave in comic literature. Parker may have become a super-hero, but he was still a high school boy at heart, a troubled human being, and the stories never forgot that. In issue #4, which introduced the great villain The Sandman (who literally can turn into grains of sand), we see Peter having to sew his own mask (who else could do it?), a minor detail normally overlooked in super-hero stories. His day-to-day problems and heartbreak over pretty classmate Liz and his mistrusted, outsider status, his double identity, and his having to endure the jeers of high schoolers, all make for a rather intense, almost moving, episode.

It's not that comic book stories in the golden age didn't necessarily deal on occasion with "real people" and the day-to-day minutiae of being a super-hero (mending distinctive outfits and the like), but Lee's classic tales revitalized a company (and industry) and influenced dozens of writers, characters, and stories, initiating the wholesale embrace of an entirely new approach in storytelling in comics. These realistic details of the early stories led eventually to the much more intense and graphic approach of modern-day comic books, from all companies. This is not to say, of course, that the fantasy didn't generally heavily outweigh the "reality." These were still "super-heroes," after all.

Meanwhile, artist Steve Ditko's work on *Amazing Spider-Man* got better and better. Issue #16 of the comic, which guest-stars Daredevil and features the villainous Ringmaster and his Circus of Crime, boasts some excellent compositions and real flair and fluidity in action sequences, as Spider-Man twirls under and around the Big Top dodging attacks from human cannonballs, trapeze artists, and circus strongmen.

Over the years, the writers threw a lot of heartbreak and turmoil into Parker's personal life—hoping to maintain the realistic edge that separates Spider-Man from so many of his earthbound peers, including the tragic death of his girlfriend Gwen Stacy at the hands of archenemy Green Goblin, Aunt May's health problems, and messed-up relationships with friends, lovers, employers, and coworkers. But as Parker graduated from school, went to college, quit college, and acquired some fame as a photojournalist, it became harder and harder to sympathize.

For one thing, puny Parker filled out. He was no longer the skinny youth with the hangdog look and spectacles, the sunken chest. The artists turned him into a hunk with a terrific build (although at least one illustrator drew him with a lankier frame and a longer, bonier face that was "cute" without being handsome). At one point, he was even torn between *two* gorgeous girlfriends, and he had a career as a photographer for a leading paper in New York City.

If there was ever any proof that not all comic readers were nerds it was that so many Spider-Man fans wrote in requesting the writers to give Peter a break. Any true nerd would have wondered what Peter's problem was! Good looks, great body, glamorous job, gorgeous gals—who cared if his aunt got indigestion now and then? Gwen Stacy's death was a tragedy, but that had happened years ago. Poor Peter eventually got married to Mary Jane Watson, who transformed over the years from a funky, flighty chick into an alluring fashion model and star of a TV soap opera.

In spite of all this, Parker has remained fairly two-dimensional and, in some ways, a schnook. Great powers and a beautiful wife aside, he can be insecure and seems the very picture of a candidate for a stress-induced ulcer. Things never go all that smoothly for the fellow, but then isn't that true for just about everyone? Which is maybe why the book works.

Other reasons are interesting writers and artists and a wonderful group of villains. One of the best is the late Green Goblin's successor, Hobgoblin, who pestered Spider-Man and tried to destroy him through many exciting issues, even framing one of Parker's friends for his own crimes. The writers milked as much suspense as possible for several years over the identity of this malevolent masked Halloween figure, who really kept Spider-Man hopping. When we finally learned his identity, it was anticlimactic, however, for Hobgoblin, aka Ned Leeds (Peter's associate and the husband of his old girlfriend, Betty Brant), was already dead, and a final confrontation never materialized. A new, more supernatural-based Hobgoblin flew in to take up the slack but hasn't quite captured the readers' fancy the way his predecessor did.

Spider-Man first made it onto the small screen in 1977 in a CBS made-for-TV movie, *The Amazing Spider-Man,* which was chopped down from 94 minutes to be squeezed into a 90-minute time slot. The screenplay skips over Peter's early years and doesn't have him gain his powers until he's a graduate student. The origin with the radioactive spider is the same, but Peter has a part-time job in a laboratory when he's bitten. A carryover from the origin story has him suddenly learning of his wall-climbing abilities when he's forced to jump out of the path of a car.

As played by Nicholas Hammond, Peter Parker is fey and vaguely epicene and more bumbling than Parker ever was in the comic books. David White is miscast as J. Jonah Jameson, the newspaper publisher to whom Peter tries to sell photographs and who has been a fixture of the comic for almost thirty years. White looks the part but lacks the character's almost manic gruffness and bluster. Peter's Aunt May is much too young and fussy, more unpleasant than motherly. "Robbie" Robertson, the city editor, another character carried over from the comic book, is a younger and slicker version and is much less believable. Spider-Man himself was played by a stuntman.

Various methods were employed to show the arachnid hero climbing up, down, and around tall buildings. Sometimes a stuntman would climb up nearly invisible wires placed on a wall, or be pulled up by similarly thin wires while mimicking the motions of climbing. There were occasional process shots—the bottom half of the screen would show Spider-Man walking over a prop wall (with the camera looking downward) while the top half would have a shot of streets and traffic presumably far below, an effective use of split screen. Less effective were the tacky shots showing Spider-Man walking over obviously projected backgrounds and pretending to grab on to cornices, window ledges and the like, all of which were two dimensional. Occasionally the old *Batman* TV show method would be employed: a hunched-over stuntman would climb over props while the camera was turned on its side.

The various stuntmen not only performed well as Spider-Man, but also provided some excellent point-of-view shots taken with cameras at great heights and unusual angles. More than once, the viewer is given a gargoyle's-eye view of the city or shown a close-up from the amazing arachnid's harrowing perspective. Spider-Man's other abilities are briefly shown: superstrength, a sixth sense, and webshooters with palm controls. The webs look and function just as they do in the comics, "sticking up" baddies and helping Spider-Man literally swing around the city from building to building. The costume Parker wears is a virtual copy of the one in the comic book.

The main story line has to do with the charismatic cultist Edward Byron (well played by the distinctive Thayer David), who has come up with a doozy of an extortion plan. He lets the authorities know that he has given ten prominent citizens a posthypnotic suggestion to kill themselves at a certain time if he isn't paid $50 million. In order to prove that he can do what he threatens, he hypnotizes other respectable New Yorkers, all of whom are

unsuspecting members of his self-help group, into committing robberies. Each is then instructed to crash his or her getaway car and completely forget what has just occurred. Before the police can arrive, someone has usually spirited away the money.

Spider-Man gets involved when Peter Parker meets Judy Tyler, the daughter of one of the victims and a budding love interest. (None of Parker's girlfriends in the comic were carried over.) Judy swears by Edward Byron, whose doctrine seems to be the happiness of pursuit as opposed to the pursuit of happiness, but Parker is leery. When he investigates Byron's headquarters as Spider-Man, he is driven off by three Oriental bodyguards with staves, and when he shows up again as Parker, Byron mesmerizes him and makes him one of the "ten" who are fated to die. Parker is just about to jump from the observation deck of the Empire State Building when the shirt-cuff button through which Byron broadcasts his orders is snagged on a part of the metal fence and pulled off. Now in his right mind, Parker changes to Spider-Man, pulls down Byron's transmitter with his webbing, and saves the lives of nine other imperiled New Yorkers before turning Byron's hypnotic devices on Byron himself and ordering the villain to surrender to the authorities.

The telefilm occasionally captures the flavor of the Spider-Man comic book, particularly in a scene when a cabdriver refuses to give him a ride ("I don't see any pockets in that costume") and our hero has to hitch a ride back home in the back of a dumpster. Alvin Boretz's teleplay has a sound premise and lots of action, but E. W. Swackhamer's direction does little more than cover the proceedings. "Horrible miscasting, dull acting, boring plot, glacier slowness, and a total lack of imagination makes this one of the worst film adaptations of a comic book ever," ranted *Cinefantastique*. In addition, Johnny Spence's musical score—the boppy pseudo-rock that was popular for telefilms at the time—is just awful. What's sad about *Spider-Man* is that with proper treatment, the script could have been turned into a nail-biting suspense film, particularly as the seconds tick by and Parker and others prepare to hurl themselves to their doom. As it stands, *Spider-Man* is only acceptable kiddie fare.

Above: A stuntman helps set up a shot behind the scenes of *The Amazing Spider-Man.*

The ratings for the telefilm were good enough for it to engender a brief series in the seventies. Afterward, plans were set in motion to bring the web-swinger to the theater screen. The first producer to option the character was Roger Corman, who ultimately could not envision *Spider-Man* as his kind of low-budget film. Cannon Films then acquired the rights and went through a number of story treatments (one would have cast an actual spider as Spider-Man!) and potential directors (*Texas Chainsaw Massacre*'s Tobe Hooper

was the front-runner at one point) before settling on a script by Ted Newsom and John Brancato and assigning Joe Zito as director. Zito had been responsible for a number of mediocre horror and action films, but was excited by *Spider-Man*'s potential, which might have been his ticket to the majors. Script doctors were called in to "improve" the screenplay and made the usual mess of it. Spider-Man creator Stan Lee was appalled with the results but kept bucking for the role of J. Jonah Jameson in none-too-subtle fashion. The finished film would have focused on the battle between Spider-Man and archenemy Dr. Octopus (possibly Bob Hoskins).

Spider-Man—The Movie never came about for a variety of reasons. In the interim, Marvel Comics had been bought by New World Pictures, who wanted to do their own version of Spider-Man and seized the opportunity to get back the rights when someone at Cannon was slow in sending in a payment. But Cannon probably wouldn't have made *Spider-Man* anyway; Cannon producer Menachem Golan decided to put all the company's chips on the expensive production of *Superman IV*, once the rights were obtained from the Salkinds. There was no money left over for the *Spider-Man* budget. Months of preproduction work were wasted.

Stan Lee was still determined to put his popular creation on the big screen. And Cannon wasn't about to give up the film rights to New World so easily. As Stan Lee rejected script after script—they either didn't capture Spider-Man's flavor or were just badly written—Cannon announced that the hapless Albert (*Captain America*) Pyun would direct the *Spider-Man* feature. Pyun claimed that he was working with Stan Lee and the film would be out in time for Christmas 1988. It never materialized.

As it stands, *Spider-Man—The Movie* is to be directed by Stephen Herek, and is set for a late 1991 release.

Above: Marvel Comics unveiled a new *Spider-Man* #1 series in the nineties, written and drawn by Todd McFarlane, and it was an immediate sensation. Copyright © 1990 by Marvel Entertainment Group, Inc.

Top: Spider-Man faces some Oriental adversaries.

THE HULK/DAREDEVIL

Those who are familiar only with the television incarnation of The Incredible Hulk may not be aware that the green goliath debuted in the comic pages of *The Hulk* in 1962. This tells the story of Dr. Bruce Banner, who invented a unique new gamma bomb. On the fateful day when the bomb is to be tested, Banner looks through his binoculars and sees a teenager who has driven out to the test area in his car on a dare from friends! Banner arrives just in time to hurl him into a nearby foxhole (it's hard to imagine just how much real safety that would have provided), but is unable to save himself from the full effects of the gamma blast. The teen is miraculously unhurt, but hours later Banner mutates into a big gray monstrosity (he didn't turn green until later) with much raw strength and ferocity and an extremely limited intellect and vocabulary.

This introduction to the Hulk also offers Banner's lady friend, Betty Ross (who is inexplicably in the bomb control room), as well as her father "Thunderbolt" Ross, who was to become the Hulk's nemesis until dying twenty-five years later in *The Incredible Hulk #330*.

The Hulk's origin is a compelling Jekyll-and-Hyde variation for all its simplicity. The story is nicely drawn by Jack Kirby, who provides a clever segue from the explosion of the bomb to a recovery room much later by repeating slightly modified panels of Banner's screeching, tormented face. "Thunderbolt" Ross, originally a caricatured blustering general, was to be humanized over the years. Betty eventually became Banner's wife, suffered numerous mental breakdowns (who could blame her, married to the Hulk?), was briefly turned by monstrous Modok into the Hulk-hating flying green Harpy (from gamma radiation, of course), and even entered a convent at one point.

During the brief run of the original *Hulk* comic, the character went through quite a few changes as writer Stan Lee explored all the possibilities. In spite of some good stories and artwork, the book was canceled after only six issues.

Not much later, a new Hulk series shared the bill with The Astonishing Ant-Man (later Giant-Man) in *Tales to Astonish*. The Hulk met his archenemy, the Leader, who was also exposed to gamma rays. He turned green, but developed massive intelligence and an outsized cranium to go with it instead of superstrength. The two would tangle many times over the years.

The Hulk proved so popular that he soon took over the book; its title was changed to *The Incredible Hulk*. During the following years, the character went through many writers, artists, and changes, but the basic concept remained the same. The Hulk was

Above: The grotesque Modok battled *The Incredible Hulk* in issue #167. Copyright © 1973 by Marvel Comics Group.

Opposite: The Incredible Hulk grins for the camera.

the star—but it was really the story of Robert Bruce Banner, a pitiable scientist whose life (such as it was) has been turned into a nightmare because of his alter ego. "Thunderbolt" Ross tried all kinds of plans to wipe out the Hulk or to turn the Hulk permanently back into Banner. The relationship between Betty and Bruce ran hot and cold, with both Banner and even the Hulk himself becoming involved with other women. Along the way there were many memorable stories, slants, and characters.

One of the most engaging Hulk stories appears in issue #142 (August 1971) and is entitled "They *Shoot* Hulks, Don't They?" The inspiration for this was not the film about a dance marathon, but Tom (*Bonfire of the Vanities*) Wolfe's nonfiction book, *Radical Chic*. Wolfe himself even appears in the story, which is a delightful satire about Malicia and Reggie, a wealthy Manhattan couple, who want to do the trendy thing (as well as *out*do their friends) by holding a fund-raising bash for some socially oppressed group that hasn't been done before. They decide to throw a party for the always misunderstood and much eleaguered Hulk and have their daughter Samantha talk him down from the Statue of Liberty, where he's sulking.

The members of New York's social register fawn and goggle over the Hulk at the party, while feminist Samantha has her mind possessed by the Enchantress, the ubiquitous Marvel Comics villainess, and turns into the Valkyrie, who decides the Hulk is a Male Chauvinist Pig and battles him to a virtual standstill, wrecking Malicia and Reggie's apartment in the process. As Tom Wolfe says, "I'd compute that the Radical Chic season for the year 1971 just ended on the Upper East Side." Roy Thomas scripted this amusing minimasterpiece, and the art was provided by Herb Trimpe and John Severin.

Gradually we discovered more about the psychological reasons for the creation of the Hulk. Radiation turned Banner into a monster, but if we learned one thing from the Hulk's series, it was that gamma rays affected everyone differently. Why did Bruce turn into such a bestial, raging horror (even if the Hulk did on occasion show a gentle, tender, righteous side)? The answer was provided by writer Bill Mantlo, working with artists Mike Mignola and Gerry Talaoc, in *Hulk #312* (1985). It tells how Bruce Banner's father was a deeply disturbed man who worked on atomic research for years and was convinced that, due to his own affected genes, his child could only be a monster. He physically abused his son and wound up murdering his wife, the boy's mother. Banner was later cruelly picked on by unthinking students who, as his father did, saw the boy genius as a freak. Banner's Hulk persona is, of course, the manifestation of years of unexpressed rage, an identity that is capable of protecting him from all assaults and abuses, a hard, impenetrable shell inside which Banner can hide and heal. The script and art for this story are particularly outstanding.

The Hulk first reached the small screen in a 1977 telefilm entitled, appropriately enough, *The Incredible Hulk*. Bruce is now David Banner (Bill Bixby), a widower whose wife, Laura, was killed in an accident. Working with a colleague, Elena (Susan Sullivan), he *exposes himself* to gamma radiation but makes an error in calculations and absorbs too much. Later he's trying to change a tire in the rain, getting increasingly frustrated and angry, when he transforms for the first time into the Hulk (Lou Ferrigno). He and Elena try to recreate the circumstances in the lab, but Banner reverts to the Hulk only after falling asleep and having a nightmare about Laura's death. The lab explosion that results from his rampage kills Elena and leads people to believe that Banner is dead, too. He becomes a man on the run, a slave to his Hulk-blackouts, and is pursued by a reporter, Jack McGhee (Jack Colvin), who suspects the truth.

In a sequel, *The Return of the Hulk* (1977), and the successful weekly series that followed, Banner would keep running from himself, interact briefly with other outcasts and losers, then run away again when the Hulk caused hysteria or McGhee got too close to his trail. Now and then he would contact another scientist or professional and try to affect a cure. In one case, a serum turns both the Hulk and Banner into dark, diabolical creatures, and in another, Banner marries a hypnosis-therapy researcher (Mariette Hartley) with a terminal illness who tries to help him but dies in the Hulk's arms.

The TV episodes were mostly padded human-interest dramas, some of which could be modestly moving and effective. The Hulk's appearances were generally limited to the climax, where he functioned has a *deus ex machina*. The TV Hulk as a "sweet" side to his nature, an eye for the ladies, and is not quite as strong as he is in the comics. His feats of superstrength are depicted in slow motion, which vitiates whatever thrills they might have possessed. As the Hulk, after bursting out of Banner's clothes, Lou Ferrigno wears shorts and what looks like a green shag rug. Episodes of the long-lasting series had Banner becoming a firefighter, befriending a midget wrestler, and winning a lottery that he has a heck of a hard time claiming because he has used an assumed name. Bland Bill Bixby never gives any intensity or depth to the role of haunted David Banner, and as the Hulk, Lou Ferrigno just looks silly.

A reunion film in 1988, *The Incredible Hulk Returns*, also served as a pilot for a series based on the Marvel hero, Thor, but had little to do with the comic. A second reunion film, *The Trial of the Incredible Hulk*, also served as the pilot for a Marvel TV series, but this time stuck much closer to its source, the *Daredevil* comic book.

Daredevil's origin was told in 1964 in *Daredevil #1*: Young Matt Murdock pushes a blind man from the path of a truck and pays a terrible price for his heroism: he not only is run down but is blinded himself. The radioactive materials that were being carried in the truck compensate for his impairment by making his other senses so incredibly acute that he develops a "radar sense" that in some ways is more accurate and vivid than sight. While

Above: David Banner (Bill Bixby) faces his nemesis, The Hulk (Lou Ferrigno).

avenging his father's murder at the hands of the Fixer, he develops the costumed identity of Daredevil, the Man Without Fear. "If I could see what I was doing, I'd probably be petrified," he remarks on more than one occasion, such as when using his billy club to whirl around and down a skyscraper's elevator cable.

Daredevil's first costume was a striking yellow and red, which he later exchanged for a less blatant dark red outfit. Marvel hoped that lightning would strike twice and that DD would become as popular as Spider-Man. Although that hasn't quite happened, DD has been published consistently for almost three decades; it is hardly a loser in the comics sweepstakes.

Murdock started out as a lawyer, and soon became one of the comics' biggest bleeding-heart liberals. (The stage for this was set as far back as Issue #3 when Matt insists on defending the infamous Owl over his partner's objections.) His major antagonists include the obese Kingpin and the insane hired assassin Bullseye. The early, lighthearted but colorful stories with such foes as the Owl and Purple Man eventually gave way to grimmer sageas with Daredevil as a legal aid attorney ministering to the victims of society's indifference in the ghetto.

The greatest DD stories appeared in a running epic in Issues #227–233 by Frank Miller and David Mazzucchelli, an absolutely terrific, twisting, cinematic tale of the Kingpin utterly crushing Murdock/Daredevil in both of his guises and on all counts. Shocking episodes included DD's old girlfriend, Karen Page, now a junkie, selling the secret of his double identity for drug money. Although this story is at times confusing, due to Miller's style and breakneck pace, it boasts good writing and vivid characterizations, and is certainly an example of the comic book at its artistic height.[2]

What makes *The Trial of the Incredible Hulk* an above-average Hulk movie is that the green goliath is only a supporting player in what is essentially the story of Matt Murdock. The telefilm presents a Daredevil that is very much like the one in the comics—Murdock is still a blind lawyer by day and vigilante by night, for instance—but made radical changes to his uniform. DD's outfit is a black ninja-like costume with a mask covering the top half of the head down to and over the eyes; slick black knee boots complete the ensemble. Stan Lee was not amused.

[2]These Daredevil stories are superior to Miller's *The Dark Knight Returns*.

Above: Daredevil (Rex Smith) guest-starred in *The Trial of the Incredible Hulk*.

"Whoever designed [DD's] nowhere costume should be stranded on a desert island with nothing to read but DC mags until he begs for mercy!" he wrote.

DD's origin is the same as in the comic, except that he works with a Captain Tenelli, who knows there is widespread corruption in the city and helps Daredevil combat it because the masked vigilante isn't hamstrung by the law. (This resembles Commissioner Gordon's relationship to Batman.) The teleplay also gives Murdock a new female partner and a black associate. Murdock/Daredevil is played with charm and flair by talented actor-singer Rex Smith.

The story line has Banner getting arrested after becoming involved when two creeps try to assault a woman in the subway. (The Hulk also makes an appearance, which doesn't help matters.) The woman, Ellie Mendez, has been intimidated by men in the employ of Wilton Fisk, Daredevil's primary adversary, into saying that Banner was her attacker. Although inspired by the comic book's Kingpin, named *Wilson* Fisk, this ruthless character is British, dissimilar-looking, and a pallid imitation.

Matt Murdock is Banner's court-appointed attorney. David can't tell Matt that he's afraid to be taken to the courtroom because he might turn into the Hulk under all the pressure. This is exactly what happens in a terrific sequence a short while later. Banner responds to a verbal beating on the witness stand by transforming into his hated alter ego, after which he chokes the prosecutor, tosses several guards around, and lifts up the entire jury box (with the jury still in it). The fact that it turns out to be a dream sequence doesn't lessen the impact.

Daredevil gets involved in the action when Ellie Mendez is kidnapped by Wilton Fisk. Banner escapes from jail by turning into the Hulk. (Bixby, who also directed, handles this in a clever—and cheaper—fashion by showing only the aftermath of the Hulk's destructive path instead of the escape itself.) When DD is ambushed trying to save Ellie, and is severely beaten, Banner nurses him back to health and helps him regain psychological strength by revealing his own dark secret. The climax has DD rescuing Ellie and forcing Fisk and his right-hand man into a hasty departure in a fancy kind of helicopter. The Hulk doesn't even appear at the finale.

Daredevil's "moves" came in for some criticism from the folks at Marvel. "Daredevil moved somewhat generically," wrote executive editor Mark Gruenwald in *Marvel Age*. "Not specifically Daredevilish enough for my tastes." However, DD's fight with a homicidal nurse who wants to kill Ellie is extremely well choreographed. In spite of its differences from the Marvel comic, this adaptation of Daredevil might have made a good weekly series, particularly if Rex Smith remained in the title role.

The next Hulk TV movie, *The Death of the Incredible Hulk*, had no special super-hero guest stars and could have used some. In this, Banner is working as a janitor in a genetics lab when he's caught playing with the computers by one of the scientists, who learns his secret. The two decide to work together not only to rid Banner of the curse of the Hulk, but also to use the secrets of the transformation to heal serious tissue injuries and the like. Jasmin, a lady spy, forces her way into the lab during an experiment and the havoc that results puts the scientist in a coma and places Banner under suspicion for the accident. He's on the run again.

Jasmin was pressured into the assignment because she believed her sister was the captive of the man who gave the orders. When she learns that her sister, Bella, is really the bad guy's superior, she joins up with Banner out of guilt. A romance develops between the two, illustrated by very soft-core love scenes focusing on the lady's naked back. Meanwhile, the scientist comes out of his coma, only to be kidnapped along with his wife, by evil Bella. There's a fairly exciting climax when David and Jasmin effect a rescue almost under the noses of Bella, her subordinate, and a sadistic underling with a handsome face, an earring, and slicked-back hair. Although the Hulk is capable of crashing through walls, he is unable to keep a small private plane (holding the villains) from taking off, and is apparently killed by a simple fall to the ground, the most unconvincing "death" in the history of the series.

In publicity releases and stories, Bixby claimed that all on the set had tears in their eyes when they filmed the "death" scene, even Ferrigno. Ferrigno thought Bixby had brought out "the most emotion I've ever seen myself act." If there were tears, they were undoubtedly tears of laughter, for *The Death of the Incredible Hulk* is a pretty boring and silly piece of TV trash. Bixby's performance as both actor and director is perfunctory, and the limited effects are cheesy, although the film looks slick for the most part. Joe Harnell's musical "score" offers a 1970s-style obligatory "rock" beat to compensate for the lack of any real, well-edited action, and the "sweet" pop song that plays over the Hulk's death scene is even worse. By this time, the Hulk had switched to an auburn Dutch boy fright wig that looks as if it came from Frederick's of Hollywood and makes the green goliath look more comical than frightening.

Was the Hulk dead? Hardly? The dust had barely cleared before there was an announcement of a new telefilm, *The Revenge of the Incredible Hulk*.

WONDER WOMAN

Wonder Woman is the only female comic book character to be published continuously since her debut in *All Star* #8 in 1941. She quickly got her own strip in *Sensation* comics, and her own magazine in 1942. She was "created," with Athena's help, by Hippolyte, Queen of the Amazons, from a statue embued with the breath of life, but her real creator was "Charles Moulton." Moulton was the pen name of William Moulton Marston, a psychologist who invented the lie detector. Marston put all his knowledge of human sexual psychodynamics into his stories, which were heavily into "bondage and discipline." Children responded to the stories on one level; adults on another. An undeniable homoeroticism permeated the stories, as well as the all-female society on "Paradise Island." A "girl-roping" contest in *Sensation* #6 is particularly blatant. But this aspect of the series wouldn't be dealt with, let alone admitted, until several decades later. Wonder Woman often grappled with Gestapo agent Paula Von Gunther (changed to Paula Van Gunta in the sixties), and her primary artist was Harry G. Peter.

As the emphasis shifted from Paradise Island to "Man's World" in the fifties and sixties, Wonder Woman stories became wilder and more outrageous. Typical tales would have the Amazin' Amazon tied up in Oriental archfoe Egg Fu's mustache or battling Giganta, the Gorilla Girl. Flagging sales and the popularity of TV spies necessitated a drastic change in 1969: Diana Prince (Wonder Woman) was stripped of her Amazonian abilities and turned into a kind of *Girl From U.N.C.L.E.* Writer-artist Mike Sekowsky teamed her up with a blind Oriental named I-Ching and pitted them against an inspired villainess, Dr. Cyber. For several exciting issues (#179–188), Wonder Woman would do her best to block the heinous plans of Cyber and her murderous henchladies. It all came to a head in a two-parter entitled "Earthquaker," in 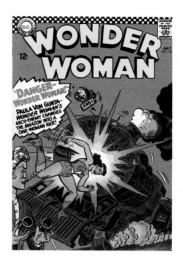 which an accident costs Cyber her beautiful looks. True to form, Cyber blames Diana for her disfigurement and chains her up in her headquarters (shades of 1940's Wonder Woman), while her earthquake machine lays waste to much of Hong Kong. Although the concept was a far cry from Marston's original idea, Sekowsky did supply some entertaining stories chock full of female-female cat fights and a lot of sadistic action. During his run, Sekowsky also had Diana square off against a bitchy witch, Morgana, and a butch trio of S&M streetwoman called "Them."

The first *Wonder Woman* telefilm, which aired on ABC in 1974, combined both Marston's and Sekowsky's vision, and featured former athlete Cathy Lee Crosby as a specially endowed secret agent. Very little from the comic book was carried over, aside from stalwart boyfriend Steve Trevor (Kaz Garas) and some references to an Amazonian heritage. Wonder Woman's star-spangled one-piece "bathing suit" was traded in for a more traditional uniform with stars on the sleeves.

The story line has WW trailing a spy named "Mr. Evil" (a monicker as corny as "Egg Fu," if not more so), played with his usual suave assurance by Ricardo Montalban. The proceedings are never more than dreary under prolific Vincent McEveety's pedestrian direction, which misses some opportunities for outlandish excitement provided by the script. Anitra Ford offers some sizzle as Wonder Woman's archrival, and the other performances are adequate. "Cathy Lee Crosby," wrote critic Robert L. Jerome, "appears a bit green and ill at ease in a role which calls for more pizzazz than poise. Yes, she can throw a javelin with skill, yet she can't quite hurdle the banalities of a Saturday morning script which goes from A to B in routine fashion." It didn't matter; this *Wonder Woman* never went to series.

Still, ABC wasn't ready to give up. Maybe it would be a good idea to go back to the basics. In 1975, they tried again with a telefilm so christened as to make it clear—or utterly confusing—to everyone: *The New, Original Wonder Woman.* This second attempt was far superior to the first.

The setting is the 1940s, and Wonder Woman is back in her red, white, and blue bathing suit. As portrayed by voluptuous Lynda Carter, the Amazin' Amazon is a knockout, and Cloris Leachman makes a fine, if unexpected,

Above: *Wonder Woman #163* pitted the "Amazin' Amazon" versus Paula Von Gunta. Copyright © 1966 by National Periodical Publications.

141

Queen Hippolyte. The script sticks very closely to the origin and concept of the super-heroine, although too much of it borders dangerously on camp; the best scenes are the ones played straight. An amusing sequence has Carter playing "bullets and bracelets"—knocking bullets aside with the metal bands on her wrists, a carryover from the comic. There is also a creatively executed fight sequence between Carter and Stella Stevens and a hilarious scene featuring a little old lady with a submachine gun. Lyle Waggoner is an okay Steve Trevor, and Leonard Horn's direction is more than adequate. Stanley Ralph Ross was the writer.

The telefilm's ratings were high enough to prompt a series, with Carter and Waggoner retaining their roles. Stories still took place back in the forties, although the period atmosphere was always distinctly limited. Cartoon Nazis and cardboard characters were in abundance, but the series wasn't much worse than others. Debra Winger made a perfect "Wonder Girl" with her deep voice and forceful manner. After two years, a ratings dip necessitated a move from ABC to CBS—and into the present time. Now WW traveled the world to take on cases of nuclear sabotage and other late-seventies concerns. The programs lasted a year or two more.

Lyle Waggoner had been a second banana on the *Carol Burnett Show* before taking the part of government agent, Steve Trevor (and later, Steve Trevor, *Jr.*) on *Wonder Woman*. According to him, the statuesque, gorgeous—if minimally talented— Lynda Carter had "the biggest boobs in Hollywood." Waggoner thought, however, that the program lost "all of its charm and humor" when it went from the forties to the seventies.

The Wonder Woman comic plodded along throughout the seventies and eighties. There were occasional spurts of interest—several 1982 issues written by Roy Thomas and drawn

Lynda Carter poses as *Wonder Woman*.

by Gene Colan, for instance—but basically the Amazin' Amazon was duller than Superman. DC had to do something about the number-one super-heroine in the world, a character that had been featured on the cover of *Ms.* magazine and which had become a symbol of feminine strength and women's rights (Lyle Waggoner notwithstanding). When Superman and Batman were "streamlined" in the mid-eighties, it was decided to do the same to Diana Prince.

The new *Wonder Woman* debuted in February 1987, and was written by Greg Potter and George Perez, with artwork by Perez and Bruce Patterson. The first tale is a complex and inspiring story that presents the "birth" of

Diana and casts the Amazons as the lost souls of women wronged by man's "fear and ignorance." Vivid sequences show how creepy Hercules betrays the women and rapes and kills their queen, Hippolyte. A bow to the "old" Wonder Woman has Diana being tested by playing "bullets and bracelets" (not referred to as such, however). Issue #2 began a five-parter in which Wonder Woman saves the world from the bloody machinations of the war god Ares.

A far cry from the ludicrous series of old, the new *Wonder Woman* shows a rare intelligence and maturity (and has one of the most literate "letters" pages in comics). The characterizations of the supporting cast, both new and old, are excellent, and the stories generally combine action with some other thought-provoking aspect. Although the naïve and inexperienced WW seems inclined toward men (a relationship with Superman went nowhere, however), the thorny question of the Amazons' sexuality has been answered: some abstain, some please themselves, and others have relationships with other Amazons. Or as one of them puts it when questioned by a minister who has visited Paradise Island in *Wonder Woman* #38: "[Some] have sworn themselves to Artemis, the virgin hunter, and Athena, the chaste warrior. Others choose the way of Narcissus. But most of us find satisfaction in each other—three thousand years *can* be a long time, Reverend." ("Oh," says the minister.)

You can bet that when and if Hollywood gets around to making a major motion picture about Wonder Woman, this particular aspect—which is highly realistic for an all-woman society—won't make it past the cutting-room floor. Here is another example of how comic books can be more "adult" than their big screen counterparts.

Top: Wonder Woman chases after a suspect.

Bottom : DC Comics introduced a new *Wonder Woman* #1 in the eighties. Copyright © 1986 by DC Comics, Inc.

Fans of the CBS prime-time adventure series, *The Flash*, may not be aware that there have been three heroes named the Flash—and the TV character is a combination of two of them.

It all began back in the golden age of comics in the 1940s. The first Flash—who wore a winged helmet modeled after Mercury's—was Jay Garrick, a superspeedster who belonged to the Justice Society of America and had his own comic as well. This first Flash was created by Gardner Fox and gained his powers from inhaling hard-water fumes.

When DC Comics revived many of their super-hero characters in the late 1950s, the first to come out of mothballs and get an overhaul was—the Flash. This Flash was a police scientist named Barry Allen, who acquires superspeed when a bolt of lightning hits shelves of beakers in his lab that douse him with a million-to-one combination of chemicals. Barry had been a comics fan as a child, and decides to call himself the Flash as a tribute to his boyhood hero. Later stories revealed that the "comic book" Jay Garrick actually existed in an alternate Earth, and the two Flashes had several adventures together in the sixties. Barry became a member of the new Justice *League* of America.

The second Flash's comic ran for many years and featured a bizarre assortment of villains, a veritable rogues' gallery: Mirror Master, the Pied Piper, Gorilla Grodd, Captain Boomerang, Captain Cold, Professor Zoom, the Reverse Flash. Stories usually would revolve around some inescapable doom trap and Flash's ingenious ways for getting out of any and all predicaments. If need be, he could manipulate the very molecules of his body, such as he did when the evil Abra Kadabra turned him into a puppet in the classic *Flash* #133 (December 1962). The final issues of his series in the mid-eighties had him on trial for the murder of Professor Zoom, who in turn had killed his wife and longtime girlfriend, Iris. These issues were as zany and entertaining as they were contrived. Flash wound up reunited with his wife—who had been snatched to a future time period and was still alive—and had a few weeks of happiness before giving his life to save the world in *Crisis on Infinite Earths* #8. It was a moving episode, particularly for longtime Flash fans who didn't want to see the old and beloved character go.

The third Flash—star of a brand-new series in 1987—had been introduced at least two decades before. He was Wally West, Iris Allen's nephew, who had become Kid

Above: The first collector's item issue of the new *Flash*, which was the old Kid Flash all grown up. Copyright © 1987 DC Comics, Inc.

Opposite: The Flash poses before his stylized lightning insignia.

Flash when (incredibly) he, too, was doused by lightning-struck chemicals. He and Barry had many adventures together before Kid Flash grew up, joined the Teen Titans, and developed a kind of attitude problem worse than Robin's.

As a child, Wally had been a lovable, heroic Boy Scout. As a young man in his twenties, he was a cynical, disillusioned, reluctant hero trying to live up to an impossible standard: Barry Allen. He learns that his father is part of a sinister secret society and has tried to kill his mother. His mother moves in with Wally when she learns

he's won a lottery. Wally gets involved with an older woman, Tina McGhee, with a jealous husband. (Some prudish Bible Belt fans complained to the publishers that Wally slept around too much, when in truth he's a lot less promiscuous than many real-life twenty-year-olds.)

The TV series decided to make its Flash character a blend of Barry Allen and Wally West. *The Flash* is named Barry and works in a police lab. But his main girlfriend and associate is Tina McGhee instead of Iris West. Like Wally, the TV Flash can't run nearly as fast as Barry Allen

could, and has to eat great quantities of food to maintain his energy. Other elements were created specifically for the series.

The show premiered with a two-hour pilot in 1990. Barry is disturbed because his father (M. Emmet Walsh) disdains his work as a police scientist and praises brother Jay[3] (Tim Thomerson), the head of a police motorcycle squad, as a "real" cop. Barry has a girlfriend, Iris, who creates computer art, but a new woman, genetic scientist Tina McGhee (Amanda Pays), comes into his life when she examines him after he's hit by lightning. Exit Iris.

The villain of the piece, Pike (Michael Nader), is Jay's former partner, who was thrown off the force because he ran a hijacking operation. Now he's the head of a group of disaffected lowlifes and motorcycle bums who feel that the cops have failed to protect them. Pike's idea of improving things is to wipe out the police and take over. (This whole group is implausible and somewhat ridiculous—today's urban areas are rarely plagued by white motorcycle punks.) These creeps also have high-tech weapons (not enough money to buy food but enough to buy weapons?) such as green glowing globes that cause explosions when thrown.

Barry is given a believable motivation for becoming the Flash. His brother is killed by Pike, the police are helpless against Pike's mob, and only Barry's powers can turn things around, as well as get justice for Jay. Where the show excels is in depicting the Flash's superpower: regular "fast-motion" is combined with a slicker

Left: The Earth-1 Flash and Earth-2 Flash teamed up in *The Flash* #151, a collector's item for all Flash fans. Copyright © 1965 by National Periodical Publications.

Right: A great, campy, collectible cover of *The Flash* #177 of the sixties. Copyright © 1968 by National Periodical Publications, Inc.

[3]"Jay" was obviously an homage to Jay Garrick, the first Flash.

superspeed effect that leaves a blur of red afterimages;[4] also employed are fast-motion point-of-view shots (from Barry's perspective) of highways swishing by, as well as occasional cuts and process shots showing Barry standing before a fast-motion background. Sometimes the effects are quite ingenious, as when Flash boxes three opponents at once, then runs circles around Pike, creating a whirlwind that sends the villain soaring into the air.

According to executive producer Danny Bilson, "The Flash's image is literally streaked in a video paintbox technique. The computer does that." A double of the actor playing Flash is occasionally employed, filmed at the same time as he is, in order to give a speed sequence extra effectiveness. The pilot film featured 103 effects shots, far more than usual for a TV movie and more than in each weekly episode thereafter.

The Flash's costume has thirty foam rubber appliances, most of which slightly exaggerate the physique of the character in true comic book style. Durability was provided by nylon coating and a special electrostatic process. But when the actor complained that wearing the suit was like being in a sauna, a cooling vest, filled with tubes, was added. Between takes, the tubes are filled with water from a hose to make things a little more comfortable for the man inside.

That man happens to be a former soap opera actor named John Wesley Shipp, who not only is excellent as Barry Allen and his alter ego but was singled out for a special *TV Guide* "Cheers" for his performance: "Shipp runs circles around his competition and brings a self-effacing charm, subtle sense of humor and genuine sensitivity to his square-jawed Scarlet Speedster." Shipp never camps up or plays down to his audience, and he looks great in the uniform.

As for the villainous Pike in the pilot episode, Michael Nader, another soap star, gives a good performance, but can't overcome the fact that Pike is essentially a one-note and colorless opponent. Alex Desert barely registers as Barry's black lab assistant, Julio Mendez, whose casting seems a bit of trendy tokenism and whose hairstyle resembles Whoopi Goldberg's. Danny Elfman's rousing, at times pretentious, scoring and some slick photography don't always compensate for a slow pace and directorial slackness.

The main problem with subsequent *Flash* episodes is that the stories are generally mediocre and below the level of the dramatic music and effects. Worse, a camp element occasionally creeps in, especially in the performances, such as that of the drug lord Belasco who wants to spray "Paradise" all over the city and make everyone an addict. The ghettos in Central City are always sanitized and neon pretty, even when a genetic engineer runs about turning the homeless into mutants.

There have been some interesting episodes, however. In one, a crooked politico hires a lady private investigator to uncover the Flash's secret identity—which she does. In another—a *very* comic bookish story—a villain from the 1940s revives from suspended animation and renews his war on Central City and on a now-retired vigilante, Nightshade. At one point Flash is caught in a death cone, formed by "entrapment lasers," that is very much like

[4]The actor is filmed against black velvet and the camera undercranked; this is later composited into the action. This was not the first time the effect was used: superspeed "blurs" can be seen in *My Secret Identity*, a television series, and in the Christopher Reeve Superman features.

the doom traps of the old Flash comic. Although the actor playing "the Ghost" is fatally miscast, the villain causes a lot of problems by attaching himself to the communications system of the city and blackmailing it. Another comic-inspired sequence has the Ghost putting his and Flash's minds *into* a TV screen and subjecting our hero to psychic brutality. Lois Nettleton is very good as the Ghost's now "aged" girlfriend.

Generally, though, the show is still too much of a kiddie program in many respects, and the scripts are often colorless and predictable. *The Flash* can't keep relying on the special effects men, Elfman's exciting musical themes, and Shipp's performance to keep it going. It needs to develop some truly dramatic impact and some "flashier" direction if it's going to become the program that it could be.

In the meantime, *The Flash* is one of the most expensive television series ever produced, with each episode costing $1.5 million. Each costume—and there are eight per season—costs $25,000. Shooting at night for extra atmosphere jacks up the price, as do all those fancy effects. Danny Elfman's indispensable music (he did the score for the 1989 *Batman*) didn't come cheap, either, nor should it have. When the music combines with the effects—as when Flash revolves his hand around and around at dizzying speed to drill himself out of a vacuum chamber—the series really soars.

The series has been well received by critics, as have the effects. "Who'd thought that so much visual capital could be made of a superpower that, in real life, would render the hero invisible to the naked eye?" asked *Cinefantastique*.

DR. STRANGE

Dr. Strange was not the first comic book sorcerer, but he's easily the most successful and longest running. "Dr. Strange, Master of Black Magic" was first introduced in *Strange Tales* #110 (1963). He wore a sort of blue-black dressing gown with a black collar, orange sash, and gold amulet below the neck. Later, he was to gain a flowing red and gold cape and flamboyant red ruff. This first story provided a quick introduction to the sorcerer (his origin would come later), as well as to "The Master" (aka "The Ancient One"), the time-withered wizard who taught Strange everything he knows. We also met Nightmare, master of a dream dimension who is determined to murder Strange for trespassing (as well as to expand his own territory).

Some time later we were to learn that Dr. Stephen Strange, a gifted surgeon, was frittering away his life and career on a boozy, hedonistic existence and, after complete ruin, had wandered away to nowhere in search of something, some spiritual guidance, which he found in the form of "the Master." The Ancient One spent years teaching Strange all manner of arcane lore, all knowledge of spells and other dimensions.

148

Opposite: *Dr. Strange* (Peter Hooten) ponders his next move in his battle with the forces of evil.

At first, Strange's name is only "spoken in whispers," his existence a secret to all but a few, but in later stories he seems to be a bit of a celebrity; even the man on the street knows who he is. *Strange Tales* #111 introduced Baron Mordo, Strange's nemesis, once the Ancient One's other pupil, who decided to devote his newfound talents only to evil. Strange and Mordo would clash many times over the years until Mordo was eventually eclipsed by other, more malevolent foes and beings. One of their best encounters had Mordo allied with a powerful demon and using the resulting extra powers to turn Strange into a fugitive, hunting him down wherever he ran. These early stories were written by Stan Lee and drawn by Steve Ditko.

Strange spent years battling demons, living houses, and creatures of the night in *Strange Tales* and was eventually awarded his own magazine. After it was canceled, a new series began in *Marvel Premiere* in 1972. Over the years, the doctor went through several changes, both cosmetic (a mask which hid his features) and conceptual (a secret identity). The Ancient One died, passed the torch, and Strange became "Sorcerer Supreme" of the Universe. Occasionally employed were concepts and creatures created by H. P. Lovecraft which pitted the doctor against slithering "Old Gods" and their minions from an alternate dimension, gods that had once ruled Earth and wanted to again. These stories were quite creepy and effective for the most part, employing sinister-looking New England towns, secret sects, portals through universes, and unseen, unspeakable monstrosities called up through shadowy rituals and other Lovecraftian paraphernalia.

Eventually, Dr. Strange got his own series back, and it had a lengthy run. One of the most interesting Dr. Strange tales appeared in issue #76 and was written by Peter Gillis and illustrated by Mark Badger, Chris Warner, and Randy Emberlin. "What Song the Sirens Sang" presents the case of an old colleague of Strange's, Darryl Berenson, who has a very successful practice, an attractive wife, a beautiful home, and lots of money, but is deeply dissatisfied. He compares his safe, comfortable life to the constantly stimulating and dangerous existence of Stephen Strange, and finds his own wanting. When he is called on by Iuriale, ruler of an other-dimensional realm, who is dying and needs communion with a human soul, he is more than ready to respond. Iuriale is exotically beautiful, with tresses composed of snakelike creatures, and open, toothed maws in her palms, but, as Dr. Strange warns, she sucks away the life force of her victims and leaves them "withered husks."

Darryl doesn't care, since Iuriale represents everything missing in his life: sensuality, romance, excitement. Dr. Strange sends Iuriale back to her realm before she can finish feeding off Berenson, but Darryl can no longer be content with his everyday existence. In spite of all his advantages in life, he commits suicide. The story illustrates how some people would rather be dead than lead lives devoid of passion and adventure, and how, indeed, many pursue excesses of sex and drugs in a search that often leads ultimately toward self-destruction.

Dr. Strange was canceled not long after this story was published, but reappeared shortly in a new, revamped *Strange Tales*, sharing the bill with the teenage drug-fighters, Cloak and Dagger. It wasn't long before he again got his own comic, the current *Dr. Strange*, as well as a slightly new direction: in the interim Dr. Strange has

Above: *Dr. Strange* #12 became highly collectible again with a new series in the eighties. Copyright © 1989 Marvel Entertainment Group, Inc.

developed a devil-may-care, slightly flippant attitude, possibly because some of the more popular comic books of the time feature heroes of this nature. While this seems a touch out of character for our Sorcerer Supreme, the book, with stories by Roy and Dann Thomas, is nevertheless quite entertaining and makes good use of an interesting supporting cast, including Doc's "apprentice," the lovable Rintrah, who is basically a green-horned bull that talks; Morgana Blessing, who has written a best-seller about the doctor; Vic, Strange's vampiric brother; and many others. A five-part "Vampiric Verses" (DS #14–18, 1990) reintroduced vampires to the Marvel Universe and employed such guest stars as Brother Voodoo and Morbius, a scientific blood-drinker.

For the record, Dr. Strange was also a member of *The Defenders* for several years, and got involved in some pretty wild adventures with that loosely structured superteam, which originally consisted only of Dr. Strange, the Incredible Hulk, and Namor, the Sub-Mariner, before becoming a haven for cast-off, second-string characters from other books. (The Defenders first began in *Marvel Feature* in 1972, and got their own book later the same year. It had a long run but was eventually canceled.)

Dr. Strange became the subject of a television movie in 1978. In this, the Sorcerer Supreme is still practicing medicine, as well as sorcery, and is portrayed as a playboy by Peter Hooten. His assistant, Wong (Clyde Kusatsu), is a more modern, less subservient interpretation of the Oriental sidekick. The story by writer, director Philip DeGuere only touches on the macabre aspects of the comic book. John Mills plays an older sorcerer who enlists Strange's aid in stopping the witch Morgan Le Fey (Jessica Walter) from laying claim to the souls of many men.

Dr. Strange became the subject of a television movie in 1978. In this, the Sorcerer Supreme is still practicing medicine, as well as sorcery, and is portrayed as a playboy by Peter Hooten. His assistant, Wong (Clyde Kusatsu), is a more modern, less subservient interpretation of the Oriental sidekick. The story by writer, director Philip DeGuere only touches on the macabre aspects of the comic book. John Mills plays an older sorcerer who enlists Strange's aid in stopping the witch Morgan Le Fey (Jessica Walter) from laying claim to the souls of many men.

Walter makes an attractive if too restrained villainess. She has the hots for Dr. Strange, though her lust is unrequited.

Although Hooten is appealing as the doctor, *Dr. Strange* is at best a clumsy, pedestrian attempt to adapt the comic to a visual medium. DeGuere's uninspired direction isn't helped by slow pacing, obvious padding, and some terribly inappropriate musical backgrounds. The special effects are uneven: there are some poor sets supposedly portraying the "astral plane," but a stop-motion[5] demon who confers with Morgan Le Fey is nicely animated. The telefilm was surprisingly well received by critics who admired its tongue-in-cheek tone.

As of this writing, Dr. Strange is currently in development as both a theatrical feature and a second, separate TV movie. The ubiquitous Albert Pyun had been mulling over the possibility of directing the feature, but the fate of his *Captain America* movie would seem to make that an unlikely possibility.

[5]Stop-motion or three-dimensional animation employs small puppets that are moved one frame at a time to approximate realistic movement; this process was used to animate the 1933 *King Kong* and many other creatures before and since.

Above: Dr. Strange looks up some mystical spells.

SWAMP THING

The Swamp Thing first appeared in a one-shot short story in DC's anthology horror comic *House of Secrets*. The readers responded so enthusiastically to the character that it was decided to revive him on a more permanent basis and provide an all new origin as well. The *Swamp Thing* comic started publishing in late 1972. The creators were Len Wein, Berni Wrightson, and Joe Orlando.

The first issue told the story of scientist Alec Holland and his wife. They come afoul of an evil man named Arcane who wants Holland's "bio-restorative" formula. The wife is killed and Holland, doused with the formula, runs into the swamp. He merges with the mossy vegetation of the swamplands and turns into a mutated creature, Swamp Thing.[6] Subsequent adventures would have the scientist, who is still sentient, following around his security agent Matt Cable and other associates and saving them from assorted monsters. Each tale was embellished by the Wrightson-Orlando artwork; their full-page drawing of a werewolf in *Swamp Thing #4* (April–May 1973) is particularly striking.

The comic had already been canceled by the time the film adaptation was made, with the idea that it would appeal to both comics and horror fans. Alec's wife was changed into a sister so that a new love interest could be added: Matt Cable became Alice Cable, played by Adrienne Barbeau. Berni Wrightson's basic design for the creature was used in the movie.

The basic premise is the same: Alec Holland (played by Ray Wise) and his sister, experimenting with recombinant DNA (they've come up with a vegetable cell that has an animal nucleus), develop a formula that not only has inadvertent explosive properties, but can "amplify your essence, make you more of what you are." As in the comic, the government lab is attacked by minions of Arcane (Louis Jourdan), and Holland turns into a sentient plant man. The rest of the film has Swamp Thing (now played by stuntman Dick Durock) assisting Alice in escaping Arcane's thugs and bringing him to justice.

Although the Swamp Thing costume is well designed, particularly in the facial area, the green latex outfit is not very convincing. Instead of appearing organic—it's supposed to be Holland's "skin" to all intents and purposes—it never looks like anything but a suit. (While filming on location, the rubber in the suit began to erode from an acid secreted by all the cypress trees; an antacid had to be sprayed onto the costume.)

---

[6]Swamp Thing is not to be confused with Marvel Comics' similarly muck-encrusted Man-Thing, who only retains the barest vestiges of his former identity. Both characters were probably inspired by the golden-age character, the Heap.

Above: The fiftieth "anniversary" issue of *Swamp Thing*. Copyright © 1986 DC Comics, Inc.

Opposite: *Swamp Thing* peeks out at his pursuers.

Bruno (Nicholas Worth), one of Arcane's thugs, is fed the formula at a sumptuous dinner party in Arcane's elegantly appointed mansion, and turns into a piglike midget. Arcane himself, in the film's most ludicrous moments, becomes a campy-looking, shaggy-haired boar creature. His battle with Swamp Thing in a foggy swampland environment is visually pleasing but none too exciting. The locations are great, however, and one sequence, in which Barbeau is chased by Arcane's men and they all come across Swamp Thing in the middle of the road, is nicely done. Barbeau's energetic performance is matched by that of a feisty black kid who runs a gas station, agrees to help her, and quips, "There goes the neighborhood," when he catches his first sight of the transformed Alec Holland.

Director Wes Craven keeps the proceedings at a fairly absorbing and entertaining level for about the first three quarters of the picture, but by the time Swamp Thing meets the Arcane-Monster—the scene is a sort of miniature version of *Godzilla vs. the Thing—Swamp Thing's* credibility goes out the window. (*Swamp Thing* was followed by a barely released 1989 sequel, *Return of the Swamp Thing*, aka *Swamp Thing 2*, in which Arcane is magically returned from the dead and the whole dopey struggle continues.)

Adrienne Barbeau did not have a good time making *Swamp Thing*, and does not appear in *Return of Swamp Thing*.

A TV series premiered on cable in 1990 and was generally well received. At this writing, it still is in production. In 1991, an animated version of *Swamp Thing* premiered on Saturday morning television in syndication.

THE PUNISHER / MASTERS OF THE UNIVERSE

The Punisher first appeared in *Amazing Spider-Man* #129 in 1974, as a villain of sorts. He was duped into believing that Spider-Man was a killer and decided to target the web spinner for assassination. From the beginning, the Punisher was different from other heroes: he, too, fought a war on crime, but rarely took prisoners and didn't take care only to wound instead of kill when fighting adversaries. He was a one-man army against merciless drug lords and the like. The chest of his black uniform was emblazoned with a huge white grinning skull. He had no special powers, aside from an impressive armament of guns and technological weaponry.

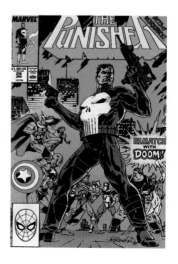

Above: His participation in the cross-comic "Acts of Vengeance" storyline made *The Punisher* #29 extra collectible. Copyright © 1990 Marvel Entertainment Group, Inc.

The Punisher soon became a recurring character in the Marvel Universe, basically a good guy—but his vigilante, often violent methods brought him up against other heroes such as Captain America and Daredevil (who were real bleeding hearts to begin with but certainly so in comparison to the Punisher). His presence was tolerated, his help grudgingly appreciated, but he never won approval.

Except with the fans. He soon became one of Marvel's most popular supporting characters, and then a star in his own right. First came a five-issue limited series that was heavy on the sex and violence (though within the boundaries of good taste). He was awarded his own unlimited series, a companion book, and a black-and-white magazine shortly thereafter, and continued to battle his own set of villains as well as Marvel Universe mainstays such as Dr. Doom. The more popular he became, the more he interacted with other Marvel heroes, in the same way that Nick Fury[7] did years before. Nick Fury also "interacted" with Frank Castle (The Punisher's real name) although the two did not get along well. In fact, Fury threatened Castle with prosecution.

The Punisher is assisted by a bespectacled buddy named Microchip, who, as his name suggests, is a whiz at computers, a fact that not only comes in handy in their war on crime, but has initiated several story ideas as well. So far the Punisher has outlasted by years a somewhat similar character, *The Vigilante*, published by DC (and not to be confused with their golden age Vigilante), whose book had a short, but respectable life and ran some excellent, hard-hitting stories. The tone of *The Punisher* is less cerebral and focuses squarely on action for the most part.

A film adaptation starring Dolph (*Rocky IV*) Lundgren as *The Punisher* was made in 1989. When his wife and children are killed by the mafia, Frank Castle takes to the sewers to organize his revenge campaign against all of New York's "godfathers."

---

[7]Nick Fury started out as the star of *Sergeant Fury and His Howling Commandos*, a Marvel comic published in the sixties but which took place during World War II. In modern continuity, he became *Nick Fury, Agent of SHIELD*.

Above: Dolph Lundgren in *Masters of the Universe* ; he played the generic "He-Man."

The rest of the story has the Japanese mafia, run by icy Lady Tanaka (Nancy Everhard), coming to Manhattan to try to wrest control from the Punisher-decimated mobsters. When they fight back, a brutal war ensues that tears the city apart. The Punisher sits back and lets these scumbags knock each other off, until he's forced to intervene when some children are kidnapped by Tanaka's underlings.

"Lundgren looks just as if he's stepped out of a comic book," said *Variety*. "All that's missing from his actions is the 'pow!' 'bam!' or 'wham!' Thankfully, he breezes through the B-grade plot with tongue firmly placed in cheek, and the script allows him some nice one-liners that indicate no one is really taking this caper seriously." The paper's critic also noted: "The Punisher has killed 125 people before the film even begins, and the ensuing ninety minutes are crammed with slaughters of every conceivable kind," while predicting that the "over-the-top" violence would neatly serve to prevent the target audience of teens from ever seeing the film. Made by the now-defunct Australian branch of New World Pictures, *The Punisher* features shots of a New York that looks suspiciously like North Sydney. No domestic distributor was found and New World considered going direct to video. (Reportedly, the powers-that-be at Marvel wanted to disavow the picture.)

The Punisher was not the first time Lundgren had played a comic book hero. In 1987, armed with a drama coach, a speech coach, a personal trainer, and his own personal hair stylist, Lundgren essayed the role of "He-Man" in *Masters of the Universe*. These characters had started out as Mattel toys for children and became so popular that they engendered live theater programs (including one at Radio City Music Hall), an animated cartoon series (that was said to be as interesting for adults as for the tots), and two comic book series, one from Marvel and one from DC (not concurrently, however).

Whatever the merit of the cartoon show, the comic book series was strictly for very young children. It was practically a "generic" comic, with one-dimensional characters and exceedingly simple stories of good versus evil. "Good" was personified in the muscular He-Man; "evil" in the wicked Skeletor. They fought for the possession of the power to be found in Castle Greyskull in the far-off land of Eternia. Never had a comic book been quite so juvenile and dull.

The film version was a slight improvement over the comics (but not, reportedly, over the cartoon series). It begins in the middle of the action, with Skeletor's forces taking over Castle Grayskull and the war between opposing sides already in progress. Skeletor is played by Frank Langella in hood, cloak, and pasty skull mask. Meg Foster is his associate, Evil-Lyn.

The trouble has started because a lovable dwarf (played winningly by Billy Barty) has invented a key through which one can cross dimensions. He-Man and company inadvertently wind up on Earth with this key in their possession. To retrieve it, Skeletor sends Evil-Lyn and her underlings to Earth. A young student (and hopeful musician) and his pretty girlfriend are embroiled in the action and nearly killed by Evil-Lyn's minions, while Skeletor himself arrives on our "primitive and tasteless" planet to get the key himself and leave He-Man and his associates stranded. Barty manages to send them all back to Eternia so they can heal the Earth girl's injury and stop Skeletor once and for all.

While all of this is undeniably silly stuff, it is made palatable by convincing performances, good special effects (mostly light shows), a fast pace and Bill Conti's music. The screenplay was written by David (*Supergirl*) Odell and the director is Gary Goddard.

Dolph Lundgren makes a visually perfect He-Man, although the actor is given little to say. He-Man exhibits great strength in the climax (when Skeletor transforms himself into an eyebeam-shooting demon) but his powers are otherwise rarely illustrated. There's no reason why Lundgren can't some day have the kind of career that Arnold Schwarzenegger has. The other actors all are to be commended for doing everything reasonably well with straight faces. The movie, however, was not a big box office success.

The direction of a perhaps ill-advised sequel, *Masters of the Universe 2*, was entrusted to (again!) Albert Pyun. He was supposed to shoot it back to back with *Spider-Man —The Movie*. By the time *Masters 2* was completed, it had somehow been transformed into a film called *Cyborg* (1989) starring kick-boxer Jean Claude Van Damme.

Hollywood is sometimes stranger than the funny books.

HOWARD THE DUCK

Howard the Duck is probably the strangest hero (of the nonsuperpowered variety) in Marvel's stable. The duck, sort of a spoof on Donald and Daffy, first appeared in a story starring Marvel's muck-monster of the swamp, Man-Thing (*Fear* #19, continued in *Man-Thing* #1). Although Howard was last seen hurtling into infinity in the climax of that story, fan reaction was so strong that he was brought back for short backups, ran for president in an amusing mock campaign, and eventually was awarded his own magazine.

The premise was simple: Unlike Daffy and Donald, Howard's being a duck was not treated matter-of-factly (comparatively speaking, that is). People would hear him talk, and screech: "But... you're a duck! To which Howard might reply (as he did in a backup in *Giant-Size Man-Thing* #2, written by Steve Gerber), "There ain't no justice! Ya save the universe an' what does it get ya? 'You're a duck!'—that's what it gets ya!" In this story, "Frog Death," Howard squares off with the terrible Garko, the Man-Frog. Needless to say, his brief battle against a man turned into a giant amphibian (and who later shrinks and is squashed by a car) is played strictly for laughs. Satire for grown-ups would come a little later.

Howard came from a world where ducks were the dominant species and human beings couldn't talk (a duck version of *Planet of the Apes*). He was a lovable, hapless, sometimes formidable stranger in a strange land, a lonesome fowl who meant no harm but found himself lost in bizarre adventures with weird and sometimes terrible people and adversaries, though not all were as far out as one might imagine. For instance, in issue #21 (February 1978), Howard battles the Sinister Soofi, a group dedicated to eradicating immorality, even if it means *killing* all those who "trespass." The leader of the group, who wears a covering headpiece shaped like an orange, turns out to be a "female hairless ape" from the Sunshine State. This story came out while Anita Bryant was waging her war against homosexuals, and while hardcore conservatives were not amused, others felt the timely story was a riot.

In *Howard the Duck*, the satire was broad and often brutal, the tone as oddly dark as it was comical, and the shenanigans squarely left of center to nonsensical. Howard was rewarded with a human girlfriend, the lovely Beverly Switzler, and eventually faded into the sunset, only to reappear in the nineties in *The Sensational She-Hulk*[8] comic (second series).

When *Howard the Duck* was made into a movie in 1986, it got one of the worst critical drubbings any film has ever received. While it is certainly not without its flaws, much of the attack on it could be attributed to "big buck film bashing." Had *Howard* been a small, low-budget, barely advertised "little" film, critics might have responded to its charm and whimsy, instead of in effect booing it off the screen.

In the film, Howard is mysteriously sucked from his home planet to Cleveland, Earth, where he meets a rock singer named Beverly Switzler (Lea Thompson). As in the comics, the two have a strange romance and even a soft-lit love scene which borders on—in fact which *is*—bestiality. Nevertheless, the sequence seems perfectly "natural" in this movie.

Things take a turn for the worse when a scientist named Dr. Jenning (the always reliable Jeffrey Jones) is possessed by an alien force while trying to send Howard back to his own planet. First, Jenning starts making funny faces and noises; then he exhibits telekinetic and other powers in a diner and causes a riot. Finally, in the film's climax, Howard and Beverly—along with likable lab assistant Phil (Tim Robbins)—square off against the alien invader come to Earth. This last scene is a knockout special effects sequence featuring a scorpion-like "Dark Overlord" that is as big as a bus and brilliantly brought to three-dimensional life by animator Phil Tippett. Tippett's lively, scuttling, horrific creation is one of the finest monsters to ever engulf the screen, and the whole climax is eye-popping and exciting.

All but the more reasonable critics failed to see it that way, ignoring the effects, the fine acting, and John Barry's rousing musical score. Much of the film's failure was blamed on Howard himself, who many felt was not as sharply delineated as in the comic, and poorly brought to "life" besides. Howard was not a special effects creation, which may or may not have been more appropriate, but a little man in a duck suit. Ed Gale and various other actors took turns playing the part.

Now that time has passed, people may look more kindly on *Howard the Duck*. It will never make—or deserve to

Above: *Howard the Duck* #21 had a strong satiric slant in the seventies; issues are now collector's items. Copyright © 1978 Marvel Comics Group.

[8]The She-Hulk, Jennifer Walters, became a female green goliath when she received a blood transfusion from her infamous cousin, Bruce Banner (the Hulk).

Opposite: *Howard the Duck* a duck lost in a world of "hairless apes."

be on—anyone's "ten best" list, but neither is it entirely worthless. Such hard-to-please critics as film historian Lawrence Quirk find the picture more than acceptable for what it is meant to be. "It's interesting, different, and holds the attention," says Quirk, "which is a lot more than you can say for a lot of pictures." Producer Gloria Katz (George *Star Wars* Lucas was executive producer) and director Willard Huyck had planned another Howard the Duck picture—until they saw the reviews and the box office returns.

DICK TRACY

Dick Tracy was introduced with a bang as a daily newspaper comic strip in 1931. The first story has him dining with sweetheart Tess Trueheart and her parents when gunmen burst in with shattering suddenness. The felons kidnap Tess after murdering her father and stealing his savings. Tracy swears to save his girl and bring the killers to justice. From that moment on, Dick Tracy becomes an avenger determined to bring evil men and wrongdoers to their just deserts.

Dick Tracy was the first police strip. It was created by writer/artist Chester Gould, whose violent, often bloody, stories were occasionally based on the headlines and featured characters with descriptive names like Mumbles and B. O. Plenty. Still, there was a hard, realistic edge to the early strips, and Gould's storytelling was skillful and absorbing; his artwork simplistic but effective and well-composed.

Dick Tracy continued on into the forties, when several serials (see chapter seven) and features were based on the character. The daily and Sunday strips were as good as ever, and read particularly well if an entire story (several weeks' worth) is absorbed at one sitting. That way one can really appreciate Gould's breakneck pacing and suspenseful intercutting. A good example is a 1945 tale in which Tracy tracks an escaped drug runner, Measles, to a flooded farming community, and Measles's efforts to get away by boat and by horse are intercut with attempts by Tracy and his men to find him. Justice always prevails in Dick Tracy, if nowhere else.

The first feature film was released by RKO in 1945, with two the following year, and a final one in 1947. The credits would consist of caricatures of each of the characters, with the final sketch a drawing of the opening shot of the movie. This sketch would be superimposed over, and eventually fade into, the shot of the actor—usually the villain—in the scene. This was an effective way of introducing the picture, but it occasionally had peculiar results. For instance, in the second film, the superimposed sketch makes the actor playing Cueball look as if he's wearing clown makeup—a face over a face. All were good, solid "B" pictures, nothing more.

Opposite: Warren Beatty doing his best to impersonate *Dick Tracy*.

Dick Tracy (1945)[9] starred "stone-faced contract player Morgan Conway...simply because he was already on the payroll," according to Charles Lee Jackson II in *Filmfax*. Conway is an acceptable Dick Tracy, but hardly an inspired one. His antagonist in the film is the murderous Splitface. Mike Mazurki plays the killer, with Jane Greer as a lovely femme fatale, and Anne Jeffreys as Tess Trueheart. The film, directed by William Berke, boasts a fast pace and some reasonably eerie and suspenseful sequences.

Dick Tracy Versus Cueball (1946), directed by the dependable Gordon Douglas, also stars Conway as Tracy and features the villainy of a large, malevolent baldie named Cueball. Cueball has been hired to steal some jewels by at

least one person in a jewelry firm, who may be Mr. Little, the nervous chief suspect, or perhaps his friend Rudolph, who looks like a living ventriloquist's dummy. By far the most vivid character—and performer—is Filthy Flora, a grizzled old lady who owns a waterfront café called the Dripping Dagger.

Tracy closes in while Cueball disposes of anyone who gets in his way. This includes Flora, whose death scene is the liveliest sequence in the film. She makes the mistake of trying to palm the jewels Cueball stole from a courier (whom he murdered at the opening) and attempts to hold off an angry Cueball with a broken beer bottle. He advances on her, whips her face a few times with his hand—then strangles her. Cueball's many strangulations are always presented with eye-bulging closeups of him and his victims. Flora, and the antique store owner who is the third victim, scream quite piercingly as they croak. (Only in the movies can somebody scream while being choked to death.)

Anne Jeffreys again appears as Tess Trueheart, who bravely puts herself in danger by pretending to be a mysterious potential buyer of stolen jewels and nearly gets done in when Cueball realizes her deception. Jeffreys is quite good and animated in the role.

Cueball is not a very bright villain. When his foot gets caught in the tracks at the end of the film, it never occurs to him to simply *take off his shoe*. Instead he stands there struggling until a train runs over him. *Dick Tracy Versus Cueball* is a slight improvement over its predecessor, with as fast a pace and that same slick "B" movie know-how that makes the most of a low budget.

The next feature, *Dick Tracy's Dilemma* (1947), would be memorable if only for bringing Ralph Byrd back to the role of Tracy, which he had played in four serials. Byrd is the quintessential Tracy, with the square jaw, forthright

---

[9]*Dick Tracy* is now widely known as *Dick Tracy, Detective*, to avoid confusion with the first serial, also titled *Dick Tracy*.

Above: Jane Greer confronts Morgan Conway as *Dick Tracy*, as young Mickey Kuhn looks on.

manner, quiet good looks, and determination we associate with the character. As *Filmfax* writer Charles Lee Jackson II explained, "The title rather reflected a real-life situation. Ralph Byrd had been away from Tracy long enough that he missed the star's life. Tracy had haunted his career for five years, working against his talent. Casting directors shied away from him, knowing that audiences would look at Byrd and see Tracy. So now, when RKO offered him the role again, he had to choose between accepting, and reinforcing, his typecasting, or pass on a new star turn. He accepted."

Dick Tracy's Dilemma has some similarities to the previous film, in that it not only centers on a robbery that's an "inside job" but also has a lot of action revolving around a sleazy saloon. The villain is the Claw, who has been hired by an unknown person to pull off the robbery of a safe, causing an insurance firm to start wondering if fraud might be involved. John Rawlins's direction is occasionally cinematic: One murder sequence is shot partially through the revolving blades of a portable fan, and there's a tense sequence in an alley when a fake beggar called Sightless is pursued and nearly killed by the Claw—who manages to finish the job later.

The picture has a great deal of genuine suspense and humor. Much of the latter is supplied by the supporting characters, including saloon gal and gambler Longshot Lillie, and the amusing, effeminate Vitamin, who appeared in the previous film but is used to better advantage here. Tracy and The Claw have a neat duel at the end in which the Claw's metal hook (from which he gets his nickname) accidentally grabs onto a power line and gives its owner the juice. So much for the Claw.

John Rawlins also directed the final Tracy feature, *Dick Tracy Meets Gruesome* (1947), which costars Boris Karloff. The clever premise has the hoodlum, Gruesome (Karloff), using Dr. A. Tomic's (sic) special gas to "freeze" everyone in a bank so that he and his gang members can simply walk in and rob it without fuss. Tracy's secretary is in a phone booth in the bank at the time and isn't affected. This segment is very well handled, with seamless freeze-frame effects combined with moving figures.

Karloff is fine in the role of Gruesome, and looks quite sinister and disreputable. He tries to send Tracy up a conveyer belt into an incinerator, but almost winds up flash-fried himself before Tracy saves him—and ends his criminal career.

Above: Ralph Byrd (center): the very best Dick Tracy.

Ad for *Dick Tracy's Dilemma* with Ralph Byrd.

Dick Tracy not only continued as a strip in the newspapers, but became a TV show (starring Ralph Byrd) in the fifties, a (dreadful) cartoon series in the sixties, and a multimillion-dollar Hollywood spectacle in the summer of 1990, courtesy of producer-director Warren Beatty, who also took the starring role.

Unfortunately, Beatty's *Dick Tracy* is a triumph of art direction and scenic design and a major disappointment in almost every other area. Beatty, a limited actor, should be great as the one-dimensional Tracy, but somehow comes off less believable than Ralph Byrd, who was also a limited actor but who really looked the part. Beatty just seems like—well, Warren Beatty trying to do an impersonation of Chester Gould's world-famous detective. An insurmountable problem is the Jim Cash and Jack Epps, Jr., script, which provides few thrills or cliff-hangers and hasn't a strong enough plot on which to build suspense. Beatty's direction muffs what few tense moments there are, or should have been, as when Tess Trueheart is tied up at the finale and likely to be crushed to death at any moment. Every now and then Beatty throws in a shot to remind us that Tess is in a predicament, but the editing doesn't wring a single drop of juice out of what should have been a nail-biting sequence.

The 1930s art deco look of the movie is top-notch, however, with most of the city comprised of Harrison Ellenshaw's superb matte paintings. The entire film was shot on the Universal backlot, so Ellenshaw's incredibly detailed work had to provide an approximation of a living comic strip that looks better than anything ever done by Chester Gould. An older process employing a yellow screen and sodium vapor lamps was used instead of the usual blue-backing technique. Several miniatures also were used: a two-foot-high, forty-foot-long scale train which weighed a ton, and a ferryboat and drawbridge built over "water" made of Plexiglas.

John Caglione, Jr.'s, makeups are also excellent and deliberately grotesque without necessarily looking nonhuman. Even under a ton of makeup, Al Pacino scores as Tracy's prime antagonist (he got an Oscar nomination for his portrayal), but Dustin Hoffman only manages to irritate as Mumbles. As nightclub singer Breathless Mahoney, Madonna gets by all right, but doesn't give her lines the kind of delivery that would indicate a genuine actress. (The twist ending in which Tracy learns that Breathless is "The Blank" is an inspired touch, though. Tess Trueheart and "Kid" (Junior) are well played by Glenne Headly and Charlie Korsmo, respectively, but the sentimental moments, particularly between Tess and Tracy, don't work because neither character has been well developed. Danny Elfman's score does what it can to drum up some pathos and excitement.

The effects, makeups, and particularly Vittorio Storaro's cinematography are awe-inspiring, but wasted on a film that just doesn't move or involve the viewer. *Dick Tracy* must be chalked up as an artistic, if not commercial, failure. Though it did not achieve the sensational grosses of *Batman,* whose box office it wished to emulate, it did do quite respectably.

Above: Beatty's *Dick Tracy* was a visual feast if little else.

COMIC STRIP DELUXE:
MANDRAKE, MODESTY, POPEYE, AND THE REST

A variety of additional comic strip characters have made it into theatrical features and telefilms, including the following:

Mandrake the Magician was created by Lee Falk in 1934 and appeared as a TV movie in 1979. Here, Mandrake (Anthony Herrera, who appears to be dubbed) is orphaned in a plane crash and raised by wizards who give him an amulet with strange powers. He can cause hallucinations (creating animals to frighten assailants), start motors, even project his photographic memory onto a polaroid snapshot. (Some okay effects work features phantom snakes, tigers, etc.) Mandrake has a pretty female assistant, as well as a hulking sidekick, Lothar, a carryover from the comic strip, who is a tall, striking-looking black fellow with a shiny bald head.

The plot has to do with an extortionist (Peter Haskell) who's blowing up amusement parks owned by the wealthy Arcadian (Robert Reed) in an attempt to get a huge cash payoff. Haskell has a slew of "mind slaves" whom

he has hypnotized into planting bombs. *Mandrake*'s mediocre script, one-dimensional characters, and perfunctory direction (by Harry Falk) make it an effort to sit through. It has not one memorable scene or aspect.

Modesty Blaise was based on Peter O'Donnell and Jim Holdway's mildly risqué British comic strip about a female superspy. Monica Vitti is Modesty and Terence Stamp is her associate, Willie Garvin. The leads are attractive, and Dirk Bogarde adds a little class as the smooth villain, Gabriel, but this lethargic disaster of a movie has to be the prime embarrassment in director Joseph Losey's career. *Modesty Blaise* was made in 1966, the height of the mod-camp craze, and looks it. Besides being silly and boring, the movie is badly photographed and scored. The strip, character, and movie are more or less forgotten today.

At the other end of the spectrum is *Flash Gordon*, which began as a comic strip (drawn superbly by Alex Raymond) in 1934, was made into several serials, and got the big-budget Hollywood treatment in 1980. Sam J.

Above: Terence Stamp and Monica Vitti starred in *Modesty Blaise*.

Jones makes a creditable Flash Gordon, and the story is essentially the same as the first comic strip adventure and the original serial: Flash, Dale Arden, and Zarkov traveling to Mongo to confront Ming the Merciless (beautifully played by the versatile Max von Sydow). The wonderful credit art looks like original Alex Raymond panels or excellent facsimiles.

Flash Gordon, directed by Mike Hodges, is generally good-humored and handsomely produced, and has several exciting sequences. The best has Flash and Prince Barin (pre-007 Timothy Dalton) fighting a duel on a floating round silver platform suspended in an open area in a city in the clouds. The battle is complicated because the weapons are whips and the platforms tilt up and down continuously as spikes periodically erupt from the surface. There is also a very nice montage as Dr. Zarkov's mind is drained of everything it knows and we see his life in frenetic clips from recent events all the way back to the womb. And there are splendid shots showing Vulcan's winged forces attacking Ming's ship in skies of orange and purple. Parts of the film seem inspired by everything from *Star Wars* (the Darth Vader masks on the soldiers) to *The Prisoner* (strange, unemotional "agents" in strange outfits watch everyone on monitors) and even *Barbarella*.

Barbarella, made in 1968, is based on a saucy French comic strip. This is another campy, art deco movie, in which a space heroine (played by Jane Fonda) is assigned to track down a renegade scientist who has made off with a dangerous secret weapon. Along the way Fonda runs into small killer robots with sharp metal teeth, as well as parakeets who nibble inhospitably on her when she's locked in a glass enclosure. She has "old-fashioned" sex with one man, and futuristic sex—via pills and hand-touching—with David Hemmings. She finds her quarry in a strange city built over a *living* lake (or blob) called the "matmus" which feeds literally and figuratively on evil. A blind angel (John Phillip Law) flies her into this city where she falls into the clutches of the sinister queen (Anita Pallenberg) who rules it.

The effects in *Barbarella* are fairly minor-league by today's standards but were considered eye-popping at the time of the picture's release. Despite striking moments and effective scenes, it

Above: The French comic strip came to life in *Barbarella* with a winged John Phillip Law and Jane Fonda.

is directed in an unexceptional manner by Roger Vadim.

Last but not least, we have one of the most unusual and likable heroes of them all, the inimitable *Popeye*, whose incredible cartoon feats certainly put him in the "superhuman" category. Popeye first appeared in Elzie Segar's strip *Thimble Theatre* about six decades before director Robert Altman made the 1980 movie of his exploits. Although some of Altman's directorial peculiarities are still in evidence, such as muffled dialogue and lots of aimless business, the picture combines great effects and stunt work to create an elaborate live-action cartoon in which nothing is impossible. Robin Williams makes an excellent Popeye, with fine support from Paul Dooley (Wimpie), Shelley Duvall (Olive Oyl), Ray Walston (Pappy), and of course Paul Smith as his perpetual adversary, Bluto. Little "Swee' pea" is one of the cutest babies to ever make an appearance on a movie screen.

Popeye recreates the kind of comical, exaggerated action that appeared in the classic imaginative cartoons from the Max Fleischer Studios: wild fistfights and boxing matches, zany expressions and voices, stunts and feats of superstrength, and the like, that would indicate superhuman abilities in the real world but in *Popeye* are just business as usual.

Robin Williams as *Popeye*.

Popeye probably loves his spinach more than he does Olive Oyl (Shelley Duvall).

CHAPTER SIX
SUPER-HEROIC TV SHOWS

If "super-heroes" means anything, it means *action*. No wonder there have been so many feature-length films, TV programs, and serials devoted to the genre. So many, in fact, that when the major comic book characters were exhausted, and then some of the minor ones, producers started churning out their own variations, characters that came not from a comic book but strictly from a screenwriter's imagination. Several programs and serials were based on radio programs. And there were still a few comic books and comic strip characters left for adaptation. This chapter will explore TV programs in the comic book tradition; the next focuses on several of the "superhuman" serials that have not already been covered.

One of the earliest super-hero TV programs would never have come about were it not for an imaginative movie entitled *The Incredible Shrinking Man* (1957). This science fiction classic, based on Richard Matheson's short novel, details the harrowing fate of a man who is exposed to toxic gas and is slowly reduced in size until he's smaller even than a doll. The special effects in the picture—the protagonist battling a cat and a spider, floating on a match in a fantastic cellar flood while his "enormous" wife stands inches away on the stairs but cannot see him— are spectacular and hold up today. Many outsized props were also built for the film, and these found their way into a syndicated TV series entitled *World of Giants* in 1959.

World of Giants starred Marshall Thompson (*Daktari*) as the country's most unusual spy. He is only six inches tall, and can be carried around in a briefcase by his government liaison, Arthur Franz. Left behind in offices, on tabletops or in desk drawers, Thompson can eavesdrop like a figurative and literal "bug." The series eschewed the astounding effects of its inspiration for budgetary reasons, but was reasonably engaging for its fairly brief run.

World of Giants may have helped inspire two successful comic series that both debuted in the early 1960s.[1] DC Comics' *The Atom* (the second DC character to be so christened) could utilize the power of a white dwarf star to shrink so drastically that he could play hopscotch with electrons. Normally, he remained at a six-inch level and at that height battled a variety of colorful foes, including the Plant Man and Chronos. The Atom's writers and artists put him in an amusing and always appropriate series of death traps: almost consumed by a Venus's-flytrap, caught inside the glass-enclosed face of a watch, captured and pinned like a butterfly, placed inside a see-through bowling ball containing poison gas,[2] and so on. After his comic concluded its lengthy run, the Atom had a brief career as a "barbarian" in an outpost of miniature aliens in a secluded jungle, then had a stab at a second short-lived U.S.-based series. He is now an undercover member of *The Suicide Squad*.

The Astonishing Ant-Man was Marvel Comics' entry into the super Ken doll sweepstakes. Henry Pym invented a shrinking gas that could reduce him to the size of one of his beloved insects. Flying over the city on a faithful flying ant, he battled crime with his partner, the Wasp, for several issues of *Tales to Astonish* and *The Avengers* before turning into Giant-Man, then Goliath, then Yellowjacket. Now he is simply known as Dr. Pym and works with the West Coast edition of the Avengers.

[1]This may well have been inspired by the *Dollman* comic series of the forties.

[2]This doom-trap was actually featured in the classic *Justice League of America* #14 (September 1962), in which the Atom first joined the Justice League.

Opposite: *The Six Million Dollar Man* straddles a torpedo.

The success of the Batman television series in the sixties led to the other networks coming out with their own super-heroic programming. NBC's entry was the silly *Captain Nice* (1966), about a wimpy chemist who comes up with a formula to transform himself into a super-hero. The captain was played by that sharp-featured actor with the nasal voice, William Daniels, and was one of his more obnoxious performances. As his superhuman alter ego, Daniels would wear a black cape, sneakers, and striped red-and-white pants that looked like rejects from the Ice Capades. Ann Prentiss, Paula's less funny sister, played Daniels's girlfriend, a cop named Candy Cane. That was about the level of the humor on the series.

Meanwhile that same season, CBS came out with *Mr. Terrific*, starring Stephen Strimpell as gas station owner Stanley Beamish, who, when he took a special pill that was formulated by government scientists, turned into a super-hero. "The principal difference between Beamish and Captain Nice," Gary Gerani wrote in *Fantastic Television*, "was that Stanley flapped his arms when he flew, while the captain glided." Mr. Terrific wore a kind of gold lamé flying suit with a goggle mask and baggy pants. Neither program lasted for more than a season, and their jokes and effects were lame even for the youngsters.

The television program with Strimpell was unrelated to the DC Comics character, Mr. Terrific, "the defender of fair play," who first appeared in the golden age, made the transition to the silver age with the rest of the Justice Society, and was murdered by his archfoe, the Spirit King, in *Justice League of America* #171–172 (October/November 1979). His garish outfit—red ski mask and tights with green pants and suitcoat—was a model of taste and restraint compared to Strimpell's.

Although *The Champions* was a British series, its first ten episodes (out of thirty) were telecast in the United States in 1968 by NBC. Comic book fans were excited by the premise of the show, but not its execution, and it garnered few hard-core fans during its run. The Champions were definitely super-heroes—they had gained special powers from a lost Tibetan race and went on important missions—but they didn't act like super-heroes. They looked and dressed like ordinary people, and their mostly mental abilities were fairly prosaic. What special effects there were, were extremely limited. Two of its stars, British actors William Gaunt and Alexandro Bastedo, came from and returned to obscurity, but American Stuart Damon had played Prince Charming in the second TV version of Rodgers and Hammerstein's *Cinderella*, had appeared on Broadway in the Rodgers–Sondheim

Above: *Mr. Terrific* (Steve Strimpell) models his not so terrific outfit, which looks like something Andy Warhol might have come up with if he were into fashion.

collaboration *Do I Hear a Waltz?* and is currently a soap star. *The Champions* is not a highlight of his resumé. There are endless comic book characters, before and since, who have had powers similar to those of *The Champions*.

The Immortal began life as a seventy-five-minute movie-of-the-week on ABC in 1969, and did double duty as a pilot for the short-lived 1970 series. In this, Christopher George plays Ben Richards, a race car driver whose blood contains special antibodies that make him immune to all diseases, and to the aging process. Most critics agreed that there were aspects, ideas, and subplots that badly needed to be developed, and the resulting weekly series tried to take care of them. Richards becomes a fugitive when a ruthless billionaire wants to turn him into his own personal blood supply. Apparently allergic to unsolicited transfusions, Richards spent one season dodging attacks and persuasions by people in the billionaire's employ. It was certainly an interesting idea, but the series failed to catch on or expand beyond its extremely limited scope. Other actors in the pilot film included Jessica Walter, Ralph Bellamy, Barry Sullivan, and Carol Lynley. Directed by Joseph Sargent, it was based on a novel by James Gunn.

The theme of a villain wanting to exploit, steal, or siphon off the powers and abilities of a superhuman character is an old one in the comics. Superman's strength has been "borrowed" via some infernal device on countless occasions, for instance. A story line in the *X-Men* comic series had the inhabitants of Genosha turning their mutants (people born with special abilities) into slaves for the good of the state. Blood transfusions can play a part in the transfer of powers, also. Jennifer Walters became the She-Hulk after her cousin Bruce Banner, the Hulk, gave her some of his blood in a medical emergency. When Captain America's blood was tainted by a new street drug, he had to have a complete transfusion, with the result that the superserum that gave him his powers so many years ago was washed out of his system. Luckily, he retained most of his abilities, as his athletic prowess, honed over many decades, is and always has been his chief strength.

Perhaps the most popular prime-time super-hero show debuted on ABC in 1973 as a TV movie. *The Six Million Dollar Man* is the story of Steve Austin (Lee Majors), who crashes his jet and is left in a pretty messy state. Scientists in a top-secret government agency get him on the operating table and start rebuilding his shattered body—with "bionic" or mechanical parts modeled on human appendages. In other words, the new Steve Austin is part human, part machine—a cyborg (the project was inspired by Martin Caidin's sci-fi book *Cyborg*). His bionic parts give him incredible capabilities: superstrength, and the ability to outrace an automobile, for instance. His legs, one arm, and one eye are all at least partially artificial.

This series about a low-grade Superman became surprisingly popular and ran for several seasons, in spite of severe deficiencies in virtually every category. Lee Majors was of the sniff and grunt school of acting, a blunt-faced piece of poor man's beefcake who seemed incapable of breathing and thinking at the same time. The second lead, Richard Anderson, who played Austin's boss, Oscar Goldman, was no less bland. Austin's foes were fairly ordinary spies and criminals, and the effects were mediocre. Austin's running at superspeed, and all of his powerful acts, from hurling javelins for miles to overturning automobiles, would be depicted in *slow motion*.

Not only would this serve to slow the action, but it gave no legitimate sense of power, speed, or energy. What's worse, this slow-mo method of suggesting superhuman abilities would become *de rigueur* in films and on TV for many seasons to come. Gil Mellé's background music was no help, either. It consisted of the usual pseudo-rock score (with the beat supposed to provide the energy that the direction and editing were lacking) that was pretty ineffective. *The Six Million Dollar Man* was just plain *bad,* with none of the color, excitement, originality, or comparative relevance of the comic books of the period.

This didn't stop audiences from lapping it up. (Presumably the programs that were on against it were even worse.) And in 1976 a spin-off program debuted on ABC: *The Bionic Woman.* Lindsay Wagner was cast as Jaime Sommers, an old girlfriend of Steve's who is nearly killed in a sky-diving accident. She gets the cyborg treatment too and spends half her time teaching grade school and the other half working for the O.S.I. (Office of Scientific Investigation). Many people felt that Wagner was the only reason to watch the show. She won an Emmy for the role in 1977.

By this time *The Six Million Dollar Man* was in its fourth season and needed some new blood. The answer was to make the antagonists a little more far out. Steve already had an archadversary, a bionic "Bigfoot" played by Ted Cassidy (Lurch of *The Addams Family*). For this fourth-season debut, the producers added "a ruthless gang of space aliens," who wanted to use Bigfoot for their own nefarious purposes. The Bionic Woman joined Steve in the struggle against these aliens, and the story was continued later in the week on her show. The following year the show took its cue from *Jaws* and had Steve battling a woman who could command trained sharks as he swam down to investigate the disabling of a nuclear submarine.

The "bionic" formula didn't stop there. For her third season premiere (the show moved to NBC at that time), the Bionic Woman played host to Max, the bionic dog, a handsome German shepherd that had been used to test the devices later implanted in Jaime. Devices that were *failing;* Jaime survived to have at least another season of adventures. Meanwhile the Six Million Dollar Man was befriending a bionic boy played by Vincent Van Patten. By 1978, both programs were off the air, a casualty of overkill and competing programs featuring characters that had already been popular in comic books. (Both *The Six Million Dollar Man* and *The Bionic Woman* were given their own comic books for a brief period in the seventies.)

Above: Steve Austin (Lee Majors) practices his super-fast running.

Almost a decade later the two characters were brought back in a successful 1987 NBC telefilm entitled *The Return of the Six Million Dollar Man and the Bionic Woman.* Colonel Steve Austin is retired and sitting on his fishing boat when the O.S.I. puts out a call for his services: a conservative organization is responsible for the sabotaging of several munitions plants. A subplot has Steven's son Michael getting trashed in a highly coincidental jet crack-up and having to be rebuilt bionically à la his father. A new series with Michael Austin carrying on in his dad's bionic footsteps never materialized, fortunately. Instead there was a second telefilm reteaming Wagner and Majors, *The Bionic Showdown: The Six Million Dollar*

Man and the Bionic Woman, in which Steve and Jaime tie the knot after all those years.

Although the ratings for both movies were good enough for NBC to consider yet another installment, it is unlikely that Lindsay Wagner will participate. She told *TV Guide*: "I'd only do a Bionic Couple again if its context was something important, something that deals with a vital issue. I haven't heard anything from them about the project since."

Bionic characters are quite popular in films and comic books. Misty Knight, a supporting character in various Marvel comic books, is a private detective with a bionic arm. Marvel has also had two characters named Death-lok, both of whom are cyborgs. In some ways *Robocop* is an offspring of the Six Million Dollar Man as well. The monster in *Alien* is a biomechanical creature, and Dean R. Koontz's early novel *Demon Seed,* which was filmed in 1977, presented a supercomputer that mates with a human female and sires a half-human, half-mechanical baby. There remains a fascination with things that are part flesh and part metal in all forms of popular fiction. Of these all, *The Six Million Dollar Man* and *The Bionic Woman* are probably the *least* interesting variations on a theme.

Another recurrent theme in film and fiction is invisibility, which of course dates back to H. G. Wells's brilliant novel *The Invisible Man.* One of the first television programs to have an invisible lead character was *The Invisible*

Above: Lee Majors poses with the Abominable Snowman on *The Six Million Dollar Man.*

Man in the fifties, a British series that had a successful run on American TV near the end of the decade. The hero, Dr. Peter Brady, was a victim of backfiring experiments which turned him permanently invisible. He was pursued by the authorities and evil forces, whom both wanted to use him for their own purposes. Brady was kept invisible in more ways than one: you never saw him, and the identity of the actor playing him was never revealed.

American television tackled the theme again in 1975. *The Invisible Man* began as an NBC telefilm starring David McCallum as Dr. Daniel Weston. Weston is experimenting (in what he thinks is the private sector) with transporting matter from point to point at the speed of light when he discovers an incredible side effect: invisibility. The trouble is that his boss (very well played by Jackie Cooper in a self-serving manner that's both menacing and amiable) wants to develop military applications for the process, which McCallum will have none of—although the military is putting up some of the money. Weston winds up smashing his equipment—not a wise thing to do as he later finds he cannot go back to his normal state. He is forced to return to work so that he can affect a "cure," setting up the situation for the subsequent series.

The special effects are quite good; the best bit has McCallum's disembodied eyes appearing, floating in space, when special contact lenses are placed over them. Weston has a handy plastic surgeon friend (Henry Darrow), who covers him with "dermaplex," a latexlike coating, so that he can become visible; apparently a simple makeup won't work as well. Although being in an invisible state would certainly cause blindness in a subject, this aspect of the situation is simply ignored. Anything McCallum takes in (eats or is injected with) becomes invisible, while anything he emits, such as blood, becomes visible.

The telefilm, directed by Robert Michael Lewis, is a suspenseful and entertaining update of Wells's classic, though by no means on the level of James Whale's superb 1933 *The Invisible Man*. As Dr. Weston, however, David McCallum is perfunctory and outclassed by his supporting players. In the series, Jackie Cooper was replaced by Craig Stevens, who could probably never be accused of outacting anyone. The show had its entertaining moments, but it lasted for only a season.

Nevertheless, NBC decided to try again, and the following year brought out *Gemini Man*, which also began life as a made-for-TV movie. This time, Ben Murphy is the one who can turn invisible. He plays a think tank researcher and troubleshooter named Sam Casey who is accidentally given the power to turn invisible after being caught in an explosion of radioactive material. The main difference between this and the McCallum series was that *Gemini Man* placed more emphasis on the super-hero shtick: Casey can stay invisible for only fifteen-minute periods each day, and he has a special wristband through which he activates his power. An associate, Dr. Abby Lawrence (Katherine Crawford), would watch the clock and bite her nails as the quarter hour of invisibility neared its conclusion. Casey worked for an organization called Intersect, which sent him on his various missions. Richard Dysart played their boss, Leonard Driscoll (William Sylvester had the role in the brief series that followed). It came from the producers of *The Six Million Dollar Man*. Despite the new formula, viewers didn't take to *Gemini Man* any more than they did to *The Invisible Man* with David McCallum.

Invisibility pops up frequently in comic books. The best-known character is Susan Richards, the Invisible Girl of *Fantastic Four* fame. *The Legion of Super-Heroes* also had a member called the Invisible Kid. While the kid's powers were standard stuff, Susan Richards is now able to create invisible energy fields, force bubbles, air pockets, and the like, making her one of the most versatile members of her long-running combo. The idea of being able to pass among others unsuspected, to simply eavesdrop or get away with all manner of crimes, has always been a seductive one.

The Man From Atlantis started out as a series of telefilms and then became a weekly program in 1977. Patrick Duffy (later of *Dallas* fame) first came to limited national attention portraying a presumed survivor of the lost continent of Atlantis, whose inhabitants apparently adapted to life underwater when the continent sank. Mark Harris, the Atlantean, can breathe underwater, swim like a fish, has webbed hands and feet—and superstrength. He is pitted against man-eating jellyfish, deadly spores, and madmen who want to control the world or just the ocean.

On land, Harris is quite literally a fish out of water. If he's away from the sea too long, he becomes deathly ill. This was only one of the similarities between *The Man From Atlantis* and DC Comics' *Aquaman* series, which predated the TV show by many years. Bill Warren in *Cinefantastique* felt that "the entire premise seems to be

derived from...*Aquaman*. The similarities go way beyond just coincidence." While never a classic, the *Aquaman* comic, however, was also never as bad as *The Man From Atlantis*. Critic Dave Schow nailed it down in his review: "It is poisonously dull, snail-paced, and has yet to produce an hour-long show that doesn't appear to be a severely padded five minutes worth of material." The only fairly interesting aspect of the original telefilm was the relationship between the lady scientist, Dr. Elizabeth Merrill (Belinda Montgomery), and waterlogged Mark Harris—she's nearly heartbroken when he almost leaves for good at the end of the film—but the subsequent series rarely delved into this odd romance between woman and fish-man.

The Man From Atlantis was also very similar (and inferior) to the Marvel Comics series *Sub-Mariner*. Created by Bill Everett, *Sub-Mariner* goes back to the golden age of comics, where he was a sometime villain, declaring war on mankind before becoming a reluctant hero to the surface world during World War II. Prince Namor is the son of a human father and an Atlantean mother, and is suitably dashing, imperial, and patronizing. Sub-Mariner has become a Marvel mainstay for decades, with different series, approaches, and chroniclers over the years. His latest series, *Namor, the Sub-Mariner,* written and drawn by John Byrne, presents the sea hero as a covert corporate executive battling an evil brother–sister duo of financiers, as well as whatever menaces these two can throw at him.

As for *The Man from Atlantis*, it had a brief run as a Marvel Comic itself in 1978, beginning with an oversize premiere issue and continuing for six more installments. The final story is still awaiting a resolution.

Above: Patrick Duffy played *The Man From Atlantis* but found more porpoise years later on *Dallas*.

NBC had one more idea for the great science fiction "boom" of the seventies engendered by the success of *The Six Million Dollar Man*, but it never got beyond the pilot stage. *Exo-Man* was a 1977 telefilm starring David Ackroyd as a paralyzed college physics professor who builds a superstrong exoskeleton. This suit carries his maimed body to where he can wreak vengeance on the baddies who crippled him. Richard Irving's plodding direction didn't do much to help the barely serviceable teleplay. *Exo-Man* may have been inspired by the exploits of Marvel Comics *Iron Man*, in which inventor Tony Stark encases himself in a metal suit to become a super-hero. The suit was an outgrowth of a special plate he wore on his chest because of a bad heart, just as Exo-Man built his suit primarily for mobility. Undoubtedly, Ackroyd would have taken after numerous villains if *Exo-Man* had become a series, but we were spared that, at least.

The Greatest American Hero had a successful run in the eighties. William Katt starred as a somewhat dorky costumed hero who acquires the ability to fly but can't quite get the hang of it. Connie Sellecca as his schoolteacher girlfriend and Robert Culp as a straight-arrow but bumbling FBI agent played his concerned confidantes. The program took a lighthearted approach to the proceedings, which were never terribly interesting, and it never really caught on with true comic book aficionados. The popular theme music by Mike Post was perhaps the best thing about the show.

ABC's *The Phoenix* was about an alien being, an "ancient astronaut," who is found in a weird-looking sarcophagus in an archaeological site in Central America. The humanoid creature, played by Judson Scott, is blond and has a perfect body (of course, it's hard to get any flab when you've been sleeping for several centuries). "Bennu is supposed to be a superbeing, worshipped by ancient beings as a god, but he comes across as a typical Californian," wrote critic Christopher Martin. Bennu spends most of his time criticizing humanity for what it's done to the ecology and environment, which did not make for riveting viewing. Comic books are full of condescending characters who feel they are morally superior to earthlings, even if they originally came from Earth themselves. The long-suffering Silver Surfer was a space alien; Adam Warlock, aka "Him," was created in a cocoon by human scientists. (Both were Marvel Comics' characters.) They and many others are appalled by humans' base nature and take off to the stars to seek their own level. Presumably the Phoenix did the same.

Peter Barton and Louis Gossett, Jr., were the stars of NBC's 1982 series, *The Powers of Matthew Star*, which was yet another dull and ill-conceived program that aped comic books without approximating one-tenth of their appeal and effectiveness. *Cinefantastique* damned it with the following notice: "Five minutes of plot excruciatingly dragged out over sixty minutes of air time, with dialogue even airheads would be embarrassed to mouth." Barton's powers were alien-based, and he was allied with the air force. The series was not very watchable.

The same was true of *Manimal*, which premiered on NBC in 1983. Simon MacCorkindale played Jonathan Chase, a professor of animal behavioral sciences who is actually able to transform himself into whichever animal he chooses: a cat or panther, a hawk, even a shark if need be. He was assisted by a lady detective (Melody Anderson) and a black associate (Michael D. Roberts). Whenever he was really in a sticky situation, Chase could simply transform himself into an elephant and burst his way out of the mess. Special effects and excitement were at a minimum, with lots of shots of ordinary, well-trained animals filling in for MacCorkindale.

Manimal was unleashed by NBC as an attempt to dethrone the top-rated *Dallas*, against which it was competing. The best thing about the series were the ads which showed a J. R. Ewing look-alike fending off the advances of a shark in his swimming pool—"Bobby! Bobbeee!"—suggesting that *Manimal* would chew on and spit out the rival network's soap opera. It never happened. *Manimal* quickly disappeared without a trace.

Men able to change into animals were nothing new. Besides all the assorted werewolves since time immemorial, there have been shape-changing comics characters such as Chameleon Kid in the *Legion of Super-Heroes* (he can also change into inanimate objects such as chairs and boxes), and Beast-boy, aka Changeling, in the *Doom Patrol* and then the *New Teen Titans* (the only disadvantage he has is that every animal he changes into is green). *Animal Man* maintains his human appearance, but takes on the powers and qualities of any animal in the vicinity. All three characters are from DC.

Misfits of Science debuted in 1985 on NBC and was a sort of miniature version of the *Legion of Super-Heroes*, as well as proof positive that material that works in a comic book won't necessarily play on TV. The late Dean Paul Martin played a doctor who takes several superhuman freaks and turns them

into a crime-fighting outfit for HIT, the Human Investigation Team. "Beef" Biefneiter can turn anything into ice, like the Iceman of Marvel's *X-Factor* comic; Johnny B. somehow absorbed electric powers from an amplifier accident and can shoot lightning bolts, just like Lightning Lad of DC's *Legion of Super-Heroes*; Gloria has the power of telekinesis, or mind over matter, like Marvel Girl of *X-Factor*; and Dr. "El" Lincoln can shrink to doll size, just like Ant-Man, Dollman, The Atom, and Shrinking Violet of *The Legion of Super-Heroes*. The lack of originality might not have mattered if there had been decent scripts and adroit direction, but most critics noted that *Misfits of Science* should have been a Saturday morning cartoon. The rock music background didn't help any, either.

Above: *The Misfits of Science* plan strategy; it didn't save their show.

It was hoped that this youth-oriented series would scrape away at the ratings of *Dallas*, which was on opposite it. But if *Manimal* failed to put a dent in *Dallas*'s numbers, how could NBC imagine that *Misfits* would? An absolute triumph of mediocre, indeed brain-dead, programming, *Misfits* barely survived the season.

Starman premiered on ABC in 1987 and was based on the 1984 motion picture of the same name. The film is about an alien (Jeff Bridges) who comes to Earth and assumes the form of a woman's (Karen Allen) late husband; she drives him to a rendezvous point while the authorities close in. The pedestrian picture does little with its interesting premise and is hardly more than an unconvincing chase film, yet it drew acclaim from many quarters. *Starman* is "comic bookish" in the worst sense of the term: contrived, underdeveloped, cliché-ridden, completely devoid of depth when it could have been moving. Only the concluding scenes ever manage to attain any sense of wonder and tenderness. Director John Carpenter—one of the most overrated in the history of the movies— stages some of the action scenes adequately, but the rest is forgettable.

Nevertheless its respectable grosses made it a candidate for TV treatment. Robert Hays has the Jeff Bridges role and, with his son by a human female, is chased around the country by an obsessive federal agent, and uses

certain "magical" devices to get out of jams. The program was more reminiscent of *The Fugitive* or *Run for Your Life* than any super-hero show. It was unrelated to the *Starman* comic book currently published by DC Comics and to the golden-age Starman who was a member of the Justice Society of America.

My Secret Identity is a syndicated series, a combination sitcom/ adventure story, that deals with a high school student who has superpowers. Andrew (Jerry O'Connell) is a baby-faced, pug-nosed teenager who trips and falls in front of a purple ray in the home of his neighbor, a sloppy professor (Derek McGrath). He gains the powers of superspeed and flight. Andrew doesn't dress up as a costumed hero, but he does use his powers for "good" on occasion. The rest of the time he just uses them to do the mundane things that teenagers do—only more quickly. In many of the episodes, there's no menace or danger to speak of, and the focus is on typical teen problems and concerns like dating, friendships, and music.

Andrew's superspeed is portrayed with fast-motion and a blurring that is quite effective (not as sophisticated, however, as on *The Flash*). One episode had him cooking up a batch of hamburgers at a fast-food place in seconds. The flying sequences, done with superimpositions and blue screening, are not as convincing. Andrew uses his powers for everything from saving a singer attacked by laser beams at a concert to rushing past a rock star's security team so that he can get an interview. *My Secret Identity* is pleasant but really too mild to be memorable.

Above: The boy-next-door hero of *My Secret Identity* flanked by best buddy and scientist/father surrogate.

One of the most interesting concepts for a super-hero program was unveiled in 1987 on ABC's *Once a Hero*. In a comic book universe, Captain Justice (Jeff Lester) is fading away because readership of the *Captain Justice* comic book is dwindling. The hero decides to cross the "Forbidden Zone" and enter our—or the real—world so that he can take part in a little self-promotion. Unfortunately, in the real world Captain Justice discovers that he no longer has any superpowers. So he remains in his secret identity and has a forties gumshoe named Gumshoe (Robert Forster) help him out.

The concept was clever and original, but perhaps a little too "cute" to sustain each sixty-minute episode—and audience interest. It wasn't long before the series—and Captain Justice—faded away for good. Recently the *Animal Man* comic book has won accolades for doing a story that also crosses the "forbidden zone" or the imaginary wall between character and reader/creator. Fed up with the tragedies that have befallen him, sensing that something beyond his control is masterminding his fate, *Animal Man* tears through the wall—out of the panel—and confront's the man chronicling his adventures. It was an imaginative and interesting series of stories, more serious and thought-provoking than *Once a Hero*, but it was nearly sunk by its pretensions and the too-big role played (literally) by the writer in (and of) the story, who placed himself on an equal or superior level to that of the hero.

Beauty and the Beast, which premiered on CBS in 1987 and went on to become a cult program, also had an interesting (and derivative) concept. Proving that popular fiction feeds off popular fiction, *Beauty* based its underground city in New York on a similar city inhabited by the "morlocks," disaffected mutants of the *X-Men* comic series. The morlocks, of course, were in turn inspired by the underground mutations of H. G. Wells's *The Time Machine*. The lion man of *Beauty*, Vincent, was the latest in a long line of human-animal hybrids possessed of both savagery and tenderness: Marvel Comics' *Wolverine*, Tigor of DC's *The Omega Men*, etc. Vincent's romance with a normal human female, Catherine (Linda Hamilton), appealed greatly to romantics, love-starved women (and undoubtedly a few men) who probably wouldn't have touched a *real* Vincent with a ten-foot pole. While Vincent was an interesting character (well played by for Ron Perlman), the stories frequently absorbing, and the proceedings bolstered by a sumptuous musical score, *Beauty and the Beast* was brought down by the limitations of its premise, the weight of its improbabilities, and the departure of half of its title characters. The creators of the show can at least be proud that it was never the out-and-out disaster people in the know predicted it would be. But it was ultimately only mediocre; it never really broke free of its comic book origins. Even with the symbiotic relationship between underground dweller Vincent and aboveground district-attorney-in-distress Catherine, their uncanny mental bond (so that Vincent always knows when she's in danger) got its cue from various comics.

Super-heroes don't always have superpowers, strange disfigurations, weird abilities, or even costumes. Under his Bat-suit, Batman is an ordinary man—well, *almost* ordinary. A "super-hero" can be someone who has no special powers but who is brave, daring, and—an essential—larger than life. Batman qualifies. And so do the characters in the following TV programs, outsize adventurers, each and every one.

Captain Midnight got his start as a radio character on September 30, 1940. Jim Albright earned the nickname "Captain Midnight" because he had to complete an extremely important mission before the clock struck twelve or all would be lost. Complete it he did—and he was known forever after as Captain Midnight. He later starred in his own movie serial and a comic book series.

Captain Midnight was still going strong in the 1950s, when he moved into the only medium he had not yet conquered: television. Richard Webb played the captain in a style that was a bit stiff but effective, forthright. Sid Melton (Ichabod Mudd, aka Icky) and Olan Soule were captain's associates, with Melton basically essaying the same role he played in virtually every film and TV show in which he appeared the lovable buddy and schnook. Captain Midnight wasn't a costumed hero, but an adventurer in a futuristic headquarters. His original adventures had been aviation-based; in the show, he probably spent more time on land than in the air. To pass the time between missions, he would take on rather mundane cases, such as investigating a jewel robbery committed by a fake swami. He would often find himself in serial and comic-influenced death traps, like being caught between closing walls in a specially rigged room. *Captain Midnight* probably is remembered best as being sponsored by Ovaltine, as well as for the secret messages sent by the captain that you needed a decoder to unscramble. The stories were mildly entertaining kid's stuff, and the show was as bland as *The Adventures of Superman*. The low-budget production values were more than adequate for the goings-on.

The Avengers, a British adventure series which aired on ABC in the sixties, was a far cry from the staid, colorless Captain Midnight. These adventurers were no Boy and Girl Scouts. They were sexy, risqué, a little outrageous. John Steed (Patrick Macnee) was teamed with a succession of lovely females; for years only the second (Diana Rigg) and third (Linda Thompson) ever reached our shores. (Belatedly, the early Honor Blackman episodes have turned up in this country on cable.)

Diana Rigg is probably why most people tuned in (although Macnee provided expert accompaniment). Her outfits consisted of a variety of multicolored jumpsuits and a lot of black leather, all very titillating and suggestive. Rigg and Macnee's opponents were foreign agents, comic book characters come to life, robots, cyborgs, and, in one absurd episode, malevolent plant life. Audiences overlooked the general silliness of the proceedings in favor of the tongue-in-cheek wit and style. Macnee and Rigg knew just how to play the material. Everything was as light, frothy, and delectable as a soufflé. The highlights of certain episodes were when Rigg would get into a stylized catfight with a female opponent. For this reason, two particular episodes stand out: one in which secretaries start

Opposite: TV sensation *Captain Midnight* had also appeared on radio, in comic books and in a Columbia serial, as advertised here.

murdering their bosses in a bizarre pseudo women's lib plot (engineered by a man, naturally); and another in which a sinister dating service figures prominently. The first has Rigg socking, chopping, and throwing around a bevy of angry female adversaries, and the second ends with her fighting off a murderous attack by two deadly witches in an office, where desks, chairs, and scissors figure in the action. Her battle with a Russian bitch in another episode is also memorable.

Eventually the proceedings got *too* silly; the light touch became heavy-handed. What started out as satire of a sort became out-and-out farce or parody. Even before Diana Rigg's Emma Peel character was replaced by Linda Thompson's Tara King, *The Avengers* was starting to fall. The introduction of a repulsively obese male liaison named "Mother" and his mute albino assistant, Rhonda, just about put the finish to the series. It briefly returned years later as *The New Avengers* with Macnee and two new cohorts.

Although not really among the better episodes, one *Avengers* story that most people remember involves a comic strip, the main character of which, a kind of birdman, is responsible for several grisly deaths. Or at least someone dressing up like him. At the end of the episode, the Avengers try to stop his latest plunder by following the panels of

the character's newest adventure—showing events that have not yet occurred or are occurring at that very instant. As Steed and Mrs. Peel race to the rescue, they flip through the large drawings, mirroring their—and the killer's—actions, to see what will happen when they arrive. Although events embroil them before they can get to the finish of the illustrated story, the "real" story ends the same way as the comic strip. The basic premise was an utterly impossible one, but that never mattered to fans of the series in its heyday.

Another incredibly popular television program of the sixties was *The Man From U.N.C.L.E.*, which starred Robert Vaughn as Napoleon Solo and David McCallum as Ilya Kuryakin, agents of the United Network Command of Law and Enforcement. Ian Fleming, creator of James Bond, initially had a hand in *The Man From U.N.C.L.E.* and came up with the name Napoleon Solo. The program, however, was more influenced by the James Bond

³We finally learned in David McDaniel's excellent paperback U.N.C.L.E. adventure, #4 in the series published by Ace Books, that THRUSH is an acronym for Technological Hierarchy for the Removal of Undesirables and the Subjugation of Humanity. McDaniel also provided an entire fascinating history for the organization.

Above: With outfits like these, it's no wonder Diana Rigg (*The Avengers*) became a TV sensation in the sixties.

Top left: Mrs. Peel (Diana Rigg) and John Steed (Patrick Macnee) were the delightful duo of *The Avengers*.

movies than it was by Fleming's more literate and "serious" novels. Gadgetry was the name of the game—gadgetry and sinister secret organizations—and that brought the program firmly into the realm of the comic book.

In most episodes, Solo and Kuryakin would battle the agents of their rival and opposite organization, THRUSH.[3] The roots of THRUSH, an international organization so large and covertly influential that it is practically a nation unto itself, go back to the pulps and to Sax Rohmer's Fu Manchu novels, with the dreaded Si-Fan and the Council of Seven. For Council of Seven, read THRUSH Central, the governing body of the evil organization. Secret societies have a rich history in pulp novels, serials, and comic books, partly because they seem so utterly fantastic. Why would anyone want to join an organization that rewards failure with horrible death? Given human nature, how could any group so vast and complex manage to remain secret, even from the world at large? Secret societies make great fiction, but they don't seem able to withstand close scrutiny.

And yet in real life, there exists organized crime, which is just as secretive, pervasive, and dangerous—even to its members—as THRUSH ever was. Drug money can easily supply the finances for armies and weaponry. Threats, blackmail, and bribery can buy a lot of silence. Perhaps THRUSH, the Si-Fan, James Bond's SPECTRE, and all the other secret organizations are mere exaggerations of groups that already exist.

Although played straight, *The Man From U.N.C.L.E.* had as light a touch as *The Avengers*, but with a strictly American style. The stories rarely veered into fantasy or illogic, as *The Avengers* did, but drew their color from outrageous gadgets and nasty antagonists. Each week a charming new THRUSH psychopath would be played by a hammy guest star. Solo and Ilya would find themselves in seemingly inescapable doom-traps. Beautiful women would threaten them with torture.

Robert Vaughn in the famous opening of *The Man From U.N.C.L.E.*

185

The program became an even bigger hit and cult favorite than *The Avengers*, and Britisher McCallum, with a shaggy, longish hairstyle, found himself an unlikely sex symbol. More and more humor was introduced into the series. By the third season, the scripts were as farcical as anything on *Get Smart*, the spy spoof that was *supposed* to be a parody. Dipping ratings got the producers to play it straight once again for the fourth season, but the show had lost too many viewers by then and was cancelled in midseason, in spite of some excellent episodes.

Despite McCallum's dull acting, the often absurd plotting, and occasionally tacky production values, the show had its share of magic and theatrical flair. Leo G. Carroll was great as U.N.C.L.E. chief, Alexander Waverly, and Anne Francis was memorable as (non-THRUSH) villainess Gervaise Ravel in two episodes. Even the third season had some exciting episodes, such as the two-part "Concrete Overcoat Affair," in which Janet Leigh[4] plays a sadistic assistant (to villainous Jack Palance) who gets into a knife-and-claw catfight with hot-blooded

Letitia Roman. The various THRUSH plots, always doomed to failure, involved everything from dogs, children, and robots to dolls and angelic boys' choirs. The lethal beauties and hard-hearted antagonists always played their parts with melodramatic relish. A typical U.N.C.L.E. scene occurs in an early episode when a man "accidentally" trips and falls into a vault that contains a secret doomsday weapon of unimaginable power. The eerie woman who was showing the vault to the unfortunate victim and several others merely says, "We can't save a man who no longer exists." (Meanwhile, sexy guest star Senta Berger keeps saying "Trush" with no first "h".) This episode and several others were expanded and shown as theatrical features and turn up on television from time to time. Gold Key came out with a comic book version for awhile, and there was a series of rather good paperback novels. A spin-off program, *The Girl From U.N.C.L.E.*, starring Stefanie Powers, lasted one season.

The Return of the Man From U.N.C.L.E., a 1983 telefilm with Vaughn and McCallum reprising their roles, captured virtually none of the magic of the original series.

The Man From U.N.C.L.E. influenced a few comic books even as it was influenced by them. Marvel took a character from one of its war books, *Sergeant Fury and His Howling Commandos*, a series of World War II adventures, and turned him into *Nick Fury, Agent of S.H.I.E.L.D.*, showing what the old warhorse was up to in contemporary times. Fury spent most of the time battling the forces of Hydra, a THRUSH-like organization run by a Supreme Hydra in a mask. Spy gadgets, weird communication devices, flying machines, death beams, superbombs, and countless agents all played a part in these early adventures by Stan Lee, Jack Kirby and Johnny

[4]In truly subtle fashion, Miss Leigh's character was christened "Miss Diketon" by a presumably homophobic scriptwriter.

Above: Alexander Waverly (Leo G. Carroll, center) gives some advice to his men from U.N.C.L.E.

Severin, appearing in *Strange Tales* in the sixties. Undeniably illogical, with gaping holes and implausibilities, they were nevertheless entertaining, fast-paced and well-told mini-spy stories that delivered on the colorful action and technological wizardry the fans demanded. The current *Nick Fury* series is a bit more sophisticated in tone without straying too far from the original formula.

The Wild, Wild West was another deservedly popular series with an inspired premise: moving the contemporary spy formula back to the 1800s; the obligatory gadgets, lethal lovelies, and master villains, but with a Western twist. Robert Conrad starred as Secret Service Agent James West, a dandy who traveled on his own personal railway car with associate and master of disguise, Artemis Gordon (Ross Martin). Their archenemy, malevolent dwarf Dr. Miguelito Loveless, deliciously played by Michael Dunn, was the bane of their existence—and vice versa—for many well scripted and entertaining episodes. If nothing else, the setting made the program a novelty. The plots and devices—earthquake-causing machines, for instance—were often as derivative as ever, but the script writers had fun with old-fashioned variations on equipment we've come to take for granted.

A less successful adventurer of the sixties was one from the past brought out of "retirement" because of the *Batman* craze. *The Green Hornet* originally had been a radio series of the 1940s, but it was thought by ABC programmers that he would make a perfect complement to the Dynamic Duo. The only difference was *The Green Hornet* was played more or less straight, as he had been in a serial and Harvey Comics' long-lasting comic book (1940–1949), both of which were inspired by the radio series.

Britt Reid (Van Williams) was a publisher moonlighting as a crime-fighter, the Green Hornet. His partner, Kato, a master in the Oriental art of fighting, was played by Bruce Lee (who hadn't yet become the international star and cult figure). The Hornet's outfit consists of a snap-brim hat and a long green coat over standard shirt, tie, and pants, with an ordinary mask covering the eyes. Kato wore a chauffeur's uniform, a mask, and a cap. The Hornet's

Above: Solo (Robert Vaughn) and Ilya (David McCallum) face the forces of THRUSH.

special equipment consists of a gas gun and a "stinger" with different settings. Williams is a bit bland as Reid/Hornet; Lee, who was given comparatively little to do, is okay, if a little mush-mouthed. However, his karate fight scenes are very convincing; he was a good, stylized fighter who looked as if he knew what he was doing, not the usual case in such staged battles.

The Green Hornet never caught on, however. It's hard to figure why the ABC brass figured he would be a good follow-up to *Batman*. The Green Hornet did not have a comic book series in the sixties, and was unknown to most comics readers of the period, as well as to the general public. He had no colorful gimmick; nothing about him would catch in the memory like Batman's costume or batcave, and unlike Batman, he was not a household name. (Even before the *Batman* series, everyone knew who Batman *was*.) *The Green Hornet* didn't have the campy humor to attract *Batman* TV fans, and the GH series was much too prosaic to appeal to comic book enthusiasts. The program should never have gone beyond the planning stages. And it didn't last very long.

Now Comics brought out a brand-new *Green Hornet* comic series in the late eighties. Actor Van Williams even wrote a few stories for it. Handsomely produced, the comic will help ensure that the character will remain alive into the nineties.

Nonsuperpowered TV adventurers of the more colorful cast were in short supply in the seventies and eighties. Only two more series barely qualify, *Sword of Justice* in 1978, and *Knight Rider*, which debuted in the fall of 1982. *Sword* is a Batman variation, with Dack Rambo as Jack Cole, who was wrongly imprisoned, and in the process of getting even with the real crooks, discovers that he likes being a "free-lance avenger." His spell in prison taught him tricks that will help him beat criminals at their own game. Cole leaves a signature playing card behind to confound authorities, frighten lawbreakers, and show where he's been. The series didn't last very long in spite of a perfectly workable premise.

Knight Rider was much more successful and lasted a few seasons. In this, the human star (David Hasselhoff) was outclassed by the hardware, a computerized, superautomobile named KITT, that had conversations with its driver (voice of William Daniels). Decked out with Ultra-Stop Emergency Decelerators, Ultra-High Frequency Degaussers, Water-Cooled Cabrillo Accelerators, and Reverse Polarity Destabilizers, KITT could probably bake a cherry pie if need be. Human drama was very limited in this show, mainly consisting of Hasselhoff hurrying to get to wherever his supercar could perform its last minute save with its none-too-exciting bag of tricks. The show was a big hit with kiddies of all ages, however.

Above: Robert Conrad of *The Wild, Wild West*.

Opposite: Van Williams played *The Green Hornet* on TV.

Before television, there were serials, five hour extravaganzas that would be played out at the local Bijou each week one chapter at a time—each ending in a cliff-hanger. From the first the super-heroic figure was the mainstay of the chapterplay. Each leading character was always larger than life and occasionally had superpowers. In addition to Superman, Batman, Captain America, and Captain Marvel, many other comic book and comic strip characters were adapted to the serial format. There were also many serials that featured superhuman or costumed heroes who were original with the chapterplay in which they starred, and not from any comics magazine or daily strip.

Blackhawk started out as a comic book in 1941 and was rather late in getting to the movie screen: 1952. *Military Comics* #1 introduced the handsome freedom fighter and his group of flying associates who owed allegiance to no particular country. Wherever they were needed, wherever freedom was threatened, they would go. They wore slick military-style uniforms that were embellished with the picture of a hawk in a circle on the chest. At first, Blackhawk himself was a Polish soldier gaining vengeance on the Nazis who murdered his family. At some point he was turned into an American, and his associates were given names and personalities: André, Stanislaus, Olaf, Chuck, and Chop Chop, the broadly caricatured Chinese, among others.

Blackhawk was a hard-fightin' man who had no compunction about killing his adversaries—after all, it was war. He often made an exception, however, when his opponents were particularly voluptuous examples of "the fairer sex." One recurring character was a female soldier of fortune named Fear, who both intrigued Blackhawk and had the hots for him. You could never be sure whose side she was on—except her own. Her penchant for shooting people for the sake of expediency became almost comical at times. She was a sexy broad with an exotic nature and a heart of stone.

The main creator of Blackhawk was Charles Cuidera, and the strip's main writer, William Woolfolk. Yet if *Blackhawk*'s success was attributable to any one person, it would undoubtedly be illustrator Reed Crandell, whose style was crisp, striking, and attractive—and easily distinguished from that of many other artists of the period. Crandell was so identified with Blackhawk that he is mentioned in the credits of the serial, but not Cuidera or any of the comic's writers.

Blackhawk stories were not only exciting—inspired by many aerial adventure films of the thirties and forties—but often suggestive, "adult" (in a juvenile kind of way), and

Above: Blackhawk as he appeared in 1950. *Modern Comics* #96. Copyright © 1950 by Comic Magazines (Quality Comics).

Opposite: Kirk Alyn (right) played *Blackhawk* in the serial.

reminiscent of hard-boiled *film noir*. The stories were certainly more saucy than the serial concocted by the writers at Columbia Pictures, including the prolific George H. Plympton, who had written a lot of the Superman serials. The same director, Spencer Bennet, was brought in, along with a codirector, Fred F. Sears.

Kirk Alyn is much more bland as Blackhawk than as a comparatively charismatic Superman. (Of course, Blackhawk *was* a more dour character.) Carol Forman, the Spider-Lady in the Superman serial, is less successful as Laska, the alleged femme fatale of the piece. Forman doesn't come on like a sultry villainess of the type that Reed Crandell drew for the comics, and there is nothing exotic about her. For one thing she never changes out of her severe-looking suit. Although Weaver Levy as Chop Chop is not as caricatured as in the comics (where he had buck teeth, a pigtail, and an outrageous color-blind outfit), he's still a very typical movie "good" Oriental of the period.

The plot has Blackhawk and company fighting sinister foreign agents, headed by Laska and an unseen "Leader." At one point, a double of Stanislaus, his evil twin brother, is planted in Blackhawk's camp, located in the southwestern United States. The first few chapters have to do with the theft of a electronic combustion ray while the last few deal with an inexhaustible new fuel called "Element X." The identity of the "Leader" doesn't come as much of a surprise (his voice is too distinctive, for one thing) or does the fact that he, too, has a double.

By 1952, the movie serial formula was really wearing thin. The writers were obviously having trouble coming up with novel cliff-hangers, as the ones in *Blackhawk* are unusually feeble. In fifteen chapters, there is only one highlight, when Stan is tied to a pole in chapter three. While the forces of Blackhawk and Laska battle on the airfield, a plane begins to move forward when a pair of headphones "conveniently" hits the controls. Chapter four has Blackhawk saving Stan from the whirling propellers by grabbing the wing and turning the plane around (a somewhat suspect development).

The serial's dopey moments are excessive, and the special effects cheesy. When Blackhawk bails out at one point, the director cuts to a shot of a doll on a parachute, although shots of real men with parachutes are used successfully elsewhere in the serial. A "flying disc" is merely an animated cartoon saucer with a TV antenna. When a car behind Blackhawk's supposedly bumps his onto a railway crossing as a train approaches, it is all too obvious that the "bump" was insufficient and someone had to *drive* the car onto the tracks. Blackhawk somehow manages to drop out of a low-flying plane and into a speeding automobile. The worst incident has Blackhawk and Chuck hiding in the back of a wagon under a load of hay. A shot clearly shows that the wagon is completely ablaze, yet the following moment we hear Chuck comment to Blackhawk in their hiding place, "Say, this thing's on fire!" By all rights both men should have been roasted by then.

Blackhawk also hits a new low in "low-budget" when it comes to Laska's many different headquarters. Blackhawk observes how each hideout or "station" looks exactly the same—which is true; regardless of whether they're located inside a cabin, a stone shack, a canyon house, or a brownstone, the interior consists of the same two rooms. Unaccountably, you must press a buzzer to go from one room to the other even though there's nothing in the latter that would need guarding.

In the Blackhawk comic, everything imaginable was tossed in to bolster flagging sales. Without a Nazi menace, the boys had to fight aliens and monsters. They developed costumed identities and wore supersuits. They plodded along until 1969 and were canceled.[1]

But nothing could keep Blackhawk down for good. His magazine was revived in the seventies with all-new adventures. (Chop Chop was given a more dignified, contemporary appearance.) When that didn't last, a new series was started with the time period moved back to World War II. These period adventures were well written and well drawn, but this series didn't last either. In 1988, *Action Comics Weekly*, an anthology comic that was an outgrowth of the old *Action* and had a brief run, presented a series with Blackhawk as a hard-fightin', hard-drinkin', hard-lovin', profane rascal in the postwar period. This characterization seemed modeled more on hardboiled detectives and Howard Chaykin's *American Flagg* character than on the original Blackhawk. This new series lasted only sixteen issues and expired in 1990. As of this writing, one of comics' oldest and most successful characters is in limbo, proving that a sexed- and souped-up version isn't always better.

Spy Smasher first appeared in Fawcett's *Whiz #2* in 1940 along with Captain Marvel. He was a wealthy sportsman named Alan Armstrong—dressed in a leather headpiece, aviator goggles, a flowing red cape, and what resembled a World War I uniform complete with tight pants, high boots, and a diamond design on the chest—who fought Nazis and saboteurs. He was extremely popular for a time but was too tied in with "the war to end all wars" to last much beyond V-E day.

A Republic serial based on *Spy Smasher*, who had earned his own title by that time, came out in 1942. Although the chapter play is only fair, it does contain some sequences that illustrate serial action at its finest. Chapter one's cliff-hanger has Spy Smasher racing down a tunnel on a railway work car. A burst of fast-moving flame is pursuing him and almost catches up to the work car, which is piled with grenades. Even if he manages to move the car fast enough, there's still a solid steel wall directly in front of him! (SS gets out of this by throwing a grenade at the fire, somehow dousing it.)

A sequence in chapter seven leading up to that episode's cliff-hanger is superb. SS races to the top of a water tower hideout to prevent a hood from using an electric ray gun on an approaching squadron of planes. The two battle their way from the top room of the tower, which contains the ray gun, down a circular staircase, and into a room on the floor below. Bullets puncture some drums there and gasoline flows out across the floor. Still slugging

[1]DC Comics acquired the rights to Blackhawk when Quality comics folded in 1956.

Above: The *Blackhawk* of the sixties #243. Copyright © 1968 National Periodical Publications, Inc.

away at his opponent, SS doesn't see the gasoline splash onto some machinery and ignite. Meanwhile, the untended gun upstairs is still aimed at the planes as they get closer and closer. *Boom!* The whole tower building blows up and collapses. (SS is seen jumping out of a window as chapter eight begins.)

Carried over from the comic book, the plot has SS battling his archfoe, the Mask. In both comic and serial, this sinister spy wears a simple flap of material over his face with eyeholes cut out; there is no attempt to keep his identity a secret from the audience. Played by Kane Richmond, Spy Smasher is the personification of a stalwart comic book hero, whereas in profile the unmasked Mask (Hans Schumm) looks curiously like *Li'l Abner's* Mammy Yokum! The serial added a look-alike brother for Alan Armstrong, David (also played by Richmond), whose function seems to be helping SS confound the enemy. Although directed by serial expert William Witney, *Spy Smasher* doesn't really start to pick up until the second half, despite

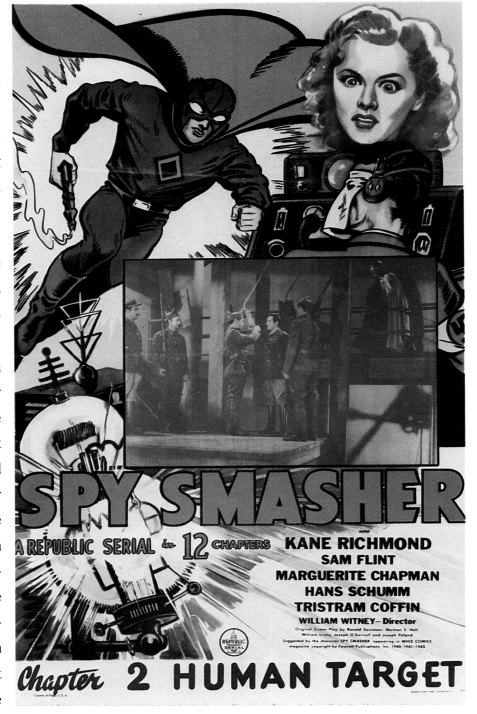

the aforementioned earlier chapter highlights. If the whole serial had been as good as chapter seven, it really would have amounted to something. The producers must have been proud of their product, however: the theme music is no less than Beethoven's Ninth!

Alex Gordon's comic strip, *Flash Gordon*, was made into several serials, based on the original stories. *Flash Gordon* (1936), directed by Frederick Stephani, recounts Flash's first encounter with Ming the Merciless (Charles Middleton) of Planet Mongo. Through a convoluted series of events, Flash (Buster Crabbe), who combines both

Above: An ad for *Spy Smasher*.

brawn and brains (he's a sportsman and Yale graduate), winds up in a rocketship piloted by one Dr. Zarkov (Frank Shannon). Zarkov plans to use the ship to offset a collision with an unknown planet that is slowly approaching—and threatening to destroy—Earth. Instead, Flash and his companions, including the lovely Dale Arden (Jean Rogers), land on the strange world, Mongo, and are immediately embroiled in incredible adventures. Mongo is full of monsters, but none worse than its ruler, Ming, who lords it over a slew of different, often hybrid warring races. By the serial's end, Flash has helped defeat Ming and restore rightful ruler, Prince Barin, to the throne. Although *Flash Gordon* is undeniably primitive moviemaking, with now comical spaceships, amusing effects, and a hilarious absence of "science," it does have a certain charm and flair all its own. It was also very influential on the "space operas" and fantasies that followed.

Flash battled Ming in three successive serials. *Flash Gordon* was followed by *Flash Gordon's Trip to Mars* (1938) and *Flash Gordon Conquers the Universe* (1940), both directed by Ford Beebe. The former has Flash investigating when someone or something starts screwing around with Earth's atmosphere to deadly effect. The latter has someone sending a purple plague across space to slaughter earthlings. Flash Gordon and company fly back to Mongo to get the antidote. Of course it is the hard-to-kill Ming behind both evil plots.

Flash Gordon Conquers the Universe is primitive and mediocre, full of stock footage, but it does feature a few hair-raising escapes and memorable scenes: Flash caught in an avalanche, trapped in a pit, and nearly fried along with Dr. Zarkov by a "Mongolian death ray." The acting is pretty bad, but nobody watches these things for the acting.

In 1939, Buster Crabbe also starred in a cliff-hanger based on *Buck Rogers*, a newspaper strip that predated *Flash Gordon* by several years. The stories were based on pulp magazine tales written by Philip Nowlan. In the serial, Buck and his little pal Buddy are caught in suspended animation from the 1930s until the year 2420, and find themselves in a war with futuristic racketeers, headed by Killer Kane. The serial was directed by Ford Beebe, but

Left: Flash Gordon captured by Ming the Merciless.

Right: A lobby card for the *Flash Gordon* serial.

is less memorable than his Flash Gordon chapterplays, with a routine plot, unimaginative effects, and tedious pacing.

Dick Tracy was the star of four serials from Republic Pictures in the thirties and forties. Chapter one of *Dick Tracy* (1937) packs more thrills and action than the entire running time of Warren Beatty's 1990 multimillion dollar epic. In it we learn of The Spider (aka The Lame One), a sinister villain who leaves a spider mark on the forehead of his victims. A young orphan, Junior, is in the vicinity when the Spider commits his latest murder at a carnival, so Tracy decides to keep the kid by his side in case he saw too much. Tracy's brother, Gordon (Carleton Young), is kidnapped by the Spider and operated on (and mildly disfigured) so that he'll obey only the archfoe's orders. When Tracy refuses to release one of the gang members, the Spider uses a vibration device to try to shake apart the newly opened San Francisco Bay Bridge. (In addition to location footage, part of the bridge was duplicated in the studio.) The chapter ends with Tracy pinned on the ground as a girder falls from the bridge and hurtles toward him.

Although it gets off to a great start, the rest of *Dick Tracy*, unfortunately, is unspectacular. It does have the usual quota of spirited fisticuffs and suspenseful sequences, and there are some decent effects and miniature work, including a wild new plane called

Above: Ad for *Flash Gordon's Trip to Mars*.

196

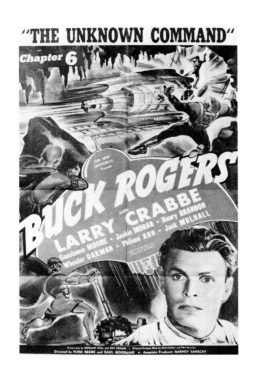

"The Wing"[2] which is used by the Spider gang and looks impressive as it soars like a hawk. (The wing span is in the front of the plane.) Tracy's associate Mike McGurk and Junior provide comedy relief, and there's a hammy hunchback named Moloch who is fond of stroking cats and assists his master, the Spider. In chapter fifteen, the Spider is unmasked as a minor supporting character the existence of whom most members of the audience had probably forgotten. Instead of saying, "*That's* who it is!" audiences doubtless wondered, "Who the hell is *that*!" The serial ends with Gordon Tracy fleeing with the Spider in a car, deliberately driving it over a cliff to save the lives of Dick and Junior, who are in the roadway. Dick Tracy was played with his usual aplomb by Ralph Byrd, who starred in all four serials. Ray Taylor and Alan James were the directors of *Dick Tracy*. In all the serials, Tracy was upgraded from police detective to FBI agent to expand his authority.

Above: Lobby card for *Dick Tracy Returns*.

Top: Lobby card for *Buck Rogers* with Larry "Buster" Crabbe.

197

In *Dick Tracy Returns* (1938), Charles "Ming" Middleton plays Pa Stark, the head of a criminal family whose sons are named Champ, Kid, Slasher, and Gunslinger Trigger. To get revenge on these homicidal cretins for bumping off his assistant Ron Merton, Tracy and his G-men systematically kill them off in chapter after chapter. *Dick Tracy's G-Men* followed in 1939. In this, our hero is after an infamous traitor and spy who "cheats death" before his execution by swallowing a liquid that neutralizes the effects of the gas used to "kill" him. Once the villain revives and escapes, Tracy spends all of fifteen chapters tracking him down.

The trouble with *Dick Tracy's G-Men* is that there is an utterly colorless villain, named Zarnoff, played by an utterly colorless actor (Irving Pichel, who later became a director). Furthermore, the serial plays more like several episodes of a TV show than a suspenseful cliff-hanger. Each episode merely features a different scheme of the master villain: sabotaging a lighthouse so that a ship will run aground and ultimately put an end to certain peace talks; stealing important government plans; blowing up a dam; etc. Zarnoff eludes the seemingly inept G-men time after time, and even outwits Tracy after being captured by him in the desert, only to be undone by his *own* actions—he takes a drink of water from a poisoned spring.

Still there are some good scenes to go with the exciting fisticuffs. Tracy is almost blown up on a radio-controlled speedboat, crushed between two piers crashing together due to agitated water (this is very similar to a cliff-hanger in *Dick Tracy*), killed by poison gas unleashed in an enclosed chamber, and riddled with his own men's bullets as he sits behind a door tied by Zarnoff to a chair. The cliff-hangers are almost always in the "missing information" category, with the following chapter including information or scenes conveniently left out of the previous week's climax. (For instance, we learn Tracy managed to get out of that chair before his men could even shoot.)

Jennifer Jones, billed as Phyllis Isley, has a very small role as Tracy's secretary. The "rousing" music is often comically quaint, particularly an action theme that is oft repeated and sounds like something an organist would play for a silent movie. You can almost see the hissable, pencil-mustached, cad overemoting as he threatens widows and orphans.

The final Tracy serial, *Dick Tracy vs. Crime, Inc.* (1941), might well be the best of the series, although two cliff-hangers are simply lifted from the first and third serial respectively, and its best sequence is comprised of stock footage. What makes it work is its better constructed plot and the mystery over the real identity of the villain, the Ghost, who has an assistant named Lucifer.

The Ghost's victims are members of an anticrime board who helped to put away the villain's brother some time

Above: Ralph Byrd (right) was the definitive Dick Tracy; he even looked like the character.

before. In his true identity, the Ghost is on this board and is privy to all he need know to destroy the members one by one. By getting rid of the board members, he hopes to form his own criminal organization without interference from anybody. Tracy does his best to stop him, but can't figure out how the Ghost—as his name would suggest— can come and go without being seen. When Tracy and associates learn after several chapters that the Ghost has a device that can turn him invisible, no one seems very awed by the information. Instead of "That's astounding!" it's more like "Hmmm, so *that's* how he does it." The Ghost wears a black leather headpiece that covers his entire face. A henchman turns on the generator that powers an invisibility medallion the Ghost wears around his neck, though there are some close calls when the Ghost nearly becomes visible at inopportune moments.

Doom-traps include having Tracy's assistant chained to the roof of a railroad boxcar while TNT is dropped into it through a hole. A trapdoor located in front of a vault sends Tracy hurtling into a pit until he manages to grab onto an outcropping. Another trapdoor figures in a sequence when a bomb lands on a shack with Tracy inside, and a huge crate almost clobbers him when it falls from high overhead. A sequence with two large ships closing in on Tracy's much smaller boat and crushing it is lifted from *Dick Tracy*. And one showing Tracy being lowered from a plane onto a remote-controlled patrol boat outfitted with

Top left: The Ghost gives some orders in *Dick Tracy vs. Crime, Inc.*

Top right: A stunt man goes into action in *Dick Tracy vs. Crime, Inc.*

Middle: How will Dick get out of this one?

Left: Or this?

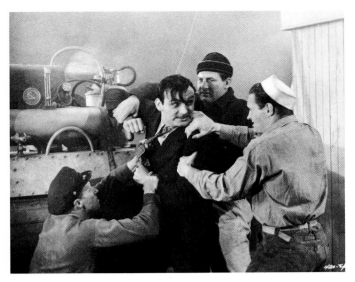

dummies and dynamite (and heading toward a dam to blow it up) is repeated from *Dick Tracy's G-Men*. A sequence from *Dick Tracy Returns* was also "borrowed."

The most elaborate sequence, in which a tidal wave caused by a bomb nearly swamps New York City, was taken from a previous Republic serial, *S.O.S. Tidal Wave*.

Nevertheless *Dick Tracy vs. Crime, Inc.* is exciting, swiftpaced, and quite entertaining. As usual, Ralph Byrd makes a great Dick Tracy. Though no Lord Olivier, Byrd is a hundred times better than the blow-dried Warren Beatty and Beatty's flat, unconvincing portrayal of the square-jawed detective. Byrd is masculine, yet warm; handsome, but vulnerable; authoritative without being overbearingly "macho" or intimidating. Whatever Byrd's private feelings about his typecasting, it was one instance where the actor met the part.

The Green Hornet[3] started out as a radio program and later became a television series. In between it was adapted as a Universal serial in the forties, with a sequel following. *The Green Hornet* was directed by Ford Beebe and Ray Taylor and starred amiable Gordon Jones as Britt Reid and the Hornet. Reid is a playboy who publishes a newspaper, the *Sentinel*, which he inherited from his father. He has a bodyguard named Michael (Wade Boteler), a former reporter, and a manservant, Kato (Keye Luke), who travels with him on safari and the like. Reid and Kato appear more like pals than employee and employer. Kato seems to do most of the tinkering in Reid's private workshop, and has helped assemble Black Beauty, a streamlined black sedan with a horn that sounds just like the "giant hornet" that Reid and Kato apparently saw in Africa.

When the city comes under the grip of a crime syndicate whose faulty construction methods are causing unsafe working conditions at several sites, a judge and the police commissioner want Reid's paper to take a stand. Reid replies that a paper should report the news, not mold it. When someone remarks that the city could use a modern-day Robin Hood, the seeds of an idea are planted in Reid's mind. He decides to use his superspeedster and other gadgets—gas guns, Green Hornet calling cards (large round buttons with a hornet imprint)—to take on the rackets in the guise of . . . the Green Hornet!

Top left: Tracy versus a gang of cutthroats. Of course, he'll win.

Right: Tracy looks as if his mind might be on romance. Forget it.

200

GH wears a stylized mask with a hornet design that covers his whole face; Kato merely puts on a pair of goggles. As the Hornet, Jones adopts a dramatic and authoritative voice in contrast to his more laid back persona as Reid. Black Beauty has an "energizer" that makes it go superfast on the highway, but the "hornet noise" it constantly makes gets pretty annoying after awhile. Since this noise *can* be shut off when GH and Kato want to sneak up on somebody, it's a wonder why they bothered with it in the first place, particularly as Reid knows the police think the Hornet is just another crook eliminating the competition and the last thing he needs is to alert them to his presence.

The Green Hornet is a pretty standard serial, but it does have some interesting elements. The syndicate has a particularly diabolical racket going in chapter three, "Flying Coffins," in which a flying school is having a suspiciously high number of fatal accidents. Young adults are persuaded by these creeps to take out insurance, which they then manage to claim by producing a bogus beneficiary. When GH busts up this heinous scheme, the Big Boss of the twelve-member syndicate orders his flunkie, Monroe, to get the Hornet or else.

The trouble with the serial is that there is no colorful villain, only a fat guy named Monroe, who rarely leaves his desk. It even turns out that Monroe himself *is* the Big Boss, and that he uses a hidden phonograph to make it seem as if he's receiving messages from a superior. The minimal suspense generated over the identity of this master criminal certainly comes to nothing.

The cliff-hangers run the gamut from the inventive to the merely stupid. Two trains racing toward each other at the end of chapter two, "The Thundering Terror," turn out not to be on the same track—a real cheat. (This cliff-hanger took advantage of the audience's expectations. It *expected* the hero or somebody to be in danger at the end of the episode so of course the trains had to be heading directly for each other. Actually a more careful look at the end of chapter two shows that the trains are really not on the same track and that no cheating occurred.)

There is, however, an exciting sequence in chapter six, "Highways of Peril," in which GH tries desperately to bring a runaway bus under control when

Top: Tracy corners a suspect.

Middle: The Green Hornet proved popular enough to come back in a second serial.

Left: The Green Hornet goes into action.

its brakes fail. The bus, full of passengers, careens down a curving road toward a bridge, but the Hornet manages to swerve the vehicle into a nearby barn instead of certain destruction in the ravine. The best scene in the serial occurs in chapter eleven, "Disaster Rides the Rails," when the Hornet and one of Monroe's henchmen have a furious battle on a train chugging its way up a mountainside. The railcar on which GH and his opponent are going at it is uncoupled from the rest of the train and the engine and begins to roll back down the mountain. As the two men continue their frantic fistfight, they are unaware that the car is heading toward another train approaching from behind. (This time it is on the same track.) A motorman in his shed anticipates the disaster and pushes a switch to move the oncoming train onto an adjacent

track, but the mechanism is frozen. He goes out onto the railway and with a hammer batters away at the frog (the device on the tracks that keeps cars on the proper rails) in a desperate attempt to shift the track. He finally succeeds, and the car with the Hornet in it goes hurtling over a cliff. All of this is cut together in breathless fashion. (Indeed the sequence is so superior to the rest of the serial that it might well have been lifted from an earlier chapterplay.)

The Green Hornet continues with a riot of stock footage in chapter twelve, "Panic in the Zoo," that shows tigers and elephants breaking out of confinement and clawing and stampeding at a carnival, panicking the crowd. The thirteenth and final chapter, "Doom of the Underworld," has the Hornet finally catching up with "Big Boss" Monroe. The serial was popular enough to engender a sequel, *The Green Hornet Strikes Agains*, with Warren Hull (later the TV game show host) in the lead.

Once the serial producers had nearly exhausted comic book, comic strip, and radio characters, they made up some of their own. Republic Pictures had to come up with a hero quickly when negotiations with National Periodical Publications (DC Comics) broke down and it was decided to turn their unmade Superman serial into *The Mysterious Dr. Satan*. The Man of Steel was replaced by the Copperhead, a masked vigilante with no real powers. Although the original Superman script that was to be filmed by Republic is said to be the basis of *The Mysterious Dr. Satan*, it seems obvious that many extreme revisions had to be made. Scientist Scott (C. Montague Shaw), his daughter Lois (Ella Neal), and his spunky secretary Alice (Dorothy Herbert) can loosely be taken as stand-ins for Perry White, Lois Lane, and Jimmy Olsen.

Above: The Green Hornet on the scene.

Opposite: The Green Hornet shows off his gas gun.

Dr. Satan is a real creep who thinks nothing of trying to blow up a planeload of passengers just to kill one victim. As usual, the doctor is after another man's scientific devices, in this case a "remote control cell" invented by Scott. The cell runs on an element called "tungite" and some of the chapters concern Dr. S's attempts to acquire the stuff through nefarious means. After awhile, the endless discussions about the cell and tungite become as tedious as all the talk about drill bits on a couple of seasons of *Dallas*

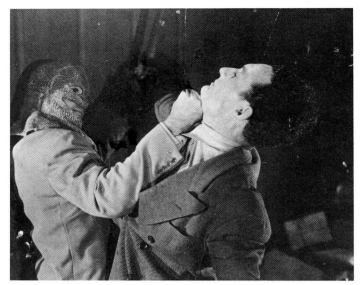

The Copperhead is really Bob Wayne (Robert Wilcox), the son of the original Copperhead, an "outlaw" who righted wrongs. He has athletic ability, is a crack shot, and wears no special costume—he simply puts a mask on with his regular clothing, whatever he happens to be wearing at the time (great for maintaining a secret identity!). Wilcox isn't much of an actor, and even Edward Ciannelli as Dr. Satan isn't much better. Ciannelli underplays to the point of dullness; his portrayal is probably more realistic, but it isn't much fun. It might have occurred to him that any guy who calls himself "Dr. Satan" is bound to be somewhat theatrical in speech and manner.

The characters act especially stupid in *The Mysterious Dr. Satan,* as when Scott, who's bigger than Dr. Satan, allows himself to be tied to a chair when none of the doctor's henchmen are around. Incredibly stupid is the scene in chapter three when Copperhead and a hood are having a lively fight on the roof of a skyscraper, while far below on the sidewalk, one of the hood's associates aims his gun, shoots at the struggling figures, and hits his buddy. It not only is ridiculous that a bullet would make it from street level to the top of a *skyscraper,* but why would the hoodlum even shoot in the first place? How could he possibly tell who was who from such a distance? The serial is full of similar idiocies.

It does have its good moments, however, such as an exciting fourth chapter, "The Human Bomb," in which the Copperhead and Scott scramble to get one of Dr. Satan's bomb-devices off an associate before the electrical power is turned back on in thirty seconds and he explodes. When the Copperhead pursues the villains, fleeing in a stolen gasoline truck, they open the nozzle and flood the road ahead of him, then set it on fire. The shot of the flames racing down the road toward the Copperhead's car is a thrilling sight. The cliff-hanger in chapter eight, in which the Copperhead falls from the back of a truck and lies helpless in the road as a car approaches at high speed, is a well edited and directed sequence; and although the device itself is prosaic, the scene in the room with the crushing walls in chapter eleven at least is dramatically handled.

One cliff-hanger is a notorious cheat. At the end of chapter ten, the Copperhead is knocked from a girder by a hoop of cable thrown by a gunsel, and we see his body hurtling by itself toward the ground. But at the beginning of chapter seven, when the sequence is repeated, Copperhead has miraculously grabbed the other end of the cable

Above: The Copperhead gives a punch to one of the hired guns of *The Mysterious Dr. Satan.*

and rides it all the way down to the street *instead* of falling—as he plainly did the week before.

The Mysterious Dr. Satan (1940) was directed by William Witney and John English, who would both helm *The Adventures of Captain Marvel* the following year. Meanwhile, Spencer Bennet of the *Superman* serials was working on what would turn out to be one of the best costumed character serials of the period, *The Masked Marvel* (1943).

Like the Copperhead, the Masked Marvel was the creation of several scriptwriters, and did not originate in a

comic book or newspaper strip. Instead of creating suspense over the identity of the villain, *The Masked Marvel* took its cue from the 1938 *Lone Ranger* and revealed only that the Masked Marvel was one of four insurance agents. These four guys are somewhat similarly built and all wear the exact same outfit, a light suit, at all times. The Masked Marvel simply puts on a black mask (that almost looks painted on) to become a "super-hero." By the penultimate chapter, two of the four suspects have been eliminated: Is the Masked Marvel the sensitive blond Bob, or the burly dark-haired Terry? The answer doesn't come as too much of a surprise because only one of the four actors seem to get more screen time than the others. The actual man behind the mask was ace stuntman, Tom Steele, unbilled.

Tom Steele's presence is probably why the fight scenes in *The Masked Marvel* are among the best and wildest ever. (Perhaps the fight scenes are better than in director Bennet's Superman serials because the opponents are equally matched as well.) The stunt men really *hurl* themselves into a fight, breaking up furniture, flinging each other over bars and counters, practically flying in

Left: *The Masked Marvel* spies on a suspect.

the air as their bodies tear apart the props and scenery. Each of the many battle scenes is frantic and energetic and expertly staged and rehearsed. Fistfights are often routine and boring in most serials; in *The Masked Marvel* they are practically the *raison d'être*.

The villain in this is a Japanese master spy, Maura Sakima (Johnny Arthur), who is responsible for many acts of wartime sabotage involving airplane factories, industrial diamonds, a special periscope, and a "television range

finder." Arthur's portrayal makes Sakima seems like a skinny Tim Conway doing an Oriental parody, and his accent sometimes sounds more Danish than Japanese. The acting in *The Masked Marvel* is generally little more than adequate.

While some of the cliff-hangers are in the "missing information" category, others provide perfectly believable escapes from their doom-traps. In chapter three, Sakima's thugs put Marvel's friend Alice Hamilton (Louise Currie) in the bottom of a large elevator shaft, but our hero saves her before the rapidly descending freight elevator can squash her to death. He pursues the felons up several stories to the top level and is himself knocked into the elevator shaft. We later learn that Alice had brought the elevator's open platform up several stories so that he hadn't far to fall. A particularly good cliff-hanger is a three-way chase cutting between a train, a dynamite-laden workcar that is heading directly toward it, and the Masked Marvel in his automobile racing to the area to either warn the engineer or stop the dynamite from hitting the train. His auto hits the workcar and explodes at the climax of this thrilling sequence.

Other good scenes include one in which MM does battle with a hood on an explosives-packed launch that runs right into a ship and blows up, and his fight with a gunsel in a house rigged to explode at midnight. He barely makes it out before the twelfth bell sounds. There's also a nice bit in chapter nine with the Marvel trapped in the back of a runaway van as it heads toward a cliff.

Amazingly, the almost obligatory dopey serial moments are kept to a minimum in *The Masked Marvel*. In a battle scene, one of Sakima's men lunges at MM , but he slips, and his knife not only goes *through* a wooden door but stabs a cohort standing against it on the other side. Marvel and company enter what has to be the cleanest-looking drainage system in history; and the climactic battle between the Masked Marvel and Sakima is rather flat and abrupt. Otherwise *The Masked Marvel* is an example of the serial at its best.

The Masked Marvel himself was basically a clone of Will Eisner's The Spirit and the Green Hornet, both of whom were among the more popular masked mystery men of the period. These fellows always wore suits and ties and hats, were great fighters and athletes, and of course knew how to really handle a gun. In real life, their extremely simple masks would never have been enough to conceal their true identities, but in the serials, comic books, and funny pages, no one ever seemed to mind.

Above : *The Masked Marvel* is ready to return the fire.

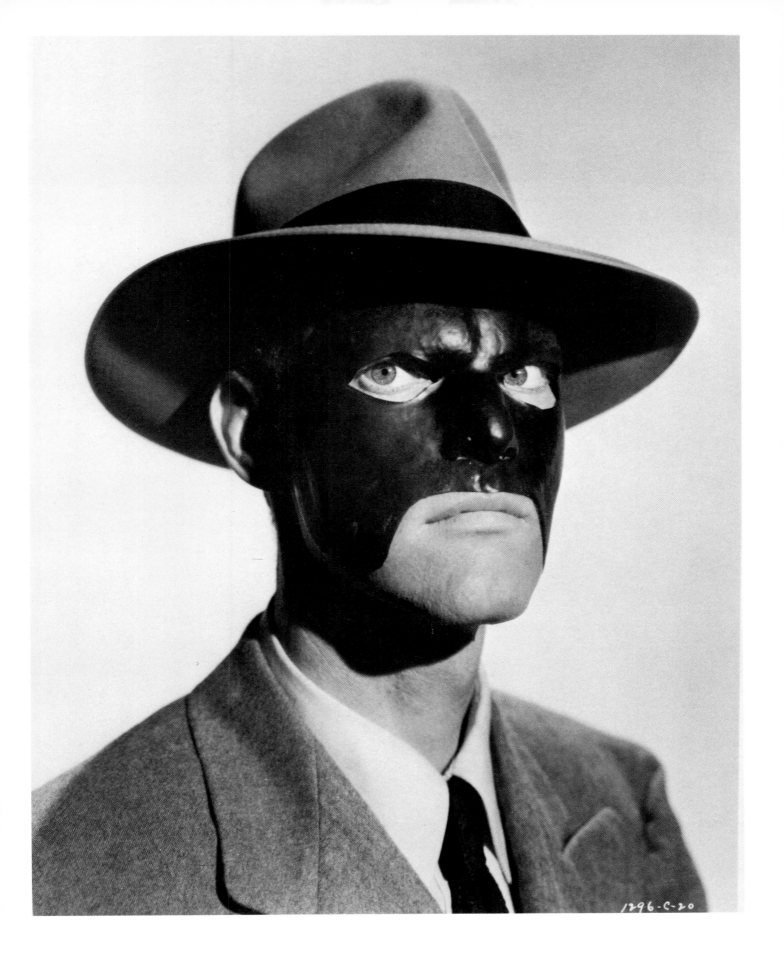

Above: Stunt man Tom Steele played the *Masked Marvel*.

CHAPTER EIGHT
BRING ON THE HEROES

A great many movies have a comic book flavor to them even though their characters are original to the screen or adapted from sources other than comic books and strips. Action heroes often proceed in a manner that is as simplistic and contrived as any old-fashioned comic book. Many have been influenced by comics whether acknowledged or not.

A popular comic book writer-artist, Howard Chaykin, who created *American Flagg!* for First Comics, believes filmmakers are influenced by comics to a greater degree than the public realizes. "Most people don't know comics exist," he told *New York Post* film critic Jami Bernard, "so a smart producer can go down to his cellar, read these things, and then use them. The film audience has no idea."

A case in point might be the *Robocop*[1] pictures, which in some aspects are similar to Chaykin's *American Flagg!* comic series. Both *American Flagg!* and *Robocop* take place in a near-future world riddled with violence and drugs that is a slight exaggeration of our own. Both are set in major cities—Chicago and Detroit, respectively—that are run by huge corporations or "plexes." Chaykin claims to have originated the devices of providing narrative and background information via television newscasts, commercials, etc., interspersed with the actual story. This device was later used in *Robocop*, Frank Miller's comic book *The Dark Knight Returns*, and *Robocop 2* (whose screenplay was written by Miller).

The basic story lines, however, are entirely different. *American Flagg!* relates the adventures of Reuben Flagg, who used to star in the risqué series, *Mark Thrust, Sexus Ranger*, but is now one of the "Plexus Rangers" policing a futuristic Chicago. Reuben has an insatiable sexual appetite and plenty of women to satisfy it. His associates include a lovable talking cat named Raul and a robot deputy with a holographic head. The stories are a riot of double entendres, political references, social satire, violence, nudity, and sex, some of it on a confused adolescent level of pure self-indulgence. If nothing else, *American Flagg!* is different from your average super-hero comic and has certainly provided some colorful stories since its debut in 1983.

The 1987 film *Robocop* is the story of Murphy (Peter Weller), a cop who is blasted apart by members of a Detroit drug ring, clinically dies, and is "brought back" as a half-mechanical cyborg and supercop. He wears a metal outer casing and helmet with visor and computer banks and is more reminiscent of *Iron Man* and the Marvel Comic cyborg (complete with computer), *Deathlok*, than of Reuben Flagg. *Iron Man*, also

---

[1]*Robocop* became a Marvel Comics series in 1990, three years after the film was released, but just in time for the sequel.

Above: The first issue of the *Robocop* comic book. Copyright © 1990 Orion Pictures Corporation. Published by Marvel Comics.

Opposite: Peter Weller as *Robocop*.

published by Marvel, features a genius inventor, Tony Stark, who dons a golden metal suit that gives him fantastic abilities. *Deathlok* is a cyborg from the future with two brains—one human, one computer—and a face only a mother could love: part metal, part disfigured human skin. *Robocop*'s basic concept of a hero who is half man and half machine owes a lot to Deathlok. (Ironically, the success of *Robocop 2* helped bring about a revival of the Deathlok character at Marvel, a bizarre case of a clone giving rebirth to the original.)

Robocop was directed by Paul Verhoeven and is an effective piece of super-heroic science fiction with a lot of style and "cyber-punk" coldness. Edward Neumeier and Michael Miner's screenplay eschews depth for a tongue-

in-cheek approach a little too often, but generally *Robocop* is fast-paced and entertaining. The highlight of the film occurs when our hero faces off against a hulking, all-machine security robot, ED-209, a stop-motion model animated by Phil Tippett. Tippett embues his creation with a lot of personality and perverse "appeal." The film boasts good performances, particularly from Ronny Cox as the villainous Jones, with Verhoeven's direction ladling on the gore pretty thick at times.

Neumeier and Miner came up with a rough draft of a script for *Robocop 2* that, if a report in *Cinefantastique* is any indication, borrowed even more heavily from Chaykin's *American Flagg!* than the first film did. When their script was ultimately rejected, Frank Miller was brought in to come up with a new one. Even his screenplay was greatly revised when the producer found it rather grim. Like Miller's *The Dark Knight Returns*, it, too, is clearly Chaykin-influenced. *Robocop 2* was released in 1990.

In the sequel, Robocop is undergoing an emotional trauma, remembering some of his past life and even driving out to the suburbs to watch his wife and child at play. Although a sympathetic psychologist tries to explain to him what's happening, his superiors are alarmed, furious and impatient. They just want their machine-man to get back to work. Had the picture expanded on these early scenes, really developed the situation of a man with a past life turned into a robotic monstrosity, and the conflict it engenders in both the cyborg and his creators, *Robocop 2* might have had some depth and subtext to go along with the mayhem. Instead it's merely an acceptable but unmemorable action-adventure film with some classy but rather unexciting special effects work.

Top: Ronny Cox poses in front of the formidable ED 209 in *Robocop*.

Bottom: *American Flagg!* #1: a strong influence on *Robocop* and other films? Copyright © 1983 First Comics, Inc. and Howard Chaykin, Inc.

The movie takes potshots at corrupt politicians, Madison Avenue, crooks, and everything else, but is oddly skittish in one regard. How is it that, aside from one black child in a group of otherwise white kids robbing a store, all of the criminals, junkies, drug dealers, and prostitutes in *Robocop 2* are Caucasian? In *Detroit*, where the inner

city is today almost exclusively black? (This is a situation that probably won't change even by *Robocop 2*'s near-future time period.) Admittedly, *Robocop 2* is a fantasy, but its conception of "Detroit" is naïve and laughable.

Yet what is frightening about this "fantasy" is that it is really not that farfetched. What with the beatings, crack-crazed killings, machine gunnings of innocent youngsters in our world today, *Robocop 2*'s milieu is "science fiction" only to the inhabitants of small, all-white, middle-class towns in Ohio or New Hampshire.

Robocop 2 got extremely mixed reviews. "Irredeemable trash—deadly boring and surprisingly cheap-looking," wrote David Denby in *New York*.

The problem with the movie is that it basically reworks the plot of the original without developing its old characters or creating new ones we could sympathize with. And Irvin Kershner's direction is neither sharp nor tight nor good enough to overcome these deficiencies. One watches the climactic battle between Peter Weller and "Robocop 2" (another wonderful Phil Tippett creation) with admiration for the effects but without ever getting caught up in the conflict.

The human antagonists of *Robocop 2* are an almost mythical drug dealer, his girlfriend, and a small, murderous

boy who takes charge when the leader is captured (and converted into Robocop 2), as well as a bitchy lady scientist who has the morals and scruples of a road slug. But these are caricatures, not characters. Ultimately *Robocop 2* betrays its comic book influences and fails to rise above it.

As for Howard Chaykin, the first *Robocop* was enough to get him thinking about leaving the comic book business. "That's one reason I want to get out of comics—I'm tired of providing reference and source material for filmmakers."

Top: *Robocop 2* is caught in the middle of a war zone.

Bottom: The hulking monstrosity of *Robocop 2*.

The influence for Steven Spielberg's three "Indiana Jones" movies was obvious: the serials of the thirties and forties. The basic plot for the first film was taken from the 1943 Republic serial *Secret Service in Darkest Africa,* which also has an American battling Nazis over certain artifacts that might help shift the balance of power. In *Raiders of the Lost Ark* (1981), the American is Indiana Jones (Harrison Ford), an archaeologist who races the Nazis to find the sacred ark of the covenant, which Hitler believes has magical powers.

The film opens with an exciting action sequence as the hero faces treachery, angry natives, a slimy villain, and all sorts of deadly traps to steal a golden statuette from a South American tomb. The rest of the picture is full of equally thrilling feats of derring-do, one or two of which seem to defy the laws of science (in true serial—and comic book—fashion). In one scene, Indiana somehow manages to survive a voyage on the outside of a submerged submarine, for instance.

Although *Raiders of the Lost Ark* is not quite a great "classic" film, it does boast some well-crafted action sequences, courtesy of director Spielberg. Ford makes a convincing, down-to-earth hero, and Karen Allen is fine as the plucky heroine, Marion Ravenwood. The climax, when the Nazis are gruesomely dispatched by the magical powers of the ark, their faces literally melting, practically started the soon-tiresome practice of the eighties of ending every action epic with a special effects "light show." John William's musical score is wonderful embellishment in every scene.

The sequel, *Indiana Jones and the Temple of Doom* (it predated the events of *Raiders*), was even better, and featured hair-raising stunts "lifted" from over a half dozen old-time chapterplays such as *Drums of Fu Manchu, Spy Smasher,* and *Tiger Woman*. None of those old serials, however, had the production values of an Indiana Jones feature. Spielberg's movies are also arguably more cinematic, not just fast-paced, but well edited and directed as only the very best sequences in the cliff-hangers of the thirties and after were. *Temple of Doom* proceeds at an especially breathless pace with each startling sequence topping the one before.

Among the knockout sequences in *Temple of Doom*: damsel-in-distress Willie Scott (Kate Capshaw) plunging her hand into a niche full of an utterly grotesque assortment of living insects in an attempt to free Indiana and his youthful sidekick Short Round (Ke Huy Quan) from a chamber full of descending spikes; Willie lowered by cage into a sacrificial pit of fire in the hidden caverns of a demented religious cult; Indiana in a frenetic chase through a

Opposite: Harrison Ford is Indiana Jones.

Above: The snakepit of *Raiders of the Lost Ark*.

mine tunnel in coal cars with a torrent of onrushing water in wet pursuit; and a marvelous one in which Indiana avoids the clutches of a bunch of homicidal thugs by severing the supports of the suspension bridge on which they and he are standing. The fact that Zorro and Nyoka did the same thing in their long-ago serials didn't spoil the

enjoyment of the sequence one bit. It was as if Spielberg was determined to make a film without one single dull *second*.

Surprisingly, the third installment of the series, *Indiana Jones and the Last Crusade* (1989), was quite a letdown. It is perfectly acceptable, entertaining film fare, but a step backward from the *Temple of Doom*. Spielberg abandoned the frenetic editing of *Temple* in favor of a more leisurely style that is not appropriate to the subject matter. *Last Crusade* is, in fact, a virtual remake of *Raiders of the Lost Ark*, with more Nazi villains and yet another search for a mystical treasure. There are very few stand-out sequences in *Last Crusade* and only one really thrilling moment—when Indiana has a battle on a runaway tank heading straight toward the edge of an exceedingly high cliff. The most noteworthy aspect of the picture is that Sean Connery plays Indiana's father, a bit of inspired casting.

Surprisingly little is spectacular or at least original about *Last Crusade*. Scenes in underground catacombs lack chills and suspense. Everything is professional and workmanlike, but nothing more.

The ending, when Indy finally finds the Holy Grail, is perhaps the most disappointing thing about the picture. The tone of the film nearly becomes sanctimonious, as if Spielberg thought that giving Indiana religion would stamp a lofty tone over the whole silly enterprise. Considering the mindlessness of the proceedings, the ploy really backfires.

Indiana Jones was briefly turned into a Marvel comic book. Although his adventures were as exciting and

Left: Indiana gets ready for trouble in *Raiders of the Lost Ark*.

Right: *Indiana Jones and the Temple of Doom:* the best in the series.

outrageous as ever, Indiana himself came off colorless up against the likes of Superman and Captain America. Maybe it was the costume.

Robert E. Howard virtually invented the "sword and sorcery" genre in the 1930s, and his most famous creation was Conan, the Cimmerian, whose adventures appeared in many pulp magazines of the day. When the stories were released in paperback in the 1960s, they were discovered by a whole new audience. This led to the unveiling of a Conan comic book that is still being published in the 1990s. The success of the paperbacks and comic book put together engendered the making of a multimillion dollar *Conan the Barbarian* from director John Milius in 1982.

A chief reason why musclebound Arnold Schwarzennegger was cast in the role of Conan was that he looked exactly like the character as drawn by famed illustrator Frank Frazetta on the paperback covers: brutish, anthropoidal, supermuscular. Arnold was wisely given only about a dozen lines of dialogue, as his accent was not what one would call "Cimmerian" (nor "Hyborian," the period from which our sword-wielding hero hails). James Earl Jones was a splendid choice for his adversary, Thulsa Doom, and Amazonian Sandahl Bergman an effective Valeria.

Yet every aspect of the picture is overwhelmed by Ron Cobb's stunning scenic design and Duke Callaghan's cinematography. With the special effects men, they re-created the Hyborian era in all its thunder and glory. There are many lavish sets and atmospheric trappings, richly enhanced by Basil Pouledoris's musical score.

The plot has Conan vowing to get revenge on Thulsa Doom, the cult leader who put him in chains and slaughtered his people. This isn't going to be easy, of course. For one thing, Thulsa has a giant serpent that just loves to snack on Barbarians or anyone else who gets in his way at dinner time. This serpent looks more convincing in still shots than in the movie, in which it is a 300-pound rubber prop combined with a mechanical eighteen-foot head (complete with movable mouth, fangs, and forked tongue) and a thirty-six-foot-long hydraulic body made of duraluminum and steel cables. The snake cost $20,000 to build.

Although *Conan* has many slow moments and weak spots, it is still entertaining and beautiful to look at. Its lack of cerebral content caused many critics to ignore its obvious artistry and visual appearance. It was successful

Top : *Conan the Barbarian* #141. Certain issues of this series have become highly prized collector's items. Copyright © 1982 Conan Properties, Inc. Published by Marvel Comics.

Bottom : Conan raises his sword in triumph.

enough to warrant a sequel, director Richard Fleischer's *Conan the Destroyer,* in 1984, however.

Conan the Barbarian debuted as a Marvel comic book around 1970. Graced with stylish Barry Smith artwork and stories (often adaptations) by Roy Thomas, the comic was a wondrous miasma of monsters, magic, damsels-in-distress, witchcraft, fortresses and towers, slithering evil demons, and macho warriors, with the ill-mannered, thieving, if oddly righteous Conan the butchest of the lot. Conan was so successful (and so good) that it spawned a black-and-white magazine featuring the Cimmerian's medieval adventures, as well as *Kull and the Barbarians,* another Howard creation, and a second Conan comic book.

Although originally meant (in longer form) for a Conan story in the magazine *Savage Times*, "The Curse of the Golden Skull" in issue # 37 (April 1974) is typical of the kind of tales found in *Conan.* The tale was adapted from Howard's story by Thomas and features intense and stylish pencils by Neal Adams. Ancient curses, warrior cavalry, violence, and bloodshed abound—and that's before the story proper begins. Conan and his companion, the black Juma (used in the story but actually created by Lin Carter and L. Sprague de Camp), are captured by mounted Hillmen and taken to the mysterious Valley of the Sun, where monsters roam. They are brought before the revived wizard, once known as Rotath of Lemuria, who lives in a high tower that can only be reached by entering a big glass globe that is lifted high up in the air by a spout of water gushing from a fountain.

Conan and Juma are put to work in the mines, and set off into a forbidden tunnel one day. There they find an enormous dragon that tries to devour them, only to be summarily consumed itself by the occupant of a lake, a monstrous, slithering, outsize slug. This horror pursues the two men out of the mines, but what it's really after is the gold they've picked up from the shore of the underground lake. The story ends with the monster sucking up fleeing Rotath, consuming his bones, which are made of gold, and spitting out a yucky mass—or, rather, mess—of shapeless skin that's left over!

As you would expect from a barbarian, Conan is an antihero. He has his own code of honor and seems to stick up for the underdog at times—not out of any deep compassion, but out of a distrust and a lack of respect for the gentry. He isn't impressed by anyone, and he has precious little sentiment. Snooty princesses particularly come in for his scorn. When Rotath fools Conan into thinking he has slain one of these damsels, Conan is furious, not because he cared about her life but because she was supposed to be in his care and her death reflects badly on

Above: Schwarzenegger versus the giant snake in *Conan the Barbarian.*

him. He has some feelings, at least in the comics, but he is not above doing the expedient thing. He's a "good guy" by default, everyone else around him being so venal that his acts of brutality, murder, and thievery are almost noble in comparison. Most of the people Conan kills or causes to be killed really ask for it.

The same might also be said of James Bond, the master spy whose film series has probably lasted longer than any other. Many who are familiar with the character only from the movies, particularly the ones with Roger Moore, may not realize that the 007 of the screen is rather different from the 007 of Ian Fleming's literate novels of the fifties and sixties.

Bond was introduced in Fleming's *Casino Royale* in 1954. He is a far cry from Roger Moore's cartoon portrayal of him and is certainly more dimensional than any of the movie characterizations. Fleming's prose is rich and vivid, full of strong descriptions and well-researched details. (Fleming's books occasionally betray their pulp influence, but are generally on a much higher level.) *Casino Royale* shows how and why Bond occasionally exhibits contemptuous attitudes toward women: his heart is broken by one at the conclusion. Years later, the excellent book was turned into a pop-art parody with Woody Allen, David Niven, Peter Sellers, and art deco sets; it was amusing but virtually unrecognizable.

The James Bond movies have always had a comic book flair to them with their melodramatic villains, colorful gadgets, and edge-of-your-seat situations. The formula began with the first adaptation, *Dr. No*, in 1962, in which Bond is up against a megalomaniac who is destroying missiles from his base in Crab Key. Dr. No is a very typical pulp/comic character, suitably exotic in both appearance and ancestry. He is half Chinese and half German and has black, shiny, metal-crushing prosthetics in place of the hands that were lost due to radiation. He has a Napoleonic

complex and is a member of SPECTRE, the Special Executive for Terrorism, Revenge, and Extortion. His headquarters is expansive and handsomely appointed, with an aquarium whose walls of magnifying glass make the fish within seem like monsters. Dr. No is in the tradition of every archfiend and supervillain from Fu Manchu to Lex Luthor, and is wonderfully played by Joseph Wiseman.

As James Bond, Sean Connery is too cool and

Top: *Casino Royale* an unrecognizable parody.

Left: James Bond has his hands full in *Goldfinger*. (Shirley Eaton is the blonde)

217

unemotional (something the character was not in the novels). His penchant for making quips about death ("Make sure he doesn't go anywhere," he says to a man about a corpse) was carried over into all the successive films. Otherwise, Connery is probably the best film Bond there ever was. Although handsomely produced on a relatively modest budget, *Dr. No* is not especially well done nor well directed (by Terence Young).

Young's *From Russia With Love* (1963) is slightly more down to earth, while injecting some comic book aspects: Spectre Island, where live targets are used for practice and Colonel Rosa Klebb (Lotte Lenya) uses brass knuckles on the corded stomach of a towel-clad recruit; Rosa's deadly shoe-knife, which she uses on one unsuspecting victim ("one and a half seconds; someday we must develop a faster acting poison") and with which she tries to kill Bond; and a tunnel beneath the Russian embassy in Venice. Connery plays Bond with his usual smooth unflappability and Daniela Bianchi continues the tradition (started by Ursula Andress in *Dr. No*) in which all of 007's women call him "Gems."

Bond began to get gadget-happy in *Goldfinger* (1964), which has a comparatively prosaic if memorably acted villain (Gert Frobe), but a tricked-up automobile; and a great scene when Goldfinger threatens Bond's private parts with a laser beam that can cut through metal. The character of Oddjob, Goldfinger's Oriental bodyguard, is straight out of a comic book. He wears a kind of butler's uniform and has a derby with a razor edge that can slice the head off a concrete statue. One can picture him taking on Captain America with his killer hat and slick karate moves. Like many super-heroes, Bond outwits the big dope by getting him to electrocute himself in an exciting climax during a Fort Knox heist. Honor Blackman plays Pussy Galore, perhaps the most obvious name since Brick in *Cat on a Hot Tin Roof*. The picture was directed nicely by Guy Hamilton.

Thunderball (1965) and *You Only Live Twice* (1967) added an epic quality to the Bond films, with bigger climactic battle scenes and many more special effects, particularly in the latter. The most intriguing sequences of *Thunderball* (Terence Young again directed) include a precredits scene in which Bond decks a bogus widow and makes his escape on a portable jetpack; a Batmobile-like car with rising trunk plates to deflect bullets and water-shooting pipes used to overturn pursuing vehicles; and an electrified death chair in the SPECTRE conference room that lowers its unsightly fried victim into the floor at the press of a button.

Lewis Gilbert's *You Only Live Twice* is definitely in the comic book tradition, with Ernst Blofeld snatching spaceships from a Japanese base inside an extinct island volcano. Donald Pleasence is as eerie and wild-eyed as ever as Blofeld, but the actor is not at his best in escapist pictures; he lacks energy and flair and speaks in a perpetual monotone. Roald Dahl's screenplay features the obligatory death traps and dangerous women, with a

Above: Sean Connery does a little underwater investigation in *Thunderball*.

certain added color. A sadistic redhead ties up Bond in a cabin and picks up a scalpel used by plastic surgeons. "They use it to slice off skin," she tells him. Later she traps Bond in a plane and bails out, leaving him to his fate. When Bond escapes, a disappointed Blofeld has the would-be murderess walk on the bridge over the indoor lagoon

in his magnificent headquarters. A section of the bridge slides downward and the woman slips into piranha-infested waters and a grisly death.

On Her Majesty's Secret Service (1969) is one of the best of the Bond films, and one of the few to follow a Fleming novel closely (almost scene for scene). In retrospect, George Lazenby does not make a half-bad Bond, and Diana Rigg is wonderful as his beloved Tracy. The plot has Blofeld (this time played with relish by Telly Savalas) hypnotizing a score of girls into carrying out his nefarious plans at an Alpine retreat where he is supposed to be curing phobias. The best scene—one of the best in the entire series—is a superbly edited and absolutely thrilling battle between Bond and Blofeld as they career down the icy mountainside on bobsleds. The film, directed by Peter Hunt, also was courageous enough to stick with Fleming's downbeat ending, when Bond's bride Tracy is murdered at the very start of their honeymoon.

Guy Hamilton's *Diamonds Are Forever* (1971) brought Connery back to the role of Bond and added the gadgetry and technological aspects that were downplayed in the previous film. The plot—loosely based on Fleming's novel, which would have made an equally satisfying movie—is a wild blend of smuggled diamonds, high-intensity lasers, secret bases beneath the Las Vegas desert, and a Howard Hughes-type multimillionaire who has been kidnapped and replaced by Ernst Stravro Blofeld, winningly played by Charles Gray. Blofeld's scheme is to build a solar ray that is capable of wiping out cities from space. *Diamonds Are Forever* really began the trend toward making each Bond movie more of a cartoon or comic

book and less like its source material, but on its own level it is delicious entertainment. Jill St. John as Tiffany Case was carried over from the novel, as were two childishly cruel hit

Top: Sean Connery on the prowl in *You Only Live Twice*.

Center: George Lazenby in *On Her Majesty's Secret Service*, the best of the Bond movies.

Left: Diana Rigg and George Lazenby in *On Her Majesty's Secret Service*.

men whose stereotyped homosexual relationship was only hinted at in the book but is confirmed in the movie. Stand-out scenes include Bond battling two curvaceous lady bodyguards named Bambi and Thumper and later crawling through a pipeline under the desert—and Blofeld in drag is a riot. The series started taking a farcical tone with this fast-paced, well-directed entry.

Hamilton's *Live and Let Die* (1973) was the first to star Roger Moore as Bond and is perhaps the worst of the Bond films. After charismatic, intense Sean Connery, Moore seemed hopelessly pallid. The globe-spanning adventures, far-reaching plots, and dastardly archvillains of previous films were replaced by a sappy voodoo priest and some mundane black racketeers, with alleged action scenes that had Keystone Kop overtones. Even Paul McCartney's theme song was lousy.

Moore's second 007, *The Man With the Golden Gun* (1974)—Guy Hamilton again—was an improvement, with the star settling comfortably, if not perfectly, into his much lighter, almost self-mocking portrayal. Conversely, the film itself has a more low-key approach than many previous entries. Bond's opponent in this is Francisco Scaramunga, (Christopher Lee) an assassin who charges one million per hit. Although *Golden Gun* doesn't have any eye-popping or really outstanding sequences, it does have its share of thrills and comic book aspects. For instance, Scaramunga's bizarre background: He was brought up in the circus, with his only friend an elephant. When the animal's handler

mistreats the beast and causes its death, he is killed by Scaramunga. The dastardly villain has an elaborate playhouse on his private island, complete with a saloon, robots, cutouts of gangsters, and flashing red lights, in which he attempts to "psych out" his opponents. His diminutive assistant, Nick Nack, played by Herve Villechaize, is in the tradition that includes everyone from Igor in the Frankenstein films to Magneto's old sycophant, the Toad, in the *X-Men*.

Top: Sean Connery returned to the role of Bond in *Diamonds Are Forever* with Jill St. John.

Bottom: Roger Moore took over for Connery and had no trouble fitting in.

The next two Bond films really took the character into the realm of the cartoon and comic book—and fantasy—with opulent sets and high-tech special effects almost overwhelming the story. In *The Spy Who Loved Me* (1977) Curt Jurgens is archvillain Stromberg, a madman in a lavish undersea lair who steals both Russian and British submarines by swallowing them up in the bowels of his enormous tanker. His ultimate plan is to turn all the world into an underwater paradise. He has his own version of Oddjob, a grotesque bodyguard named "Jaws" (Richard

Kiel) who has sharp metal teeth and a hulking physique. At one point, Bond's car turns into a minisub, and there are death traps involving shark pools and pursuing helicopters (one of which is piloted by the luscious Caroline Munro).

By the time of the next film, *Moonraker* (1979), the James Bond series seemed more inspired by a *Nick Fury, Agent of SHIELD* comic book than by Fleming's novels (of which *Moonraker* is one of the best). Carryovers from the book include the evil Hugo Drax and the Moonraker rocket—and that's about all. In the book,, the rocket was merely to decimate London; in the movie, it carries several dozen couples to a space satellite (from there they will start a new race), and Earth itself is targeted for destruction. James Bond purists were even more appalled at *Moonraker* than they had been at *Spy*, but both films are undeniably colorful and exciting, if taken on their own somewhat limited terms.

The stunts and effects in *Moonraker* are spectacular, and some great scenes include a battle on top of a cable car, the collapse of the space station, and a highly suspenseful sequence when Bond and his associate, Holy Goodhead[2] (Lois Chiles), go after deadly gas capsules in a spaceship and try desperately to destroy them before they reach Earth and poison its atmosphere. The laser battle in space between government agents and Drax's men provides some bizarre images, and French actor Michael Lonsdale nicely underplays as the smug, neckless, pixie-ish, and petulant devil Hugo Drax. "You appear with the tedious inevitability of an unloved season," he says to Bond. The old movie serials, which they partly resemble, were never as gorgeous or expansive as *Spy* and *Moonraker*, both of which were directed by Lewis Gilbert.

Top: James Bond versus the forces of Hugo Drax in *Moonraker*.

Bottom: The James Bond series really got "spacey" with *Moonraker*.

The next few Bond films have been much more mundane. *For Your Eyes Only* (1981) was a complete reversal from *Moonraker* and a return to the more believable formula of the earliest 007 films. It is distinguished by an exciting sequence wherein Bond and a lady companion are dragged along the sea bottom by a rope tied to a speeding ship and a breathtaking mountain climb in which Bond shinnies to the top before a villain can send him and the rope to oblivion. The tight, taut editing in this sequence is almost worthy of Hitchcock. *Octopussy* (1983) again eschews the elaborate special effects of *Moonraker*, but is still a larger-than-life (and comically obvious) "male fantasy" complete with a gaggle of bosomy "Volga boatwomen" at the oars of a ship with a male captain, and the sensual Octopussy herself (Maud Adams). *Never Say Never Again* (1983) is basically a remake of *Thunderball*, with Sean Connery back in the role of Bond, but its highlight is the performance of sexy Barbara Carrera as the evil Fatima Blush, a character in the tradition of all the gorgeous antiheroines in *Blackhawk* and other comics.

Roger Moore played Bond for the last time in *A View to a Kill* (1985)—the most hair-raising scene of which is either the climax with a blimp and the Golden Gate Bridge or Moore in bed with Grace Jones. Timothy Dalton took over the 007 role in *The Living Daylights* (1987), where he played a refreshingly "serious" Bond after the tired cartoon antics of an aging Roger Moore. Dalton had to contend with a few leftover slapstick moments in *Daylights* (originally written for Moore) but came into his own in *License to Kill* (1989), in which he goes after a vicious drug lord, played with verve by Robert Davi. Dalton adds depth and dimension to the role of Bond, putting him a notch above Sean Connery, without sacrificing any of the glamor. *License to Kill* is much more along the lines of

Fleming's original vision, maybe even grittier and more realistic, and proves a Bond film can be quite compelling even without multimillion dollar sets and effects. It can't resist a few comic book touches, however, such as that pet iguana of Davi's, which always sports what is probably a priceless necklace around its neck. John Glen directed all of the Bond films beginning with *For Your Eyes Only*, aside from *Never Say Never Again*, which was helmed by Irvin Kershner.

Guy Hamilton, who directed some of the James Bond features, hoped lightning would strike twice with a new series based on an inexplicably popular bunch of execrably written paperback novels featuring the exploits of "The Destroyer." Christopher Wood's screenplay adapted the early chapters of the initial one but wisely made many changes in introducing the characters to a wider audience. It was hoped that the first film, *Remo Williams: The Adventure Begins* (1985) would spawn a whole new film series along the lines of the Bond adventures, but the

Above: Lois Chiles and Roger Moore in *Moonraker*.

picture wasn't well received enough for that to happen. It is strange that some paperback novels that were *below* the level of most comic books could be the basis of such a surprisingly good picture.

Fred Ward is excellent as a New York City cop who is unwillingly recruited by a secret organization accountable only to the president. There are only two other people in this group, whose job is to terminate criminals who are above or outwit the law. The latest target is a munitions manufacturer who tries to cover up the fact that his rifles are defective and may kill more soldiers than they save. Shanghaied by the organization without the slightest say in the matter, Remo finds himself in a rather horrifying situation, but the movie is too lighthearted and good-natured to deal with it (or anything else) on other than a comic book level.

Remo Williams is simply a code name that has been "carefully" derived from the bottom of a bedpan. Remo is trained by an inscrutable Korean named Chuin, who is played very well by Joel Grey in superb Oriental and old-age makeup. Chuin nearly drives Remo crazy with his strict diet and regimen, but teaches him how to do such things as dodge bullets with ease. A clever sequence has Remo showing Chuin what he's learned by climbing up a series of metal pipes, beams, and obstacles, and almost falling off on several occasions.

There is some excellent stunt work in a hair-raising sequence set on and around the Statue of Liberty, with Remo fighting off three rugged assailants who are determined to send him hurtling to the ground on Liberty Island. Other great scenes show Remo using the diamond filling in a villain's tooth to cut an escape exit through

the glass wall of a gas-filled death chamber, and a group of persistent Doberman pinschers who can not only pull down ladders using their own weight and teeth but also walk on tightropes. The movie boasts a fast, zany pace and good direction by Hamilton, and a nice musical score by Craig Safan. Follow-ups would have been welcome, but were not to be.

The success of the James Bond series brought a flood of other spy movies, comic books, and made-for-TV movies, one of the best of which was the British-made *Madame Sin* (1971). Bette Davis stars as an international villainess who, like Fu Manchu, kidnaps "dead" scientists to work for her. The comic book trappings of the screenplay include the nuns with stun guns who capture Sin's pawn, Robert Wagner, and Sin's art deco mansion, complete with holograms, sonic forcefields, elevators

Top: Fred Ward hugs the Statue of Liberty in *Remo Williams: The Adventure Begins*.

Bottom: *Madame Sin* James Bond-like gadgets and a villainess out of Fu Manchu.

that go sideways as well as up and down, and laboratories wherein sonic guns are tested and people are brainwashed via surgery. Wagner is a former intelligence agent who hasn't been himself since the presumed death of a lady spy with whom he was in love.

Some "clients" of Sin's, revolutionaries, want a Polaris submarine, and a reluctant Wagner is inveigled into helping her steal it by kidnapping the commander, an old friend of his. The commander is programmed to set a course that will bring the sub to Madame Sin's island. When her henchmen try to murder Wagner (his battle with thugs flying above him in a helicopter is exciting), he finally turns on her and contacts the authorities. But Madame Sin has the last laugh when Wagner's lost love reappears, only to poison him.

Bette Davis has a high old time basically playing herself, as she often did in her later period. The film has a delightful sense of humor and some real suspense, as well as stunning location shots of Scotland (and Sin's impressive castle) and adroit direction (David Greene) and editing. The only negative is the inappropriate musical score. The picture ends with Madame Sin coveting Buckingham Palace as she drives by it. "When does the lease expire?" she asks her loyal associate, Denholm Elliott.

Mel Gibson starred as "Mad Max" in a trio of hugely popular action films that got more comic bookish with each picture. *Mad Max* (1980) introduced the character, a cop in a futuristic Australia where the whole system of law and order has been overtaken by an "every man for himself" attitude that allows barbaric biker gangs to run riot. When one of these gangs runs down Gibson's wife and baby son, he swears revenge. *Mad Max* is a pretty bad low-budget picture that has a few energetic scenes and car chases, but suffers from ragged continuity, weak

[3]Film theory has it that some, generally brilliant, directors are the *auteurs*—or authors—of their films, a theory that should not apply to the likes of George Miller (who have illustrated no "brilliance"), and which has screenwriters tearing their hair. The best directors, particularly if they write their own screenplays as well, do leave a personal stamp on their pictures and can correctly be called auteurs.

Above: Mel Gibson as Mad Max.

characterizations, and a lack of story. Unaccountably, director George Miller was given an undeserved "auteur"[3] status because of this tedious bit of lowbrow macho fantasy. Even the revenge theme lacks impact, although the gruesome final sequence is fairly effective.

Mad Max returned in *The Road Warrior* (aka *Mad Max 2*), a sequel directed by Miller in 1981. In this entry, Gibson has become more of a myth than a person, the legendary hero who will come to save the people from disaster, in this case yet another savage gang that wants the fuel of an isolated colony. Although *The Road Warrior* is better than the original, and boasts a thrilling final segment with all manner of weird vehicles in a hectic chase, it is still mediocre and rather stupid. As in *Mad Max*, Miller's use of the paraphernalia and costumes of the gay leather sub-sect for the villains gives the film a homophobic subtext.

The third Mad Max film, *Mad Max Beyond Thunderdome* (1985), was directed by Miller and George Ogilvie. Chasing a thief, Max runs into Bartertown, a "sleaze-pit" ruled by Masterblaster, who is actually two people, a brainy midget strapped to the shoulders of a hulking, mindless giant. This character is very similar to Warstar of the Imperial Guard, a group that has appeared several times in Marvel's *X-Men*, except that Warstar seems more robotic than human. Tina Turner flamboyantly plays Aunt Entity, who wants Max to kill Masterblaster. Max and MB wind up fighting to the death in the Thunderdome, a grilled-in arena.

All of the above, which is exciting, takes place in the first third of the picture, leaving a slow, meandering middle section (banished to the desert, Max runs into a group of wild children who think he's a legendary captain come to lead them back to nonexistent civilization), and a disappointing chase-climax that lacks the tight cutting and continuity it cries out for. Furthermore, the inane picture is at times incomprehen-

sible, with characters, motivations, and actions frequently confused. The Thunderdome sequence—with Max and MB hanging from ropes and swinging savagely past each other—is the only highlight of the film. (You have to see Tina Turner tearing across the desert in a souped-up dune buggy to believe it.) There are some lyrical, poetic passages in the music and in the visuals, but those seeing something deep here are kidding themselves.

Miller's work has been acclaimed by people who confuse the "kinetic" pacing and editing of his pictures with good direction, but he is certainly not in the class of William Wyler, Alfred Hitchcock, Federico Fellini, or John Ford, and the Mad Max films are ultimately forgettable trash for the masses, lacking the grandeur, wonder, and positivism of the best of the superhuman features.

Above: *Star Wars* an overrated but popular "comic book" movie.

Top: The comic book-inspired character(s) "Masterblaster" of *Mad Max Beyond Thunderdome*.

The success of *Star Wars* (1977) is a perfect illustration of how the public will deride comic books, insisting they are fit only for children and morons, and yet will flock to see a film that makes many comic books seem like works of intellectual genius in comparison. The public assumes that these movies have to be *serious* because it takes so much money to make them, and anything that costs money has to be good—and *important*—according to this mentality.

Star Wars isn't a terrible picture by any means, just a vastly overpraised one. It tells the story of a young lad in a far-off galaxy who manages to save a world threatened with extinction by the nasty rulers of his universe. The film operates on a level that is scarcely more sophisticated than the Flash Gordon serials, but supposedly boasts impressive special effects work. The same critics who were nitpicking every little "resolution differential" in *Superman* were oddly blind to the less imaginative effects in *Star Wars*. Darth Vader would seem a very colorless villain without the voice of unseen James Earl Jones (what a waste!) to back him up.

George Lucas, who directed *Star Wars*, turned the directorial reins over to Irvin Kershner for the sequel, *The Empire Strikes Back* (1980), in which Luke Skywalker continues his battle with his father, Darth Vader. Having the villain turn out to be a relative or someone having some relationship with the hero is an old, old routine in comic books (Orion and Darkseid of the *New Gods* comic of the sixties provided a later example), but many were outraged when this *Empire* plot development was leaked to the press. *The Empire Strikes Back* is an energetic simple-minded picture with some great effects and a thrilling climactic battle between Luke and Vader. Princess Leia's spunkiness, which had seemed refreshing in *Star Wars*, was wearing thin, however.

Richard Marquand's *Return of the Jedi* (1983) is probably the best film in the trilogy. The title was changed from *Revenge of the Jedi* to *Return* when *Star Wars* fans pointed out that the "Jedi" were creatures of vengeance and the title was redundant. (These fans obviously have *very* little to do with their time.) The film demonstrates a lot of glitz and movie know-how, although the mechanical and puppet creatures that cavort on the sidelines, such as the bizarre, bloblike "Jabba the Hutt," are more interesting than the humans. The only halfway touching moment in

Above: Ben Kenobi (Alec Guinness) crosses light-swords with the evil Darth Vader in *Star Wars*.

the film occurs when one of these creatures is killed and his or her mate cries over its body; the human drama, in contrast, is distinctly unmoving.

While the Superman movies were just as juvenile as the *Star Wars* trilogy, at least there was a certain honesty about their origins. *Star Wars* and its sequels borrowed most of their ideas from old comics and serials while pretending to be something new, a canard bolstered by the very contemporary if at times overrated special effects. Both series were guilty of editing out most of the moments of emotional honesty and humanity that *could* be found in many comic books—and science fiction novels—of the period. *Star Wars* et al. could have replaced their one-dimensional characters with real people and have been just as entertaining.

Star Wars ushered in the era of the big-budget special effects movie that favored tricks and stunts over people, with actors who were more charismatic than talented. Isn't that the case with all "comic book" and super-hero movies? one might wonder. Yet if comic books and other works of escapist fiction can resonate with legitimate characterization and telling, honest emotion, why can't Hollywood follow suit and add some *substance* to the usual effects and scenarios?

Star Trek: The Motion Picture (1979) is not necessarily a feast for the intellect, but it seems light years beyond *Star Wars* in terms of (admittedly limited) characterization and its more thought-provoking aspects. Better actors could have made their characters come alive—really *react* to what was happening around them—and lifted the whole tone of the picture to another, worthier level. As it is, *Star Trek: TMP* is a bit of literate hokum that gets better with each viewing.

The comic book aspects are pervasive, including the basic premise. The crew of the enterprise is up against an all-powerful alien organism, called Veeger, which turns out to be a living machine. In a typical, old-fashioned comic book contrivance, this machine calls itself Veeger because it was originally a Voyager space probe and mud is now covering all but the "v," "g," "e," and "r" of its name. The Voyager probe was launched more than three-hundred years before, landed on a "machine planet" (which sounds like something out of the *Metal Men* comic book of the sixties), and was sent back in a huge ship built for it. It has gathered so much information in the intervening years that it has acquired consciousness and wants to bring its data back to "the creator," which it believes is also a machine. The crew of the *Enterprise,* those annoying "carbon units," are practically beneath its notice. Veeger—or VGER—is now possessed of a brilliant intellect, but it doesn't know its correct name is Voyager because of a little mud that it probably can't even see!

Above: The *Star Trek* crew as they looked in the sixties.

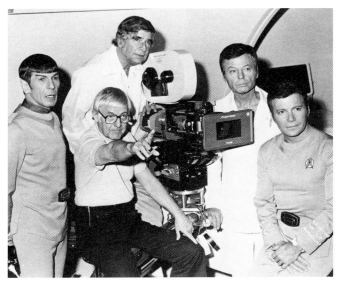

Like so many other "comic book" movies—and unlike so many comics—*Star Trek: TMP* falls short of delineating its "human drama" in both script and acting. There are moments in the film that should be emotionally powerful—Stephen Collins encountering a perfect duplicate of his now-dead lover (Persis Khambatta), for instance—that are almost tossed away in a perfunctory manner. Spock's realization that he can't give up the human side of his nature when he sees what VGER has become could also have been stronger.

Still, *Star Trek: TMP* has some fine effects work, a standout score by Jerry Goldsmith, and an occasional sense of awe and wonder. It ends with Collins and Khambatta (as VGER's duplicate of the real woman) merging together to form a new, presumably biomechanical life-form. In the best comic book tradition, this creature takes off to the stars to find its destiny—like the Silver Surfer, "Him," and countless others before it. Directed by Robert Wise, *Star Trek: TMP* probably plays better on the small screen than in the movie theater.

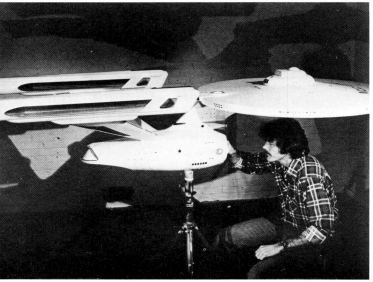

It is fitting that this volume on comic books, super-hero movies, and their progeny should wind up with a look at *Doc Savage: The Man of Bronze* (1975), directed by Michael Anderson. Although a Doc Savage comic book had been published in the forties (Street and Smith) and the seventies (Marvel) and is being published today (DC), the character was first introduced in a pulp magazine of the thirties, and hence predates the comic book as we know it. Like the Shadow, another pulp character, Doc Savage was highly influential on the super-heroes who would come later, and was one of the chief inspirations for Superman. Doc Savage worked with a band of brave

Top: Robert Wise (seated) directing *Star Trek: The Motion Picture*. Many comic book type ideas were used in the film, which has improved with age.

Lower left: The *Enterprise* in space...
Lower right: ...and how it really looks.

adventurers, specialists in their fields, and circled the globe battling dastardly villains and monstrous menaces and rescuing damsels and others in distress. The pulp stories were fast, vivid, colorful, and exciting, with *The Monsters* (giant men run amok in a town) and *The Land of Terror* (a crater filled with prehistoric monsters) among the most memorable.

Producer George Pal got the idea of coming out with a series of Doc Savage films in the 1970s and had the first novel, *The Man of Bronze*, adapted for the screen. The actors chosen to act the parts were ideal: Ron Ely made a striking Doc Savage, and Bill Lucking (Renny), Paul Gleason (Long Tom), Michael Miller (Monk), Eldon Quick (Johnny), and Darren Zwerling (Ham) all looked as if they'd just stepped out of the pulps. There was even a talented pig to play Monk's pet, Habeas Corpus.

The story, which is quite faithful to Kenneth Robeson's pulp novel, has Doc called down to Hidalgo when his father is murdered. The senior Savage had apparently just staked a claim to a treasure found in a mythical village beyond "the edge of the world," where brave men fear to go. The evil Captain Seas (a colorless villain played just that way by Paul Wexler) wants to keep Doc's hands off the treasure and employs the "green death" to do his dirty work. This is a slithering bunch of vaporous, lethal reptiles distilled from essence of snake venom and brought to life through supernatural means. The green death is portrayed by animated cartoon serpents.

Doc Savage (which turned out to be Pal's final movie) has a fine beginning in New York at our hero's skyscraper headquarters, including an exciting high-rise chase after a slippery suspect. But the second half of the picture bogs down to an unsalvageable level. There is no sense of wonder or even atmospheric music as Doc and his companions literally march (to Sousa tunes) into unknown territory, a sequence devoid of the awe and mystery of the best of the pulps. The set of the mysterious village with its pool of liquid gold was done on the cheap, and the climax involving a

Top: Ron Ely played *Doc Savage: The Man of Bronze.*

Bottom: The villainous Captain Seas (Paul Wexler) entertains a guest (Robyn Hitor) in *Doc Savage.*

minor earthquake is overly abrupt. There's a surfeit of comedy relief and a deficiency of thrills, and little of that forthcoming "Indiana Jones" movie know-how that can make this kind of stuff really come alive. Although there isn't too much camp (aside from a man who sleeps in a giant cradle, like something out of the *Batman* TV series), the approach is often *too* lighthearted, unlike the source novels. There are some good action scenes and fisticuffs mid-picture, on Seas's yacht, but they aren't enough to keep *Doc Savage* from sinking. Although a sequel, *The Arch Enemy of Evil*, was announced at the closing credits, no other Doc Savage film has materialized.

But Doc Savage and his cronies are still viable characters, some of the first superhuman heroes and most influential. Perhaps someday another enterprising producer and director will get together to do a different, better screen adaptation.

It if could happen to Batman, it could happen to anyone.

Above: The classic pulp hero in collectible comics format: *Doc Savage* #16. Copyright © 1989 The Condé Nast Publications, Inc. Published by DC Comics, Inc.

Top: The well-chosen cast of *Doc Savage: The Man of Bronze.*

SELECT FILMOGRAPHY*

THE ADVENTURES OF CAPTAIN MARVEL. 1941. Republic. *Directors:* William Witney, John English. *Associate Producer:* Hiram S. Brown, Jr. *Screenplay:* Sol Short, Ronald Davison, Norman S. Hall, Joseph Poland, Arch B. Heath. *Director of Photography:* William Nobles. *Special Effects:* Howard Lydecker. *Music:* Cy Feuer. *Cast:* Tom Tyler (*Captain Marvel*), Frank Coghlan, Jr. (*Billy Batson*), William Benedict (*Whitey Murphy*), Louise Currie (*Betty Wallace*), Robert Strange (*John Malcolm*), Harry Worth (*Professor Bentley*), Bryant Washburn (*Henry Carlyle*), George Pembroke (*Dr. Stephen Lang*), Reed Hadley (*Rahman Bar*), Nigel de Brulier (*Shazam*). Chapter One: *Curse of the Scorpion*. Chapter Two: *The Guillotine*. Chapter Three: *Time Bomb*. Chapter Four: *Death Takes the Wheel*. Chapter Five: *The Scorpion Strikes*. Chapter Six: *Lens of Death*. Chapter Seven: *Human Targets*. Chapter Eight: *Boomerang*. Chapter Nine: *Dead Man's Trap*. Chapter Ten: *Doom Ship*. Chapter Eleven: *Valley of Death*. Chapter Twelve: *Captain Marvel's Secret*.

THE ADVENTURES OF SUPERMAN (television). 1953–1957. ABC and syndication. *Directors:* Thomas Carr, Lee Sholem, George Blair, Harry Gerstad, Phil Ford, Howard Bretherton, Lew Landers, George Reeves. *Producers:* Robert Maxwell, Bernard Luber (first season only), Whitney Ellsworth. *Director of Photography:* Harold Stine, Harold Wellman, Joseph Biroc. *Special effects:* Thol (Si) Simonson. *Creators:* Jerome Siegel and Joe Shuster. *Cast:* George Reeves (*Superman/Clark Kent*), Phyllis Coates (*Lois Lane*—first season only), Noel Neill (*Lois Lane*—second and subsequent seasons), Jack Larson (*Jimmy Olsen*), John Hamilton (*Perry White*), Robert Shayne (*Inspector Henderson*).

ATOM MAN VS. SUPERMAN. 1950. Columbia. *Director:* Spencer Bennet. *Producer:* Sam Katzman. *Director of Photography:* Ira H. Morgan. *Screenplay:* George H. Plympton, Joseph F. Poland, David Mathews. *Editor:* Earl Turner. *Musical Director:* Mischa Bakaleinikoff. *Cast:* Kirk Alyn (*Superman*), Noel Neill (*Lois Lane*), Lyle Talbot (*Luthor*), Tommy Bond (*Jimmy Olsen*), Pierre Watkin (*Perry White*), Jack Ingram (*Foster*), Don Harvey (*Alber*), Rusty Westcott (*Carl*), Terry Frost (*Baer*), Wally West (*Dorr*). Chapter One: *Superman Flies Again*. Chapter Two: *Atom Man Appears*. Chapter Three: *A Blaze in the Sky*. Chapter Four: *Superman Meets Atom Man*. Chapter Five: *Atom Man Tricks Superman*. Chapter Six: *Atom Man's Challenge*. Chapter Seven: *At the Mercy of Atom Man!* Chapter Eight: *Into the Empty Doom*. Chapter Nine: *Superman Crashes Through*. Chapter Ten: *Atom Man's Heat Ray*. Chapter Eleven: *Luthor's Strategy*. Chapter Twelve: *Atom Man Strikes*. Chapter Thirteen: *Atom Man's Flying Saucers*. Chapter Fourteen: *Rocket of Vengeance*. Chapter Fifteen: *Superman Saves the Universe*.

*includes selected TV programs and serials.

BATMAN. 1943. Columbia. *Director:* Lambert Hillyer. *Producer:* Rudolph C. Flothow. *Screenplay:* Victor McLeod, Leslie Swabacker, Harry Fraser. *Director of Photography:* James S. Brown, Jr. *Editors:* Dwight Caldwell, Earl Turner. *Music:* Lee Zahler. *Cast:* Lewis Wilson (*Batman/Bruce Wayne*), Douglas Croft (*Robin/Dick Grayson*), William Austin (*Alfred*), Shirley Patterson (*Linda Page*), J. Carrol Naish (*Dr. Daka*), Earle Hodgins (*Barker*). With: Charles Middleton, Stanley Price, Kenne Duncan, Anthony Warde.

Chapter One: *The Electrical Brain.* Chapter Two: *The Bat's Cave.* Chapter Three: *The Mark of the Zombies.* Chapter Four: *Slaves of the Rising Sun.* Chapter Five: *The Living Corpse.* Chapter Six: *Poison Peril.* Chapter Seven: *The Phoney Doctor.* Chapter Eight: *Lured by Radium.* Chapter Nine: *The Sign of the Sphinx.* Chapter Ten: *Flying Spies.* Chapter Eleven: *A Nipponese Trap.* Chapter Twelve. *Embers of Evil.* Chapter Thirteen: *Eight Steps Down.* Chapter Fourteen: *The Executioner Strikes.* Chapter Fifteen: *The Doom of the Rising Sun.*

BATMAN (television). 1966–1968. ABC. *Executive Producer:* William Dozier. *Producer:* Howie Horwitz. *Director of Photography:* Howard Schwartz. *Story Consultant:* Lorenzo Semple, Jr. *Makeup:* Ben Nye. *Theme Music:* Neal Hefti. *Music:* Nelson Riddle. *Cast:* Adam West (*Batman/Bruce Wayne*). Burt Ward (*Robin/Dick Grayson*), Neil Hamilton (*Commissioner Gordon*), Alan Napier (*Alfred*), Madge Blake (*Aunt Harriet*), Stafford Repp (*Chief O'Hara*), Yvonne Craig (*Batgirl/Barbara Gordon*).

BATMAN. 1989. Warner Bros. *Director:* Tim Burton. *Producers:* Jon Peters, Peter Guber. *Executive Producers:* Benjamin Melniker, Michael Uslan. *Co-Producer:* Chris Kenny. *Associate Producer:* Barbara Kalish. *Screenplay:* Sam Hamm, Warren Skaaren. *Director of Photography:* Roger Pratt. *Production designer:* Anton Furst. *Special visual effects:* Derek Meddings. *Special effects supervisor:* John Evans. *Set decorator:* Peter Young. *Editor:* Ray Lovejoy. *Musical score:* Danny Elfman. *Songs written and performed by* Prince. *Based upon characters created by* Bob Kane *appearing in magazines published by* DC Comics. *Cast:* Michael Keaton (*Batman/Bruce Wayne*). Jack Nicholson (*Joker/Jack Napier*), Kim Basinger (*Vicki Vale*), Robert Wuhl (*Alexander Knox*), Pat Hingle (*Commissioner Gordon*), Billy Dee Williams (*Harvey Dent*), Michael Gough (*Alfred*), Jack Palance (*Grissom*), Jerry Hall (*Alicia*), William Hootkins (*Eckhardt*), Lee Wallace (*Mayor*).

BATMAN AND ROBIN. 1949. Columbia. *Director:* Spencer Bennet. *Producer:* Sam Katzman. *Screenplay:* George H. Plympton, Joseph F. Poland, Royal K. Cole. *Director of Photography:* Ira H. Morgan. *Art Director:* Paul Palmentola. *Film Editors:* Earl Turner, Dwight Caldwell. *Musical Director:* Mischa Bakaleinikoff. *Production Manager:* Herbert Leonard. *Cast:* Robert Lowery (*Batman/Bruce Wayne*), John Duncan (*Robin/Dick Grayson*), Jane Adams (*Vicki*), Lyle Talbot (*Gordon*), Ralph Graves (*Harrison*), Don Harvey (*Nolan*), William Fawcett (*Hammil*), Leonard Penn (*Carter*), Rick Vallin (*Brown*), Michael Whalen (*Dunne*).

Chapter One: *Batman Takes Over.* Chapter Two: *Tunnel of Terror.* Chapter Three: *Robin's Wild Ride.* Chapter Four: *Batman Trapped!* Chapter Five: *Robin Rescues Batman.* Chapter Six: *Target—Robin!* Chapter Seven: *The*

Fatal Blast. Chapter Eight: *Robin Meets the Wizard.* Chapter Nine: *The Wizard Strikes Back!* Chapter Ten: *Batman's Last Chance.* Chapter Eleven: *Robin's Ruse.* Chapter Twelve: *Robin Rides the Wind.* Chapter Thirteen: *The Wizard's Challenge.* Chapter Fourteen: *Batman vs. Wizard.* Chapter Fifteen: *Batman Victorious.*

BLACKHAWK. 1952. Columbia. *Directors:* Spencer Bennet, Fred F. Sears. *Producer:* Sam Katzman. *Screenplay:* George H. Plympton, Royal K. Cole, Sherman L. Lowe. *Based on the* Blackhawk *comic magazine drawn by* Reed Crandell. *Director of Photography:* William Whitley. *Art Director:* Paul Palmentola. *Set Decorator:* Sidney Clifford. *Special effects:* Jack Erickson. *Musical Director:* Mischa Bakaleinikoff. *Cast:* Kirk Alyn (*Blackhawk*), Carol Forman (*Laska*), John Crawford (*Chuck*), William Fawcett (*Dr. Rolph*), Michael Fox (*Mr. Case*), Don Harvey (*Olaf*), Rick Vallin (*Stan/Boris*), Larry Stewart (*Andre*), Weaver Levy (*Chop Chop*), Rick Stuart (*Cross*).

Chapter One: *Distress Call From Space.* Chapter Two: *Blackhawk Traps a Traitor.* Chapter Three: *In the Enemy's Hideout.* Chapter Four: *The Iron Monster!* Chapter Five: *Human Targets.* Chapter Six: *Blackhawk's Leap for Life!* Chapter Seven: *Mystery Fuel.* Chapter Eight: *Blasted From the Sky!* Chapter Nine: *Blackhawk Tempts Fate!* Chapter Ten: *Chase for Element X!* Chapter Eleven: *Forced Down!* Chapter Twelve: *Drums of Doom!* Chapter Thirteen: *Blackhawk's Daring Plan.* Chapter Fourteen: *Blackhawk's Wild Ride.* Chapter Fifteen: *The Leader Unmasked!*

CAPTAIN AMERICA. 1943. Republic. *Directors:* John English, Elmer Clifton. *Associate Producer:* William J. O'Sullivan. *Screenplay:* Royal K. Cole, Ronald Davison, Basil Dickey, Jesse Duffy, Harry Fraser, Grant Nelson, Joseph Poland. *Director of Photography:* John MacBurnie. *Art Director:* Fred Ritter. *Set Decorator:* Charles Thompson. *Editors:* Wallace Grissell, Earl Turner. *Sound:* Ed Borshell. *Musical Score:* Mort Glickman. *Cast:* Dick Purcell (*Grant Gardner/Captain America*), Lorna Gray (*Gail Richards*), Lionel Atwill (*Dr. Maldor*), Charles Trowbridge (*Commissioner Dryden*). Russell Hicks (*Mayor Randolph*), George J. Lewis (*Matson*), John Davidson (*Gruber*). With: Norman Nesbitt, Frank Reicher, Hugh Sothern.

Chapter One: *The Purple Death.* Chapter Two: *Mechanical Executioner.* Chapter Three: *Scarlet Shroud.* Chapter Four: *Preview of Murder.* Chapter Five: *Blade of Wrath.* Chapter Six: *Vault of Vengenace.* Chapter Seven: *Wholesale Destruction.* Chapter Eight: *Cremation in the Clouds.* Chapter Nine: *Triple Tragedy.* Chapter Ten: *The Avenging Corpse.* Chapter Eleven: *The Dead Man Returns.* Chapter Twelve: *Horror on the Highway.* Chapter Thirteen: *Skyscraper Plunge.* Chapter Fourteen: *The Scarab Strikes.* Chapter Fifteen: *Toll of Doom.*

DIAMONDS ARE FOREVER. 1971. United Artists. *Director:* Guy Hamilton. *Producers:* Albert R. Broccoli, Harry Saltzman. *Screenplay:* Richard Maibaum, Tom Mankiewicz, based on the Ian Fleming story. *Photography:* Ted Moore. *Production Design:* Ken Adams. *Editors:* Bert Bates, John W. Holmes. *Music:* John Barry. *Sound:* John Mitchell, Al Overton. *Cast:* Sean Connery (*James Bond*), Jill St. John (*Tiffany Case*), Charles Gray (*Ernst Blofeld*), Lana Wood (*Plenty O'Toole*), Jimmy Dean (*William Whyte*), Bruce Cabot (*Saxby*), Bruce Glover (*Wint*), Putter Smith (*Kidd*), Norman Burton (*Felix Leiter*), Bernard Lee ("*M*"), Lois Maxwell (*Miss Moneypenny*).

DICK TRACY. 1937. Republic. *Directors:* Ray Taylor, Alan James. *Producer:* Nat Levine. *Associate Producer:* Laurence Wickland. *Screenplay:* Barry Shipman, Winston Miller. *Original Story:* Morgan Cox, George Morgan. *Photography:* William Nobles, Edgar Lyons. *Supervising Editor:* Murray Seldeen. *Film Editors:* Helene Turner, Edward Todd, Bill Whitney. *Sound Engineer:* Terry Kellum. *Cast:* Ralph Byrd (*Dick Tracy*), Kay Hughes (*Gwen*), Smiley Burnette (*Mike*), Lee Van Atta (*Junior*), John Piccori (*Moloch*), Carleton Young (*Gordon Tracy*), Fred Hamilton (*Steve Lockwood*). With: Francis X. Bushman, Byron K. Foulger, Oscar & Elmer.

Chapter One: *The Spider Strikes.* Chapter Two: *The Bridge of Terror.* Chapter Three: *The Fur Pirates.* Chapter Four: *Death Rides the Sky.* Chapter Five: *Brother Against Brother.* Chapter Six: *Dangerous Waters.* Chapter Seven: *The Ghost Town Mystery.* Chapter Eight: *Battle in the Clouds.* Chapter Nine: *The Stratosphere Adventure.* Chapter Ten: *The Gold Ship.* Chapter Eleven: *Harbor Pursuit.* Chapter Twelve: *Trail of the Spider.* Chapter Thirteen: *The Fire Trap.* Chapter Fourteen: *The Devil in White.* Chapter Fifteen: *Brothers United.*

DICK TRACY. 1990. Touchstone. *Director/Producer:* Warren Beatty. *Executive Producers:* Barrie M. Osborne, Art Linson, Floyd Mutrux. *Screenplay:* Jim Cash, Jack Epps Jr., based on characters created by Chester Gould. *Photography:* Vittorio Storaro. *Production Design:* Richard Sylbert. *Special Character Makeup:* John Caglione, Jr., Doug Drexler. *Editor:* Richard Marks. *Music:* Danny Elfman. *Songs:* Stephen Sondheim. *Visual Effects:* Buena Vista Visual Effects Group. *Cast:* Warren Beatty (*Dick Tracy*). Charlie Korsmo (*Kid*). Glenne Headly (*Tess Trueheart*). Madonna (*Breathless Mahoney*). Al Pacino (*Big Boy Caprice*). Dustin Hoffman (*Mumbles*). William Forsythe (*Flattop*). Charles Durning (*Chief Brandon*). Mandy Patinkin (*88 Keys*). Paul Sorvino (*Lips Manlis*). Dick Van Dyke (*D.A. Fletcher*). James Caan (*Spaldoni*), Kathy Bates (*Mrs. Green*), Michael J. Pollard (*Bug Bailey*).

THE FLASH. 1990. Warner Bros. Television. *Director:* Robert Iscove. *Producers:* Craig W. Van Sickel, Steven Long Mitchell, Gail Morgan Hickman (Pet Fly Productions). *Executive Producers:* Danny Bilson and Paul DeMeo. *Writers:* Danny Bilson and Paul DeMeo. *Developed by* Danny Bilson and Paul DeMeo. *Music:* Danny Elfman. *Cast:* John Wesley Shipp (*Barry Allen/The Flash*), Amanda Pays (*Tina McGee*), Alex Desert (*Julio Mendez*), Paula Marshall (*Iris West*), Michael Nader (*Pike*), Priscilla Pointer (*Nora Allen*), M. Emmet Walsh (*Henry Allen*), Tim Thomerson (*Jay Allen*), Lycia Naff (*Lila*), Robert Hooks (*Chief Cooper*).

HOWARD THE DUCK. 1986. Universal. *Director:* Willard Huyck. *Producer:* Gloria Katz. *Executive Producer:* George Lucas. *Screenplay:* Willard Huyck and Gloria Katz. *Based on the Marvel Comics character created by* Steve Gerber. *Director of Photography:* Richard H. Kline. *Production Design:* Peter Jamison. *Editors:* Michael Chandler, Sidney Wolinksy. *Music:* John Barry. *Visual effects:* Industrial Light & Magic. *Alien Monster Design:* Tom Burman, Bari Dreiband-Burman. *Cast:* Ed Gale, Chip Zien, Jim Rose, Steve Sleap, Peter Baird, Mary Wells, Lisa Sturz, Jordan Prentice (*Howard the Duck*), Lea Thompson (*Beverly Switzler*), Jeffrey Jones (*Dr. Jenning*), Tim Robbins (*Phil Blumbrutt*), Paul Guifoyle (*Lt. Welker*), Tommy Swerdlow (*Ginger Moss*).

REMO WILLIAMS: THE ADVENTURE BEGINS. 1985. Orion. *Director:* Guy Hamilton. *Producer:* Larry Spiegel. *Executive Producers:* Dick Clark, Mel Bergman. *Screenplay:* Christopher Wood. *Based on* The Destroyer *series by* Richard Sapir and Warren Murphy. *Director of Photography:* Andrew Laszlo. *Production Designer:* Jackson De Govia. *Stunt Coordinator:* Glenn H. Randall, Jr. *Editor:* Mark Melnick. *Music:* Craig Safan. *Cast:* Fred Ward (*Remo*). Joel Gray (*Chiun*). Wilford Brimley (*Harold Smith*). J.A. Preston (*Conn MacCleary*). George Coe (*Gen. Scott Watson*). Charles Cioffi (*George Grove*). Kate Mulgrew (*Major Reyner Fleming*). Patrick Kilpatrick (*Stone*). Michael Pataki (*Jim Wilson*).

ROBOCOP. 1987. Orion. *Director:* Paul Verhoeven. *Producer:* Arne Schmidt. *Executive Producer:* Jon Davison. *Screenplay:* Edward Neumeier, Michael Miner. *Photography:* Jost Vacano. *Production Design:* William Sandell. *Robocop designed and created by* Rob Bottin. *Special makeup effects:* Bottin. *ED-209 designed and created by* Craig Davies and Peter Ronzani. *ED-209 sequences by* Phil Tippett. *Editor:* Frank J. Urieste. *Music:* Basil Poledouris. *Cast:* Peter Weller (*Robocop*). Nancy Allen (*Lewis*). Ronny Cox (*Jones*). Kurtwood Smith (*Clarence*). Miguel Ferrer (*Morton*). Robert Do'Qui (*Sgt. Reed*). Daniel O'Herlihy (*The Old Man*).

ROBOCOP 2. 1990. Orion. *Director:* Irvin Kershner. *Producer:* John Davison. *Executive Producer:* Patrick Crowley. *Screenplay:* Frank Miller and Walon Green, from story by Miller. *Based on characters created by* Edward Neumeier and Michael Miner. *Photography:* Mark Irwin. *Production Design:* Peter Jamison. *Animation Sequences:* Phil Tippett. *Special Photographic Effects:* Peter Kuran/VCE. *Editor:* William Anderson. *Music:* Leonard Rosenman. *Cast:* Peter Weller (*Robocop*). Nancy Allen (*Anne Lewis*). Daniel O'Herlihy (*The Old Man*). Belinda Bauer (*Juliette Faxx*). Tom Noonan (*Cain*). Gabriel Damon (*Hob*). Felton Perry (*Donald Johnson*). Robert Do'Qui (*Sgt. Reed*). Galyn Gorg (*Angie*). Stephen Lee (*Duffy*).

THE SPY WHO LOVED ME. 1977. United Artists. *Director:* Lewis Gilbert. *Producer:* Albert R. Broccoli. *Screenplay:* Christopher Wood and Richard Maibaum, based on the Ian Fleming character. *Photography:* Claude Renoir. *Production Design:* Ken Adam. *Editor:* John Glen. *Music:* Marvin Hamlisch. *Sound:* Gordon Everett. *Special Visual Effects:* Derek Meddings. *Cast:* Roger Moore (*James Bond*), Barbara Bach (*Anya*), Curt Jurgens (*Stromberg*), Richard Kiel (*Jaws*), Caroline Munro (*Naomi*), Walter Gotell (*General Gogol*), Geoffrey Keen (*Minister of Defense*), Bernard Lee ("*M*"), Desmond Llewellyn ("*Q*"), Lois Maxwell (*Miss Moneypenny*).

SUPERGIRL. 1984. Tri-Star. *Director:* Jeannot Szwarc. *Producer:* Timothy Burrill. *Executive Producer:* Ilya Salkind. *Screenplay:* David Odell. *Photography:* Alan Hume. *Production Design:* Richard Macdonald. *Editor:* Malcolm Cooke. *Music:* Jerry Goldsmith. *Special Visual Effects:* Derek Meddings. *Optical Visual Effects:* Roy Field. *Cast:* Helen Slater (*Kara/Linda Lee/Supergirl*). Faye Dunaway (*Selena*). Peter O'Toole (*Zaltor*). Brenda Vaccaro (*Bianca*). Mia Farrow (*Alura*). Simon Ward (*Zor-El*). Marc McClure (*Jimmy Olsen*). Hart Bochner (*Ethan*). Maureen Teefy (*Lucy Lane*). Peter Cook (*Nigel*).

SUPERMAN. 1948. Columbia. *Directors:* Spencer Bennet and Thomas Carr. *Producer:* Sam Katzman. *Screenplay:* Arthur Hoerl, Lewis Clay, Royal K. Cole. *Adaptation:* George H. Plympton, Joseph F. Poland. *Photography:* Ira H. Morgan. *Art Director:* Paul Palmentola. *Set Decorator:* Sidney Clifford. *Editor:* Earl Turner. *Musical Director:* Mischa Bakaleinikoff. *Cast:* Kirk Alyn (*Superman/Clark Kent*). Noel Neill (*Lois Lane*). Tommy Bond (*Jimmy Olsen*). Pierre Watkin (*Perry White*). Carol Forman (*Spider-Lady*). George Meeker (*Driller*). Jack Ingram (*Anton*). Terry Frost (*Brock*). Charles King (*Conrad*). Charles Quigley (*Hackett*).

Chapter One: *Superman Comes to Earth.* Chapter Two: *Depths of the Earth.* Chapter Three: *The Reducer Ray.* Chapter Four: *Man of Steel.* Chapter Five: *A Job for Superman.* Chapter Six: *Superman in Danger.* Chapter Seven: *Into the Electric Furnace.* Chapter Eight: *Superman to the Rescue.* Chapter Nine: *Irresistible Force.* Chapter Ten: *Between Two Fires.* Chapter Eleven: *Superman's Dilemma.* Chapter Twelve: *Blast From the Depths!* Chapter Thirteen: *Hurled to Destruction.* Chapter Fourteen: *Superman at Bay.* Chapter Fifteen: *The Pay-Off.*

SUPERMAN AND THE MOLE MEN. 1951. Lippert. *Director:* Lee Sholem. *Producer:* Barney A. Sarecky. *Screenplay:* Richard Fielding. *Photography:* Clark Ramsey. *Editor:* Al Joseph. *Special Effects:* Ray Mercer. *Cast:* George Reeves (*Kent/Superman*), Phyllis Coates (*Lois Lane*), Jeff Corey (*Luke Benson*), Walter Reed (*Bill Corrigan*), J. Farrell MacDonald (*Pop Shannon*), Stanley Andrews (*Sheriff*), Ray Walker (*John Craig*), Hal K. Dawson (*Weber*), Frank Reicher (*Hospital Superintendent*), Beverly Washburn (*Child*).

SUPERMAN. 1978. Warner Bros. *Director:* Richard Donner. *Producer:* Pierre Spengler. *Executive Producer:* Ilya Salkind. *Screenplay:* Mario Puzo, David Newman, Leslie Newman, Robert Benton. *Director of Photography:* Geoffrey Unsworth. *Production Designer:* John Barry. *Music:* John Williams. *Special Effects:* Colin Chilvers. *Cast:* Christopher Reeve (*Superman/Clark Kent*), Margot Kidder (*Lois Lane*), Jackie Cooper (*Perry White*). Marc McClure (*Jimmy Olsen*), Gene Hackman (*Lex Luthor*), Ned Beatty (*Otis*), Marlon Brando (*Jor-El*), Susannah York (*Lara*), Valerie Perrine (*Eve Teschmacher*), Glenn Ford (*Jonathan Kent*), Phyllis Thaxter (*Martha Kent*), Jeff East (*Young Clark*) Trevor Howard (*The Elder*) Terence Stamp (*General Zod*), Sarah Douglas (*Ursa*), Jack O'Halloran (*Non*), Maria Schell (*Vond-Ah*)

SUPERMAN II. 1981. Warner Bros. *Director:* Richard Lester. *Producer:* Pierre Spengler. *Executive Producer:* Ilya Salkind. *Screenplay:* Mario Puzo, David Newman, Leslie Newman. *Photography:* Geoffrey Unsworth and Robert Paynter. *Production Design:* John Barry, Peter Murton. *Editor:* John Victor-Smith. *Music:* Ken Thorne, *from original material composed by* John Williams. *Special Effects:* Colin Chilvers. *Supervisor of Optical and Visual Effects:* Roy Field. *Additional Flying Sequences and Director of Miniature Effects:* Derek Meddings. *Cast:* Christopher Reeve (*Superman/Clark Kent*), Gene Hackman (*Lex Luthor*), Margot Kidder (*Lois Lane*), Sarah Douglas (*Ursa*), Jack O'Halloran (*Non*), Terence Stamp (*General Zod*), Ned Beatty (*Otis*). Jackie Cooper (*Perry White*). Marc McClure (*Jimmy Olsen*), Valerie Perrine (*Eve Teschmacher*), Susannah York (*Lara*), Clifton James (*Sheriff*), E.G. Marshall (*President*).

SUPERMAN III. 1983. Warner Bros. *Director:* Richard Lester. *Producer:* Pierre Spengler. *Executive Producer:* Ilya Salkind. *Screenplay:* David and Leslie Newman. *Photography:* Robert Paynter. *Production Design:* Peter Murton. *Art Directors:* Terry Ackland-Snow and Brian Ackland-Snow. *Editor:* John Victor-Smith. *Music:* Ken Thorne, *with original themes by* John Williams. *Director of Special Effects and Miniatures:* Colin Chilvers. *Supervisor of Optical and Visual Effects:* Roy Field. *Cast:* Christopher Reeve (*Superman/Clark Kent*), Richard Pryor (*Gus Gorman*), Annette O'Toole (*Lana Lang*), Jackie Cooper (*Perry White*), Marc McClure (*Jimmy Olsen*), Margot Kidder (*Lois Lane*), Annie Ross (*Vera Webster*), Robert Vaughn (*Ross Webster*), Pamela Stephenson (*Lorelei Ambrosia*), Gavan O'Herlihy (*Brad*).

SUPERMAN IV. 1987. Warner Bros. *Director:* Sidney J. Furie. *Producers:* Menachem Golan and Yoran Globus. *Executive Producer:* Michael Kagan. *Screenplay:* Lawrence Konner, Mark Rosenthal. *Story:* Christopher Reeve, Konner, Rosenthal. *Photography:* Ernest Day. *Production Designer:* John Graysmark. *Editor:* John Shirley. *Music:* John Williams, *adapted by* Alexander Courage. *Visual Effects Supervisor:* Harrison Ellenshaw. *Special Effects Supervisor:* John Evans. *Cast:* Christopher Reeve (*Superman/Clark Kent*), Gene Hackman (*Lex Luthor*). Jackie Cooper (*Perry White*), Marc McClure (*Jimmy Olsen*), Jon Cryer (*Lenny*), Sam Wanamaker (*David Warfield*), Mark Pillow (*Nuclear Man*), Mariel Hemingway (*Lacy Warfield*), Margot Kidder (*Lois Lane*).

Select Bibliography

Benton, Mike. *The Comic Book in America: An Illustrated History.* Dallas: Taylor Publishing Co., 1989.

Dawidziak, Mark. "Behind-the-Scenes at 'The Flash.'" *Cinefantastique,* February 1991.

Eisner, Will. *The Spirit.* Monthly magazine published by Kitchen Sink Press, Inc. Princeton, Wisc.

Gerani, Gary, with Paul H. Schulman. *Fantastic Television.* New York: Harmony Books, 1977.

Gilpin, Kris. "Harrison Ellenshaw on Visual Effects for 'Superman IV.'" *Cinefantastique,* December 1987.

Heitland, Jon. *The Man From U.N.C.L.E. Book.* New York: St. Martin's Press, 1987.

Henderson, Jan. Interview with Frank Coghlan and William Benedict. *Filmfax,* February–March 1988.

————. "The Life and Times of Honest George." *Filmfax,* July 1988.

————. Interview with Lee Sholem. *Filmfax,* December 1988.

Jackson, Charles Lee, II. "Superman: The Early Years." *Filmfax,* December 1988.

————. "Batman: The Capsulized History of a Hero." *Filmfax,* August 1989.

Jankiewicz, Pat. Interview with Stanley "Batwriter" Ross. *Filmfax,* August 1989.

Jones, Alan. "'Batman' and Tim Burton." *Cinefantastique,* November 1989.

Littwin, Susan. "All Flesh and Substance." *TV Guide,* December 22–28, 1990.

Miller, Frank. *The Dark Knight Returns.* New York: DC Comics, 1986.

Quirk, Lawrence. *Fasten Your Seat Belts: The Passionate Life of Bette Davis.* New York: William Morrow, 1990.

Schoell, William. "All About Batman." *Quirk's Reviews,* September 1989.

Shay, Don. Interview with Richard Donner. *Cinefantastique* vol. 8, no. 4, 1979.

Siegel, Jerry, and Joe Shuster. *Superman Archives,* vol. 1. New York: DC Comics, 1989.

Steranko, Jim. *The Steranko History of Comics,* vol. 1. Reading, Pa.: Supergraphics, 1970.

————. *The Steranko History of Comics,* vol. 2. Reading, Pa.: Supergraphics, 1972.

Teitelbaum, Sheldon. "Spider-Man: The Movie." *Cinefantastique,* September 1987.

————. "Writers Sue Christopher Reeve for Flying Off with Script Ideas." *Cinefantastique,* September 1987.

White, Taylor L. Interviews with Sam Hamm. *Cinefantastique,* July 1989.

Selected Periodicals

New York Post, New York Daily News, Variety, People, Premiere, Quirk's Reviews, TV Guide, Fantazia, Amazing Heroes, Comics Scene.

About the Author

William Schoell is a native New Yorker who has written hundreds of articles for national publications. He is executive editor of *Quirk's Reviews* and a columnist for *Scream Factory*. His published novels include *Fatal Beauty, Saurian, Late at Night, The Pact,* and *The Dragon.* He worked for a New York City law firm and in the cooperative advertising department of Columbia Pictures before turning to full-time writing in the late seventies. His previous film-related book was *Stay Out of the Shower: Twenty-five Years of Shocker Films Beginning with "Psycho,"* which was published both in the United States and the United Kingdom. He is currently working on a number of projects, including a novel inspired by old serials and comics, and a "mainstream" book about a young runaway. Mr. Schoell has a choice collection of about 5,000 comics, as well as a selective video collection. His favorite writers include O. Henry, Agatha Christie, H. G. Wells, John Steinbeck, H. P. Lovecraft, Jules Verne, James Baldwin, and Tennessee Williams. William Schoell is a night owl who loves Manhattan but admits that "the creatures roaming about at two in the morning are sometimes a lot nastier than any 'supervillain.'"